Welcome to London

One of the world's great – and most visited – cities, London has something for everyone: from culture to fine food and a buzzing party scene. Its energy is intoxicating and its diversity inspiring.

This city is deeply multicultural, with one in three Londoners foreign-born. Britain may have voted for Brexit (although the majority of Londoners didn't), but London remains one of the world's most cosmopolitan cities, and diversity infuses daily life, food, music, fashion and art. It inspires festivals such as the now-famed Notting Hill Carnival, and the new annual Borough of Culture celebrations.

London is also a city of contrasts. On the one hand, it is constantly changing: witness the evolving skyline, with its statement skyscrapers; the endless stream of new restaurants, pop-up bars and concept stores; and the myriad new artists, from fashion designers to musicians, that have emerged from its creative milieu. No matter how often you visit, you'll always find something new.

On the other hand, this thirst for innovation has been facilitated by a strong sense of history and of how London came to be London. The city's buildings are striking milestones in a unique and beguiling biography, and many of them – Big Ben, Tower Bridge, the Tower of London – are instantly recognisable landmarks. Amazingly, all this history and culture leave glorious amounts of green spaces, which are a joy to explore or relax in.

> *London remains one of the world's most cosmopolitan cities, and diversity infuses daily life, food, music, fashion and art.*

View of London and the London Eye (p98)
PPTARA/SHUTTERSTOCK ©

★ LONDON ★

North London
Parks, marke
Camden and
after dark gu
glorious day
out. *(Map p2*

Hampstead Heath
(3.2km)

King's Cross

St Pan
Interna
(Euros

Euston

Kensington & Hyde Park
Three world-class museums and the largest of the royal parks in a well-heeled district. *(Map p278)*

Regent's Park

British Museum

SOHO

**Leices
Squar**

Piccadilly Circus

National Gallery

Trafalgar Squar

Paddington

Hyde Park

Buckingham Palace

**West
A**

Design Museum

Natural History Museum

Victoria & Albert Museum

Victoria

Kew Gardens
(8km)

Heathrow
(19km)

West End
The beating heart of London, with iconic sights, shopping and nightlife. *(Map p274)*

Hampton Court Palace
(13km)

Clerkenwell, Hoxton & Spitalfields
Good food and a great night out in one of London's trendiest areas. *(Map p282)*

s and
slington
rantee a
nd night
4)

◉ King's Cross
as
nal
r)

Shoreditch
◉

St Paul's Cathedral
✠

Covent Garden
r ◉

Charing
Cross
◉Ⓤ

River Thames

Tower of London
⌂

Borough Market
Ⓤ ◉ⓊⓇ
London
Bridge

Ⓤ
Tate Modern

Tower Bridge
◉

East London
Ground-zero for multicultural London; great restaurants and increasingly trendy. *(Map p285)*

Ⓤ Waterloo

⊕ **Houses of Parliament**
inster
bey

City & South Bank
Centuries of history and architecture across the Thames from a must-visit area for art lovers, theatre-goers and culture hounds. *(Map p280)*

◐ 0 — 2 km
 N 0 ——— 1 mile

Greenwich
(3.2km)

Contents

LONDON

TOP SIGHTS, AUTHENTIC EXPERIENCES

Emilie Filou, Damian Harper

4

Plan Your Trip
This Year in London

London

Culture and sports will be high on the list for 2020 – hello Euro football tournament and London Design Biennale! There are many smaller events happening too, and plenty of life's small pleasures to enjoy in the capital's ever changing eating and drinking scene.

Clockwise from above: Performer at Notting Hill Carnival; UEFA Euro 2020 official ball; Exhibit at London Design Biennale

2020

MIRCEA MOIRA/SHUTTERSTOCK ©

★ Top Festivals & Events

Brent: London Borough of Culture 2020, year-long

Wimbledon Championships, June-July

UEFA Euro 2020 Final, July

Notting Hill Carnival, August

London Design Biennale, September

FULL SPECTRUM BY FLYNN TALBOT FOR AUSTRALIA, LONDON DESIGN BIENNALE 2018
PHOTO CREDIT: MARK COCKSEDGE ©

Plan Your Trip
This Year in London

January

01

The new year in London kicks off with a big bang at midnight. London is in the throes of winter, with short days: light appears at 8am and is all but gone by 4pm.

⊙ Bridget Riley Exhibition   Oct 2019–Jan 2020

A major retrospective of the British artist at the Hayward Gallery, including her celebrated black and white Op Art works and stripe paintings, perceptual artwork and representational pieces, as well as her colour art. It features Riley's most famous work and rarer (as well as new) creations.

☆ London International Mime Festival   Jan

Held over the month of January, this festival (www.mimelondon.com) is a must for lovers of originality, playfulness, physical talent and the unexpected.

⊙ London Art Fair   22–26 Jan

More than 100 major galleries participate in this contemporary art fair (www.londonart fair.co.uk), now one of the largest in Europe, with thematic exhibitions, special events and the best emerging artists.

✲ Brent: London Borough of Culture 2020   Jan–Dec

In 2020, Brent (pictured below) will be London Borough of Culture (www. lboc2020.com). The scheme aims to celebrate London's rich diversity, history and creative industry. Celebrations will make much of the borough's migration history and its sports heritage. The highlight will be a mile-long street party.

✲ Chinese New Year   25 Jan

To usher in the Year of the Rat, Chinatown fizzes, crackles and pops with a colourful street festival, which includes a Golden Dragon parade (pictured above), feasting and partying.

DINENDRA HARIA/SHUTTERSTOCK ©

02

February

February is usually chilly and wet (sometimes even snow-encrusted). Schools break off for a week in mid-February. Londoners lark about with pancakes on Shrove Tuesday.

☆ BAFTAs   mid-Feb

The British Academy of Film and Television Arts (BAFTA; www.bafta.org) rolls out the red carpet mid-February to hand out its annual cinema awards. It's the British Oscars, if you will. Expect plenty of celebrity glamour.

♣ Shrove Tuesday   25 Feb

On Shrove Tuesday, you can catch pancake races (pictured above) and associated silliness at various venues around town (Spitalfields Market, in particular).

♟ Pint by the Fire   Feb

What better way to thaw after sightseeing in the cold than with a drink by the fire? Amazingly, London still has plenty of pubs with working fireplaces so make the most of them.

☆ A Night at the Opera   Feb

The nights are long and cold so what better way to cosy up than inside the stunning Royal Opera House to revel in a world-class opera or ballet? (Plus, it's a really good opportunity to dress up.)

Plan Your Trip
This Year in London

PAOLO BONA/SHUTTERSTOCK ©

March

March sees spring in the air, with trees beginning to flower and daffodils emerging across parks and gardens. London is getting in the mood to head outdoors again.

☆ Watch a Six Nations Rugby Game   Feb–Mar

Every year, England, Wales, Scotland, Ireland, France and Italy compete in the Six Nations tournament (www.sixnations rugby.com; pictured above), one of rugby's great competitions. Numerous pubs show the games, so grab yourself a drink and a seat and cheer along with the rest of the crowd.

✾ St Patrick's Day Parade & Festival   15 Mar

Top festival for the Irish in London, held on the Sunday closest to 17 March, with a colourful parade through central London and other festivities in and around Trafalgar Sq.

☆ Head of the River Race   late Mar

Some 400 crews take part in this colourful annual boat race (www.horr.co.uk), held over a 7km course on the Thames, from Mortlake to Putney.

◉ Flare   late Mar

This LGBTIQ+ film festival, organised by the British Film Institute (www.bfi.org.uk/flare), runs a packed programme of film screenings, along with club nights, talks and events.

FOTOMATON/ALAMY STOCK PHOTO ©

April

London is in bloom, with warmer days and a lighthearted vibe. British Summer Time starts late March, moving clocks forward an hour, so it's now light until 7pm. Some sights previously shut for winter reopen.

☆ The Boat Race
early Apr

Crowds line the banks of the Thames for the country's two most famous universities going oar-to-oar from Putney to Mortlake. Dates vary, due to each university's Easter breaks, so check the website (www.the boatraces.org).

☆ Easter
12 Apr

With Good Friday and Easter Monday both being public holidays, Easter is the longest bank holiday in the UK. Chocolate, which you'll find in many shapes and flavours, is a traditional Easter treat, as are hot-cross buns (spiced, sticky-glazed fruit buns).

☆ London Marathon
mid-Apr

Some 35,000 runners – most running for charity – pound through London in one of the world's biggest road races (www.virgin moneylondonmarathon.com), heading from Blackheath to the Mall.

☆ Udderbelly Festival
Apr–Jun

Housed in a temporary venue in the shape of a purple upside-down cow on the South Bank (pictured above), this festival of comedy, circus and general family fun (www.udderbelly.co.uk) has become a spring favourite. Events run from April to the end of September.

Plan Your Trip

This Year in London

PRETTYAWESOMEA/SHUTTERSTOCK ©

May

A delightful time to be in London: days are warming up and Londoners begin to start lounging around in parks, popping on their sunglasses and enjoying two bank-holiday weekends (the first and the last in May).

☆ Regent's Park Open Air Theatre   May–Sep

A popular and very atmospheric summer time fixture in London, this 1200-seat outdoor auditorium (www.openairtheatre. com) plays host to four productions a year – famous plays (Shakespeare often features), new works, musicals and usually one production aimed at families during an 18-week season.

☉ Museums at Night   mid-May

For one weekend in May, numerous museums across London open after-hours (www. museumsatnight.org.uk), with candlelit tours, spooky atmospheres, sleepovers and special events such as talks and concerts.

☉ Chelsea Flower Show   19–23 May

The world's most renowned horticultural event (pictured above) attracts London's green-fingered and flower-mad gardeners. Expect talks, presentations and spectacular displays from the cream of the gardening world.

☆ Shakespeare's Globe Theatre   late Apr–Oct

Watch the work of the most famous playwright in a faithful reproduction of a 17th century theatre (p216). The venue is outdoors and most of the audience is standing.

2020

LONONDUBH/SHUTTERSTOCK ©

June

The peak season begins with long, warm days (it's light until 10pm), the arrival of Wimbledon and other alfresco events.

⊙ Open Garden Squares Weekend
early Jun

Over one weekend, more than 200 gardens in London that are usually inaccessible to the public fling open their gates for exploration (www.opensquares.org).

✿ Trooping the Colour
mid-Jun

The Queen's official birthday (www.trooping-the-colour.co.uk) is celebrated with much flag-waving, parades, pageantry and noisy flyovers (pictured above). The Royal Family usually attends in force.

☆ Meltdown
mid-Jun

The Southbank Centre hands over the curatorial reins to a legend of contemporary music (eg Morrissey, Patti Smith or David Bowie) to pull together a full programme of concerts, talks and films mid-June (www.southbankcentre.co.uk).

☆ Wimbledon Lawn Tennis Championships
late Jun–early Jul

For two weeks a year, the quiet South London village of Wimbledon falls under a sporting spotlight as the world's best tennis players gather to battle for the championships (p227; pictured below).

N_FUJITA/SHUTTERSTOCK ©

⊙ Royal Academy Summer Exhibition
mid-Jun–mid-Aug

Beginning in June and running through August, this exhibition (p51) at the Royal Academy of Arts showcases works submitted by artists from all over Britain and the world, distilled to a thousand or so pieces.

Plan Your Trip
This Year in London

MS JANE CAMPBELL/SHUTTERSTOCK ©

07

July

This is the time to munch on strawberries, drink in beer gardens and join in the numerous outdoor activities, including big music festivals.

✿ Pride London early Jul
The gay community paints the town pink in this annual extravaganza (www.pridein london.org), featuring talks to live events, and culminating in a huge parade across London (pictured above).

☆ Wireless early Jul
One of London's top music festivals, with an emphasis on dance and R&B, Wireless (www.wirelessfestival.co.uk) takes place in Finsbury Park in northeast London. It is extremely popular, so book in advance.

☆ The Proms mid-Jul–early Sep
The Proms offers two months of outstanding classical concerts (www.bbc.co.uk/proms) at various prestigious venues, centred on the Royal Albert Hall.

☆ Lovebox mid-Jul
This two-day music extravaganza (www. loveboxfestival.com) in Gunnersbury Park,

☆ UEFA Euro 2020 Final 12 Jul
European football's most eagerly anticipated footballing event kicks off to vast crowds at Wembley Stadium (pictured below) , when two teams finally emerge from a pool of two dozen teams to square off for one of the beautiful game's most cherished prizes.

NINOTEE/SHUTTERSTOCK ©

West London, was created by dance duo Groove Armada. Its raison d'être is dance music, but there are plenty of other genres too, including indie, pop and hip-hop.

2020

August

School's out for summer, families are holidaying and the hugely popular annual Caribbean carnival dances into Notting Hill. The last weekend brings a bank holiday.

✈ Outdoor Swimming   Jun–Aug
London may not strike you as the place to go for an al fresco swim, but you can enjoy a dip in the Serpentine in Hyde Park (pictured above) or in the ponds in Hampstead Heath (water quality is tested daily).

☆ Summer Screen at Somerset House   early Aug
For a fortnight every summer, Somerset House turns its stunning courtyard into an open-air cinema (p65), screening an eclectic mix of film premieres, cult classics and popular requests.

🍷 Great British Beer Festival   Aug
Organised by CAMRA (Campaign for Real Ale), this boozy festival (www.gbbf.org.uk) cheerfully cracks open casks of ale from the UK and abroad at Olympia exhibition centre.

🎊 Notting Hill Carnival   29–31 Aug
Europe's biggest – and London's most vibrant – outdoor carnival (pictured below) is a celebration of Caribbean London, featuring music, dancing and costumes over the summer bank-holiday weekend.

Plan Your Trip
This Year in London

September

09

The end of summer and start of autumn is a lovely time to be in town, with comedy festivals and a chance to look at London properties normally shut to the public.

☆ Greenwich Comedy Festival   early Sep

This week-long laugh fest – London's largest comedy festival – brings big names and emerging acts to the National Maritime Museum.

🎪 The Mayor's Thames Festival   Sep

Celebrating the River Thames, this cosmo politan festival (www.totallythames.org) brings fairs, street theatre, music, food stalls, fireworks and river races, culminating in the superb Night Procession.

☉ Open House London   mid-Sep

For a weekend in mid-September the public is invited in to see over 800 heritage buildings throughout the capital that are normally off-limits (www.openhouselondon. org.uk; UCL at Here East pictured above).

☉ London Design Biennale   Sep

Some of the best, most eye-catching and exciting design works from over 40 countries are displayed at Somerset House (pictured below) on the Strand in the heart of London in this month-long festival (www.londondesign biennale.com).

10

October

The weather is getting colder, but London's parklands are splashed with gorgeous autumnal colours. Clocks go back to winter time the last weekend of the month.

🏃 Autumn Walks
Oct

London's parks look truly glorious on a sunny day when the trees have turned a riot of yellows and reds. Hyde Park and Greenwich Park are particularly beautiful at this time of year and offer great views of London's landmarks.

🏛 Affordable Art Fair
mid-Oct

For four days in March and October, Battersea Park turns into a giant art fair (www. affordableartfair.com; pictured above), where more than 100 galleries offer works of art from just £100. Plenty of talks and workshops, too.

☆ Dance Umbrella
mid-Oct

London's annual festival of contemporary dance (www.danceumbrella.co.uk) features two weeks of performances by British and international dance companies at venues across the city.

☆ London Film Festival
mid-Oct

The city's premier film event (www.bfi.org. uk/lff) attracts big overseas names and shows more than 100 British and international films before their cinema release. Masterclasses are given by world-famous directors.

Plan Your Trip
This Year in London

ALEXEY FEDORENKO/SHUTTERSTOCK ©

Oxford Street

November

London nights are getting longer. It's the last of the parks' autumn colours – enjoy them on a walk and relax by an open fire in a pub afterwards.

🎆 Guy Fawkes Night (Bonfire Night) 5 Nov

Bonfire Night commemorates Guy Fawkes' foiled attempt to blow up Parliament in 1605. Bonfires and fireworks light up the night on 5 November. Primrose Hill, Highbury Fields, Alexandra Palace, Clapham Common and Blackheath have some of the best firework displays.

🎆 Lord Mayor's Show mid-Nov

In accordance with the Magna Carta of 1215, the newly elected Lord Mayor of the City of London travels in a state coach from Mansion House to the Royal Courts of Justice to take an oath of allegiance to the Crown – nowadays with floats, bands and fireworks (www.lordmayorsshow.london).

☆ London Jazz Festival late Nov

Musicians from around the world swing into town for 10 days of jazz (www.efglondon jazzfestival.org.uk). World influences are well represented, as are more conventional styles.

🎆 Lighting of the Christmas Lights late Nov

A celebrity is called in to switch on all the festive lights that line Oxford (pictured above), Regent and Bond Sts, and a towering Norwegian spruce (an annual gift from Norway to Britain to commemorate cooperation during WWII) is set up in Trafalgar Sq.

2020

DAVE BENETT/GETTY IMAGES FOR HAMLEY'S ©

12

December

A festive mood reigns as Christmas approaches and shops are decorated. Days are increasingly shorter. Christmas Day is the quietest day of the year, with all shops and museums closed and the tube network shut.

🛍 Christmas Shopping   Dec

London has everything you could possibly want and more. Hamleys (pictured above), with its six storeys of toys, will mesmerise children. Harrods will wow you with its extravagant window display and over-the-top decorations (and prices!). The festive atmosphere should put a spring in your step.

⛸ Ice-Skating   Dec–Jan

Open-air ice rinks pop up across the city, including one in the exquisite courtyard of Somerset House (p65) and another one in the grounds of the Natural History Museum (p114).

🛍 Boxing Day   26 Dec

Boxing Day used to be the opening day of the winter sales, and one of the busiest

☆ New Year's Celebrations   31 Dec

On 31 December the famous countdown to Big Ben striking midnight is met with terrific fireworks (pictured below) from the London Eye and celebrated by massive crowds. There are parties in every pub and bar in town.

SAMOT/SHUTTERSTOCK ©

days of the year for shops. Pre-Christmas sales have somewhat dampened the rush but it remains a lively day.

Plan Your Trip
Hot Spots For...

GLITZ & GLAMOUR

⊙ **Buckingham Palace** Pomp, pageantry and a lot of gilded ceilings in the Queen's main residence. (p48)

☆ **Royal Opera House** Opera or ballet in the glittering surroundings of London's premier opera house. (p65)

☆ **Ronnie Scott's** Legendary jazz venue where all the big names have played. (p218)

🔒 **Harrods** Egyptian-themed elevator, stratospheric prices and opulent displays – it's London's most extravagant department store. (p181; pictured above)

🍷 **Dukes London** Drink where Ian Fleming of James Bond fame drank. (p207)

FOODIES

⊙ **Borough Market** Admire the foodscape and revel in the free samples. (p78; pictured below)

✗ **Chin Chin Labs** Liquid nitrogen ice-cream: sounds weird, but is more wonderful than you can imagine. (p161)

🔒 **Milroy's of Soho** For all your whisky needs, look no further. (p185)

✗ **Vanilla Black** Vegetarianism and veganism are here to stay; this is why. (p163)

🍷 **Greenwich Union** One of the best pubs to sample craft beers, from London and elsewhere. (p198)

NIGHT OWLS

⦿ **Tate Modern** Outstanding modern art gallery that's open until 10pm on Friday and Saturday. (p86)

🍷 **Fabric** One of the best clubs in town, open until the small hours. (p194)

✕ **Beigel Bake** Whatever the time of day or night, this bagel shop will see you right. (p75)

☆ **Comedy Store** The Friday and Saturday 11pm shows are as funny as the 7.30pm ones. (p218)

⦿ **National Portrait Gallery** Open until 9pm on Friday, with a bar, music and special events. (p57)

CULTURE VULTURES

⦿ **Victoria & Albert Museum** Fashion, sculpture, jewellery, photography – there isn't a decorative art the V&A doesn't cover. (p104; pictured above)

↻ **Guide London** Hire a Blue Badge guide, a know-it-all chaperone who'll tell you the stories about – as well as behind – the sights. (p224)

✕ **St John** At the forefront of the revival of British cuisine, it has brought back forgotten ingredients and traditions. (p154)

🍷 **Ye Olde Cheshire Cheese** One of the oldest and most atmospheric pubs in London. (p202)

BARGAIN HUNTERS

🛍 **Sunday Upmarket** Browse for that unique vintage piece. (p75)

⦿ **British Museum** Most museums of this calibre charge admission fees. Tours are free too. (p42)

🛍 **Hackney Walk** Large discount-fashion precinct for big brands. (p180; pictured above)

⦿ **Tate Modern** The views from level 10 of the Blavatnik Building are free – and just as good as any of the paying ones. (p86)

☆ **Shakespeare's Globe** Enjoy a world-class performance for just £5 with a standing ticket. (p216)

Plan Your Trip
Top Days in London

DAVID STEELE/SHUTTERSTOCK ©

The West End & the South Bank

Plunge into the heart of the West End for some of London's top sights. This itinerary also spans the River Thames to the South Bank, taking in Westminster Abbey, Buckingham Palace, Trafalgar Square, the Houses of Parliament and the London Eye.

❶ Westminster Abbey (p36)

Begin at Westminster Abbey to steep yourself in British history, dating back to 1066.

◐ Westminster Abbey to Buckingham Palace

🏃 Cross the road to Storey's Gate and head west along Birdcage Walk.

❷ Buckingham Palace (p48)

Peer through the gates, go on a tour of the interior (summer only) or catch the Changing of the Guard at 11am.

◐ Buckingham Palace to Cafe Murano

🏃 Stroll through St James's Park and across the Mall to St James's St.

❸ Lunch at Cafe Murano (p168)

In the heart of St James's, this busy restaurant cooks superb northern Italian fare.

◐ Cafe Murano to Trafalgar Square

🏃 Walk along Jermyn St and down Haymarket to Trafalgar Square.

Day
01

GIOVANNI G/SHUTTERSTOCK ©

➍ Trafalgar Square (p58)

Visit London's epicentre (all distances are measured from here), and explore the National Gallery (p57).

➲ Trafalgar Square to Houses of Parliament

🚶 Walk down Whitehall.

➎ Houses of Parliament (p52)

Dominating the east side of Parliament Sq is the Palace of Westminster, with one of London's ultimate sights, Elizabeth Tower (containing Big Ben).

➲ Houses of Parliament to London Eye

🚶 Cross Westminster Bridge.

➏ London Eye (p98)

Hop on a 'flight' on the London Eye. Pre-book tickets online or grab a fast-track ticket to shorten wait times.

➲ London Eye to the King's Arms

🚶 Walk down to the Imax roundabout in front of Waterloo Station; turn onto Exton St and continue until Roupell St.

➐ Drinks at King's Arms (p203

Like the streets around it, the King's Arms feels like it belongs to a different era.

From left: Changing of the Guard ceremony (p49); view from the London Eye (p98)

Plan Your Trip
Top Days in London

History, Views & a Spot of Shakespeare

Get set for more of London's top sights – once again on either side of the Thames. Visit the British Museum in Bloomsbury, climb the dome of St Paul's Cathedral, explore the Tower of London and soak up some Shakespeare.

Day

02

❶ British Museum (p42)

Begin with a visit to the British Museum and ensure you tick off the highlights, including the Rosetta Stone, the Egyptian mummies and the Parthenon Marbles.

➲ British Museum to St Paul's Cathedral

⊖ Take the Central Line from Holborn to St Paul's.

❷ St Paul's Cathedral (p90)

Don't miss climbing the dome for its astounding views of London, and save some time for the fascinating crypt. Break for lunch at Miyama (p162).

➲ St Paul's Cathedral to Tower of London

🚌 Hop on bus 15 from the cathedral to the Tower of London.

❸ Tower of London (p66)

The millennium of history contained within the Tower of London – including the Crown

Jewels, Traitors' Gate, the White Tower and its armour collection, and the all-important resident ravens – deserves at least a couple of hours to fully explore.

○ Tower of London to Tower Bridge

🚶 Walk along Tower Bridge Approach from the Tower of London to Tower Bridge.

❹ Tower Bridge (p84)

Cross the Thames via elegant Tower Bridge. Check the website for bridge lift times if you want to see it open and close.

○ Tower Bridge to Oblix at the Shard

🚶 Stroll west along the river to the Shard; the entrance is on St Thomas St.

❺ Drinks at Oblix (p202)

Round off the day with drinks, food, live music and fabulous views of London from the 32nd floor of the Shard, London's most spectacular skyscraper.

○ Oblix at the Shard to Shakespeare's Globe

🚶 Walk through Borough Market and then follow the Thames west to Shakespeare's Globe.

❻ A Play at Shakespeare's Globe (p216)

Watch one of Shakespeare's famous plays in a theatre as it would have been in Shakespeare's day: outdoors in summer months in the Globe (or by candlelight in the Playhouse).

From left: View from St Paul's Cathedral (p90); Performance at Shakespeare's Globe (p216)

ALEXEY BROSLAVETS/SHUTTERSTOCK ©

Plan Your Trip
Top Days in London

Kensington Museums, Knightsbridge Shopping & the West End

Passing through some of London's most attractive neighbourhoods, this route takes in a selection of the city's best museums and a worldfamous department store before delivering you to the bright lights of the West End.

Day
03

❶ Victoria & Albert Museum

Start your day in South Kensington. Cross off some of the Victoria & Albert's 146 galleries. Or opt for the huge Natural History Museum (p114) or the interactive Science Museum (p117) if you're of a more scientific bent.

➲ Victoria & Albert Museum to Kensington Gardens & Hyde Park

🚶 Walk north along Exhibition Rd, west along Kensington Rd and north along Broad Walk.

❷ Lunch at Kensington Palace Pavilion (P159)

Lunch on the tasty offerings at this restaurant overlooking the sunken garden of Kensington Palace. Afternoon tea is another superb option.

➲ Kensington Palace Pavilion to Kensington Gardens & Hyde Park

🚶 Kensington Palace Pavilion is on the west side of Kensington Gardens, itself alongside Hyde Park.

❸ Kensington Gardens (p102) & Hyde Park (p100)

Explore Kensington Gardens and Hyde Park. Make sure you take a look at the Albert Memorial (p103), take a peek inside Kensington Palace (p103) and stroll along the Serpentine.

◗ Kensington Gardens & Hyde Park to Harrods

🏃 Stroll through Hyde Park to Knightsbridge, on its southern edge.

❹ Harrods (p181)

A visit to Harrods is both fun and fascinating, even if you don't plan to buy anything. The food court is a great place for edible souvenirs.

◗ Harrods to Piccadilly Circus

🚇 Walk to Knightsbridge station, then take the Piccadilly Line three stops to Piccadilly Circus.

❺ Piccadilly Circus (p122)

Jump off the tube at this busy (former) roundabout to have a look at the famous

statue (Eros' brother) and enjoy a night out in Soho.

◗ Piccadilly Circus to Yauatcha

🏃 Walk up Shaftesbury Ave and turn left onto Rupert St, which becomes Berwick St, then left into Broadwick St.

❻ Dinner at Yauatcha (p169)

For the most sophisticated and exquisite dim sum, Yauatcha is unrivalled. The selection of tea is second to none. Bookings are essential.

◗ Yauatcha to Swift

🏃 Turn right on Broadwick St, then right on Wardour St, then left on Old Compton St to Swift.

❼ Drinks at Swift (p204)

Ease further into the evening with drinks at this sophisticated cocktail bar.

From left: Albert Memorial in Hyde Park (p100); Harrods (p181)

Top Days in London

JOHN BRAID/SHUTTERSTOCK ©

Greenwich to Shoreditch

You don't want to neglect sights further afield, and this itinerary makes a big dent in what's on offer. Lovely Greenwich has a whole raft of stately sights, while an evening in trendy Shoreditch is always fun.

Day

04

❶ Royal Observatory & Greenwich Park (p130)

Start the day in riverside Greenwich and make sure you visit Greenwich Park and the Royal Observatory. Stride over the Meridian and drink in the fabulous views.

◯ Greenwich Park & Royal Observatory to Goddards at Greenwich

🏃 Amble down the hill towards Greenwich, walk down King William Walk to Greenwich Market.

❷ Lunch at Goddards at Greenwich (p157)

This is the place to try the classic London dish of pie and mash (with or without eel). Go classic with mince beef or rogue with a chicken (or vegetarian) pie.

◯ Goddards to Cutty Sark

🏃 Cross Greenwich Market; the Cutty Sark towers over you.

MICHAEL PUCHE/SHUTTERSTOCK ©

❸ Cutty Sark (133)

Hop on board this splendidly restored great clipper, star of the tea trade in the late 19th century. The exhibits evoke life on board as well as the history of trade between Britain and the East.

➲ Cutty Sark to Old Spitalfields Market

🚋🚇 Take the DLR from Cutty Sark station to Bow Church and change for the Hammersmith & City line to Liverpool St station.

❹ Old Spitalfields Market (p76)

Browse the stalls (and shops) of Old Spital-fields Market. The best days are Thursday, Friday and Sunday. The surrounding streets, Brick Lane especially, are very lively and full of history.

➲ Old Spitalfields Market to Discount Suit Company

🏃 Head south down Crispin St and then Bell Ln until you hit Wentworth St.

❺ Discount Suit Company (p194)

Sample the edgy concoctions at this delightful speakeasy – in a former life, this was, you guessed it, a suit company for city workers.

➲ Discount Suit Company to Hawksmoor Spitalfields

🏃 Head back to Old Spitalfields Market, turn right onto Brushfield St, then left onto Commercial St.

❻ Steak at Hawksmoor Spitalfields (p156)

Indulge in the very best meat money can buy at this long-standing Shoreditch institution. There are plenty of fabulous wines to accompany your dinner. Bookings essential.

From left: Cutty Sark (p133); Old Spitalfields Market (p75)

Plan Your Trip

Need to Know

Daily Costs

Budget: Less than £85

○ Dorm bed: £12–30

○ Market-stall lunch or supermarket sandwich: £3.50–5

○ Many museums: free

○ Standby theatre tickets: £5–25

○ Santander Cycles daily rental fee: £2

Midrange: £85–200

○ Double room: £100–200

○ Two-course dinner with glass of wine: £35

○ Temporary exhibitions: £12–18

○ Theatre tickets: £15–60

Top end: More than £200

○ Four-star or boutique hotel room: more than £200

○ Three-course dinner in top restaurant with wine: £60–90

○ Black cab trip: £30

○ Top theatre tickets: £65

Advance Planning

Three months before Book weekend performances for top shows; make dinner reservations at renowned restaurants; snap up tickets for must-see temporary exhibitions; book accommodation.

One month before Check listings on entertainment sites such as *Time Out* (www.timeout.com/london) for fringe theatre, live music and festivals, and book tickets.

A few days before Check the weather online through the Met Office (www.metoffice.gov.uk).

Useful Websites

Lonely Planet (www.lonelyplanet.com/england/london) Destination information, hotel bookings, traveller forum and more.

Time Out London (www.timeout.com/london) Up-to-date and comprehensive entertainment listings distributed for free every Tuesday.

Londonist (www.londonist.com) About London and everything that happens in it.

Transport for London (www.tfl.gov.uk) Essential tool for staying mobile in the capital.

London Evening Standard (www.standard.co.uk) The capital's main newspaper, free at every tube station.

Met Office (www.metoffice.gov.uk) Provides weather forecasts for the UK and worldwide.

Arriving in London

Heathrow Airport Trains, the tube and buses to London (5am–midnight) cost £5.10–27. Night buses run later and 24-hour tube trains run Friday and Saturday. Taxis cost £48–90.

Currency

Pound sterling (£)

Language

English (and more than 300 others)

Visas

Not required for Australian, Canadian, New Zealand and US visitors, as well as several other nations, for stays of up to six months. Check requirements on www.gov.uk/check-uk-visa.

Money

ATMs are widespread. Major credit cards are accepted everywhere. The best place to change money is in post-office branches, which do not charge a commission.

Mobile Phones

Buy local SIM cards for European and Australian phones, or a pay-as-you-go phone. Set other phones to international roaming.

Time

GMT/UTC; during British Summer Time (BST; late March to late October), London is one hour ahead of GMT.

For more, see the **Survival Guide** (p257)

When to Go

Summer is peak season: days are long and festivals are plentiful, but expect crowds. Spring and autumn are cooler, but can be delightful. Winter is cold and often wet, with short days.

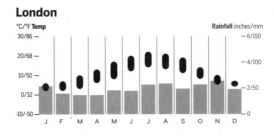

London

°C/°F **Temp**   Rainfall inches/mm

From 2020 express trains will run along the Elizabeth Line (Crossrail).

Gatwick Airport Trains to London (4.30am–1.35am) cost £10–20; hourly buses to London 24/7 from £8; taxis £100.

Stansted Airport Trains to London (5.30am–12.30am) cost £17; 24/7 buses to London from £10; taxis £130.

Luton Airport Trains to London (7am–10pm) from £14.70; buses 24/7 to London £11; taxis £110.

London City Airport DLR trains to central London (5.30am–12.15am Monday–Saturday, 7am–11.15pm Sunday) from £2.80; taxis £25–50.

St Pancras International Train Station In central London (for Eurostar train arrivals); connected by Underground lines to other parts of the city.

Getting Around

The cheapest way to get around London is with an Oyster Card or a UK contactless card (foreign cardholders should check for contactless charges first).

Tube (London Underground) The fastest and most efficient way of getting around town. Trains operate from around 5.30am to 12.30am and 24 hours on Friday and Saturday on five lines.

Train The DLR and Overground networks are ideal for zooming across more distant parts of the city. Trains run from a number of stations to more distant destinations in and around London.

Bus The London bus network is very extensive and efficient; while bus lanes avoid the worst of the traffic, buses can still be slow going.

Taxis Black cabs are ubiquitous, but not cheap. Available around the clock.

Bicycle Santander Cycles are great for shorter journeys around central London.

What to Take

o An umbrella

o Good walking shoes – the city is best explored on foot

o UK plug adaptor

o A few extra layers – it can be cool, even in summer

o A small day pack

What to Wear

o Fashion is big in London but eclectic so you're unlikely to stand out whatever you wear.

o Many top-end restaurants, bars and clubs will insist on smart attire, especially for shoes. Style is pretty relaxed elsewhere, although Londoners usually make an effort in the evenings.

o Regardless of the season always carry an umbrella or a jacket that can repel a shower or two.

Plan Your Trip
What's New

SVEN HANSCHE/SHUTTERSTOCK ©

Fourth Plinth Gets Philosophical

In 2020 Heather Phillipson takes over Trafalgar Square's fourth plinth (p60) with *THE END*. The sculpture features a giant scoop of cream, with a cherry and a bug on top, a metaphor for hubris and impending doom.

All Aboard Crossrail

The capital's most ambitious transport project (p237)in a generation is now fully operating, branching out from Reading and Heathrow in the West to Abbey Wood and Shenfield in the east, all via central London.

Spire London

London's skyline keeps evolving and this new skyscraper near Canary Wharf – the tallest residential building in Western Europe – is the latest addition to the capital's collection of eclectically named towers.

Eataly London

The international Italian food-hall brand which has taken the US, Japan and Brazil by storm is due to make its first foray into London in 2020 with a hall on Bishopsgate in the city. If you know your *orecchiette* from your *pici*, this is the place for you.

All about Raphael

To mark the 500th anniversary of Raphael's death, the V&A (p104) is launching a series of initiatives to enhance our understanding of the painter's famous 'cartoons', the designs of the tapestries made to hang in the Sistine Chapel in the Vatican.

Above: Crossrail Place on Canary Wharf, architect Foster and Partners

Plan Your Trip
For Free

Free Sights

It costs nothing to visit the Houses of Parliament (p52) and watch debates. Another institution of public life, the Changing of the Guard (p49), is free to watch. For one weekend in September, Open House London (p224) opens the doors to some 850 significant buildings for free.

Free Museums & Galleries

The permanent collections of all state-funded museums and galleries are open to the public free of charge. They include the Victoria & Albert Museum (p104), Tate Modern (p86), Tate Britain (p54), British Museum (p42), National Gallery (p57) and National Portrait Gallery (p57).

The Serpentine Galleries (p101) are also free.

Free Views

Why pay good money for a view when some of the finest in London are free? Head up to Level 10 of Blavatnik Building at Tate Modern (p88) or to the summit of Primrose Hill (p111) in Regent's Park.

Free Concerts

The beautiful St Martin-in-the-Fields (p61) church on Trafalgar Square hosts free concerts at 1pm on Monday, Tuesday and Friday.

Walking

Walking around town is possibly the best way to get a sense of the city and its history. The West End is relatively compact and a great place to walk; otherwise, follow the Thames along the South Bank for sightseeing combined with iconic London views.

Cycling

Bike-share your way around with W (p268) – the access fee is £2 for 24 hours; bike hire is then free for the first 30 minutes.

Above: View from Switch House at the Tate Modern (p86)

Plan Your Trip
Family Travel

GORDON BELL/SHUTTERSTOCK ©

Need to Know

○ **Babysitters** Find a babysitter or nanny at Greatcare (www.greatcare.co.uk).

○ **Cots** Available in most hotels, but always request them in advance.

○ **Public transport** Under-16s travel free on buses, under-11s travel free on the tube, and under-fives ride free on trains.

Museums

London's museums are particularly child-friendly. You'll find storytelling at the National Gallery (p57) for children aged three years and over, arts-and-crafts workshops at the Victoria & Albert Museum (p104), various workshops at the Transport Museum (p64), plenty of artsy activities at the Tate Modern (p86) and Tate Britain (p54), and various drop-in sessions during exhibitions at Somerset House (p65). And what's more, they're all free (check websites for details).

Other excellent activities for children include sleepovers at the British Museum (p42), Science Museum (p117) and Natural History Museum (p114), though you'll need to book months ahead. The last two are definitive children's museums, with interactive displays and play areas.

Other Attractions

Kids love the London Zoo (p110), London Eye (p98) and London Dungeon (p99). In wintertime, ice rinks glitter at the Natural History Museum (p114) and Somerset House (p65). There's also a seasonal rink further afield at Hampton Court Palace (p12).

In addition, there are exciting climbs up the dome of St Paul's Cathedral (p90) or the Monument (p72). You can also pass time watching the performers in Trafalgar Square (p58), Covent Garden Piazza (p62) or along the South Bank. Many arts and cultural festivals aimed at adults also cater for children. London's parks burst with possibilities: open grass, playgrounds,

ANTON_IVANOV/SHUTTERSTOCK ©

wildlife, trees and, in the warmer weather, ice-cream trucks.

Most attractions offer family tickets and discounted entry for kids under 15 or 16 years (children under five usually go free).

Eating & Drinking

Most of London's restaurants and cafes are child-friendly and offer baby-changing facilities and high chairs. Note that high-end restaurants and small, quiet cafes may be less welcoming, particularly if you have toddlers or small babies.

The one place that isn't traditionally very welcoming for those with children is the pub. By law, minors aren't allowed into the main bar (though walking through is fine), but many pubs have areas where children are welcome, usually a garden or outdoor space. Things are more relaxed during the day on Sunday.

★ Best Sights for Children

Natural History Museum (p114)

Changing of the Guard (p49)

Cutty Sark (p133)

Science Museum (p117)

Unicorn Theatre (p217)

Getting Around

When it comes to public transport, buses are better for children than the tube, which is often very crowded and hot in summer. As well as being big, red and iconic, buses in London are usually the famous double-decker ones; kids love to sit on the top deck and get great views of the city. Another excellent way to get around is simply to walk.

Hopping on a boat is another way to put fun (and sightseeing!) into getting from A to B.

From left: Seasonal ice rink at the Natural History Museum (p114); Science Museum (p117)

TOP
EXPERIENCES

The very best to see and do

Westminster Abbey

Westminster Abbey is such an important commemoration site that it's hard to overstate its symbolic value or imagine its equivalent anywhere else in the world. With a couple of exceptions, every English sovereign has been crowned here since William the Conqueror in 1066, and most of the monarchs from Henry III (died 1272) to George II (died 1760) are buried here.

Great For...

Westminster Ⓤ

Parliament Sq

St James's Park Ⓤ

Victoria St

Abington St

River Thames

🕀 **Westminster Abbey**

ⓘ Need to Know

Map p274; ☏ 020-7222 5152; www.westminster-abbey.org; 20 Dean's Yard, SW1; adult/child £22/9; ◷ 9.30am-3.30pm Mon, Tue, Thu & Fri, to 6pm Wed, to 3pm Sat May-Aug, to 1pm Sat Sep-Apr; Ⓤ Westminster

★ **Top Tip**

The abbey gets incredibly busy, even at opening, so come armed with patience.

There is an extraordinary amount to see at the Abbey. The interior is chock-a-block with ornate chapels, elaborate tombs of monarchs and grandiose monuments to sundry luminaries throughout the ages. First and foremost, however, it is a sacred place of worship.

A Regal History

Though a mixture of architectural styles, the Abbey is considered the finest example of Early English Gothic (1190–1300). The original church was built in the 11th century by King (later St) Edward the Confessor, who is buried in the chapel behind the sanctuary and main altar. Henry III (r 1216–72) began work on the new building, but didn't complete it; the French Gothic nave was finished by Richard II in 1388. Henry VII's huge and magnificent Lady Chapel was added in 1519.

The Abbey was initially a monastery for Benedictine monks, and many of the building's features attest to this collegial past (the octagonal Chapter House, the Quire and four cloisters). In 1536 Henry VIII separated the Church of England from the Roman Catholic Church and dissolved the monastery. The king became head of the Church of England and the Abbey acquired its 'royal peculiar' status, meaning it is administered directly by the Crown and exempt from any ecclesiastical jurisdiction.

North Transept, Sanctuary & Quire

Entrance to the Abbey is via the Great North Door. The North Transept is often referred to as Statesmen's Aisle: politicians

The Queen's Window

and eminent public figures are commemorated by large marble statues and imposing marble plaques. Above the information desk near the entrance is the **Queen's Window**, a stained-glass window designed by eminent British artist David Hockney on his iPad. It was unveiled in September 2018 and commemorates Queen Elizabeth II's reign as the longest-ruling monarch.

At the heart of the Abbey is the beautifully tiled sanctuary (or sacrarium), a stage for coronations, royal weddings and funerals. George Gilbert Scott designed the ornate **high altar** in 1873. In front of the altar is the

REX/SHUTTERSTOCK ©

Cosmati marble pavement dating back to 1268. It has intricate designs of small pieces of marble inlaid into plain marble, which predicts the end of the world in AD 19,693! At the entrance to the lovely **Chapel of St John the Baptist** is a sublime Virgin and Child bathed in candlelight.

The Quire, a magnificent structure of gold, blue and red Victorian Gothic by Edward Blore, dates back to the mid-19th century. It sits where the original choir for the monks' worship would have been, but bears no resemblance to the original. Nowadays, the Quire is still used for singing, but its regular occupants are the Westminster Choir – 30 boys and 12 'lay vicars' (men) who sing the daily services.

Chapels & Chairs

The sanctuary is surrounded by chapels. **Henry VII's Lady Chapel**, in the easternmost part of the Abbey, is the most spectacular, with its fan vaulting on the ceiling, colourful banners of the Order of the Bath and dramatic oak stalls. Behind the chapel's altar is the elaborate sarcophagus of Henry VII and his queen, Elizabeth of York.

Beyond the chapel's altar is the **Royal Air Force Chapel**, with a stained-glass window commemorating the force's finest hour, the Battle of Britain (1940), and the 1500 RAF pilots who died. A stone plaque on the floor marks the spot where Oliver Cromwell's body lay for two years (1658) until the Restoration, when it was disinterred, hanged and beheaded. Two bodies, believed to be those of the child princes allegedly murdered in the Tower of London in 1483, were buried here almost two centuries later in 1674.

There are two small chapels either side of Lady Chapel with the tombs of famous monarchs: on the left (north) is where **Elizabeth I** and her half-sister **Mary I** (aka Bloody Mary) rest. On the right (south) is the tomb of **Mary Queen of Scots**, beheaded on the orders of her cousin Elizabeth.

The vestibule of the Lady Chapel is the usual place for the rather ordinary-looking **Coronation Chair**, upon which every monarch since the early 14th century has been crowned.

Shrine of St Edward the Confessor

The most sacred spot in the Abbey lies behind the high altar; access is generally restricted to protect the 13th-century flooring. St Edward was the founder of the Abbey and the original building was consecrated a few weeks before his death. His tomb was slightly altered after the original was destroyed during the Reformation, but still contains Edward's remains – the only complete saint's body in Britain. Ninety-minute **verger-led tours** of the Abbey include a visit to the shrine.

Outer Buildings & Gardens

The oldest part of the cloister is the East Cloister (or East Walk), dating to the 13th century. Off the cloister are three museums. The octagonal **Chapter House** has one of Europe's best-preserved medieval tile floors and retains traces of religious murals on the walls. It was used as a meeting place by the House of Commons in the second half of the 14th century. To the right of the entrance to Chapter House is what is claimed to be the oldest door in Britain – it's been there for 950 years.

The adjacent **Pyx Chamber** is one of the few remaining relics of the original Abbey and holds the Abbey's treasures and liturgical objects. It contains the pyx, a chest with standard gold and silver pieces for testing coinage weights in a ceremony called the Trial of the Pyx.

To reach the 900-year-old **College Garden** (Map p274; ☏020-7222 5152; www. westminster-abbey.org; off Great College St, SW1; ☾10am-4pm Tue-Thu; Ⓤ Westminster) **FREE**, enter Dean's Yard and the Little Cloisters off Great College St.

South Transept & Nave

The south transept contains **Poets' Corner**, where many of England's finest writers are buried and/or commemorated by monuments or memorials.

In the nave's north aisle is **Scientists' Corner**, where you will find the tombs of **Isaac Newton** and **Prof Stephen Hawking**. Just ahead of it is the north aisle of the Quire, known as **Musicians' Aisle**, where baroque composers Henry Purcell and John Blow are buried, as well as more modern music-makers such as Benjamin Britten and Edward Elgar.

Facade of Westminster Abbey

The two towers above the west door are the ones through which you exit. These were designed by Nicholas Hawksmoor and completed in 1745. Just above the door, perched in 15th-century niches, are the additions to the Abbey unveiled in 1998: 10 stone statues of international 20th-century martyrs who died for their Christian faith. These include American pacifist Dr Martin Luther King, the Polish priest St Maximilian Kolbe, who was murdered by the Nazis at Auschwitz, and Wang Zhiming, publicly executed during the Chinese Cultural Revolution.

Queen's Diamond Jubilee Galleries

Located in the medieval triforium, the arched gallery above the nave, these new galleries include exhibits such as the death masks of generations of royalty, armour and stained glass. Highlights are the graffiti-inscribed Mary Chair (used for the coronation of Mary II) and the Westminster Retable, England's oldest altarpiece, from the 13th century.

☑ Don't Miss

Triforium exhibits include wax effigies representing Charles II and William III (who is on a stool to make him as tall as his wife, Mary II).

★ Top Tip

The Choir sings the daily services and evensong, which are free to attend, at 5pm on weekdays and 3pm on weekends.

MILLIONSTOCK/SHUTTERSTOCK ©

Egyptian collection in the British Museum

British Museum

Britain's most visited attraction – founded in 1753 when royal physician Hans Sloane sold his 'cabinet of curiosities' – is an exhaustive and exhilarating stampede through 7000 years of human civilisation.

Great For...

☑ **Don't Miss**

The Rosetta Stone, the Mummy of Katebet and the marble Parthenon Sculptures.

The British Museum offers a stupendous selection of tours, many of them free. There are 14 free 30-minute eye-opener tours of individual galleries each day. The museum also has free 45-minute lunchtime gallery talks (1.15pm Tuesday, Wednesday, Friday and Saturday), an Around the World in 90 Minutes tour (£14; 11.30am and 2pm Friday, Saturday and Sunday) and free 20-minute spotlight tours on Friday evenings. Audio and family guides (adult/child £7/6) in 10 languages are available from the desk in the Great Court.

Great Court

Covered with a spectacular glass-and-steel roof designed by Norman Foster in 2000, the Great Court is the largest covered public square in Europe. In its centre is the world-famous **Reading Room**, formerly the

The Great Court

British
Museum

Holborn

Tottenham
Court Rd

New Oxford St

PHILIP BIRD LRPS ©FAGE/SHUTTERSTOCK ®

❶ Need to Know

Map p274; 📞020-7323 8000; www.british
museum.org; Great Russell St, WC1; ⏱10am-
5.30pm Sat-Thu, to 8.30pm Fri; Ⓤ Tottenham
Court Rd or Russell Sq FREE

✕ Take a Break

Nearby, Queen's Larder (p206) is one of
London's most atmospheric pubs.

★ Top Tip

The museum is huge, so pick your inter-
ests and consider the tours.

British Library, which has been frequented
by all the big brains of history, from Mahat-
mà Gandhi to Karl Marx.

Ancient Egypt, Middle East & Greece

The star of the show here is the Ancient
Egypt collection. It comprises sculptures,
fine jewellery, papyrus texts, coffins and
mummies, including the beautiful and
intriguing **Mummy of Katebet** (room 63).
The most prized item in the collection (and
the most popular postcard in the shop) is
the **Rosetta Stone** (room 4), the key to
deciphering Egyptian hieroglyphics. In the
same gallery is the enormous bust of the
pharaoh **Ramesses the Great** (room 4).

Assyrian treasures from ancient Mesopotamia include the 16-tonne **Winged Bulls
from Khorsabad** (room 10), the heaviest

object in the museum. Behind it are the
exquisite **Lion Hunt Reliefs from Nineveh**
(room 10) from the 7th century BC, which
influenced Greek sculpture. Such antiquities
are all the more significant after the Islamic
State's bulldozing of Nimrud in 2015.

A major highlight of the museum is the
Parthenon sculptures (room 18). The marble frieze is thought to be the Great Pana-
thenaea, a blow-out version of a festival in
honour of Athena held every four years.

Roman & Medieval Britain

Upstairs are finds from Britain and the rest
of Europe (rooms 40 to 51). Many items
go back to Roman times, when the empire
spread across much of the continent, such
as the **Mildenhall Treasure** (room 49), a
collection of pieces of 4th-century Roman
silverware from Suffolk with both pagan
and early-Christian motifs.

Lindow Man (room 50) is the well-
preserved remains of a 1st-century man
(comically dubbed Pete Marsh) discovered in a bog near Manchester in northern
England in 1984. Equally fascinating are

artefacts from the **Sutton Hoo Ship-Burial** (room 41), an elaborate Anglo-Saxon burial site from Suffolk dating back to the 7th century.

Perennial favourites are the lovely **Lewis Chessmen** (room 40), 12th-century game pieces carved from walrus tusk and whale teeth that were found on a remote Scottish island in the early 19th century. They served as models for the game of Wizard Chess in the first Harry Potter film.

Enlightenment Galleries

Formerly known as the King's Library, this stunning neoclassical space (room 1) was built between 1823 and 1827 and was the first part of the new museum building as it is seen today. The collection traces how disciplines such as biology, archaeology, linguistics and geography emerged during the Enlightenment of the 18th century.

What's Nearby?

Sir John Soane's Museum Museum
(Map p280; ☑020-7405 2107; www.soane.org; 13 Lincoln's Inn Fields, WC2; ⊙10am-5pm Wed-Sun; Ⓤ Holborn) **FREE** This little museum is one of the most atmospheric and fascinating in London. The building is the beautiful, bewitching home of architect John Soane (1753–1837), which he left brimming with surprising personal effects and curiosities, and the museum represents his exquisite and eccentric taste.

Soane, a country bricklayer's son, is most famous for designing the Bank of England.

The heritage-listed house is largely as it was when Soane died and is itself a main part of the attraction. It has a

The Dome room of Sir John Soane's Museum

canopy dome that brings light right down to the crypt, a colonnade filled with statuary and a picture gallery where paintings are stowed behind each other on folding wooden panes. This is where Soane's choicest artwork is displayed, including *Riva degli Schiavoni, looking West* by Canaletto, architectural drawings by Christopher Wren and Robert Adam, and the original *Rake's Progress*, William Hogarth's set of satirical cartoons of late-18th-century London lowlife. Among Soane's more unusual acquisitions are an Egyptian hieroglyphic sarcophagus, a mock-up of a monk's cell and slaves' chains.

Charles Dickens Museum   Museum

(Map p284; ☏020-7405 2127; www.dickens museum.com; 48-49 Doughty St, WC1; adult/child £9.50/4.50; ◷10am-5pm Tue-Sun; Ⓤ Russell Sq or Chancery Lane) The prolific writer Charles Dickens lived with his growing family in this handsome four-storey Georgian terraced house for a mere 2½ years (1837–39), but this is where his work really flourished, as he completed *The Pickwick Papers*, *Nicholas Nickleby* and *Oliver Twist* here. Each of the dozen rooms, some restored to their original condition, contains various memorabilia, including the study where you'll find the desk at which Dickens wrote *Great Expectations*.

All Saints Margaret Street   Church

(Map p274; ☏020-7636 1788; www.allsaints margaretstreet.org.uk; 7 Margaret St, W1; ◷7am-7pm Sun-Fri, from 11am Sat; Ⓤ Oxford Circus) In 1859, architect William Butterfield completed one of the country's most supreme examples of High Victorian Gothic architecture with extraordinary tiling and sumptuous stained glass. All Saints was selected by the head of English Heritage in 2014 as one of the top 10 buildings in the UK that have changed the face of the nation, a list that included Westminster Abbey and Christ Church in Oxford.

> ★ **Top Tip**
>
> Check out the outstanding *A History of the World in 100 Objects* podcast, which retraces two million years of history through 100 objects from the museum's collections.

LEON NEAL/GETTYIMAGES ©

> ★ **Top Tip**
>
> On the evening of the first Tuesday of each month, Sir John Soane's Museum is lit by candles. It's very popular so arrive early to avoid the long queue.

The British Museum

A HALF-DAY TOUR

The British Museum, with almost eight million items in its permanent collection, is so vast and comprehensive that it can be daunting for the first-time visitor. To avoid a frustrating trip – and getting lost on the way to the Egyptian mummies – set out on this half-day exploration, which takes in some of the museum's most important sights. If you want to see and learn more, join a tour or grab an audio guide (£7).

A good starting point is the ❶ **Rosetta Stone**, the key that cracked the code to ancient Egypt's writing system. Nearby treasures from Assyria – an ancient civilisation centred in Mesopotamia between the Tigris and Euphrates Rivers – including the colossal ❷ **Winged Bulls from Khorsabad**, give way to the ❸ **Parthenon Sculptures**, highpoints of classical Greek art that continue to influence us today. Be sure to see both the sculptures and the

Winged Bulls from Khorsabad
This awesome pair of alabaster winged bulls with human heads once guarded the entrance to the palace of Assyrian King Sargon II at Khorsabad in Mesopotamia, a cradle of civilisation in present-day Iraq.

Parthenon Sculptures
The Parthenon, a white marble temple dedicated to Athena, was part of a fortified citadel on the Acropolis in Athens. There are dozens of sculptures and friezes with models and interactive displays explaining how they all once fitted together.

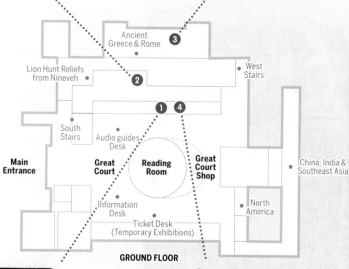

GROUND FLOOR

Ancient Greece & Rome ❸

Lion Hunt Reliefs from Nineveh ❷ West Stairs

South Stairs Audio guides Desk ❶ ❹

Main Entrance Great Court Reading Room Great Court Shop China, India & Southeast Asia

Information Desk North America

Ticket Desk (Temporary Exhibitions)

Bust of Pharaoh Ramesses II
The most impressive sculpture in the Egyptian galleries, this 725kg bust portrays Ramesses the Great, scourge of the Israelites in the Book of Exodus, as great benefactor.

Rosetta Stone
Written in hieroglyphic, demotic (cursive ancient Egyptian script used for everyday) and Greek, the 762kg stone contains a decree exempting priests from tax on the first anniversary of young Ptolemy V's coronation.

monumental frieze celebrating the birth of Athena. En route to the West Stairs is a huge **④ Bust of Pharaoh Ramesses II**, just a hint of the large collection of **⑤ Egyptian mummies** upstairs. (The earliest, affectionately called Ginger because of wispy reddish hair, was preserved simply by hot sand.) The Romans introduce visitors to the early Britain galleries via the rich **⑥ Mildenhall Treasure**. The Anglo-Saxon **⑦ Sutton Hoo Ship Burial** and the medieval **⑧ Lewis Chessmen** follow.

EATING OPTIONS

Court Cafe At the northern end of the Great Court; takeaway counters with salads and sandwiches; communal tables.

Gallery Cafe Out of the way off Room 12; quieter; offers freshly baked pizzas.

Great Court Restaurant Upstairs overlooking the former Reading Room; sit-down meals.

Lewis Chessmen
The much-loved 78 chess pieces portray faceless pawns, worried-looking queens, bishops with their mitres turned sideways and rooks (or castles) as 'warders', gnawing away at their shields.

Sutton Hoo Ship Burial
This unique grave of an important (but unidentified) Anglo-Saxon royal has yielded drinking horns, gold buckles and a stunning helmet with face mask.

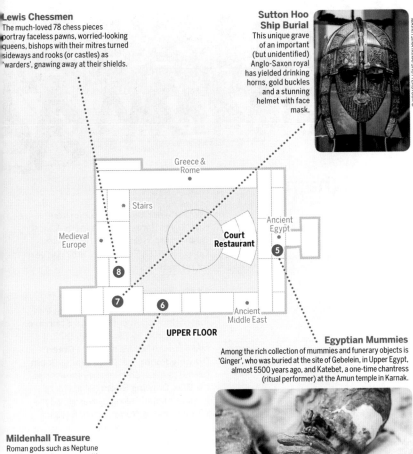

MAVRITSINA IRINA/SHUTTERSTOCK ©

Greece & Rome

Stairs

Ancient Egypt

Medieval Europe

Court Restaurant

⑤

⑧

⑦   ⑥

Ancient Middle East

UPPER FLOOR

Egyptian Mummies
Among the rich collection of mummies and funerary objects is 'Ginger', who was buried at the site of Gebelein, in Upper Egypt, almost 5500 years ago, and Katebet, a one-time chantress (ritual performer) at the Amun temple in Karnak.

ILEANA_BT / SHUTTERSTOCK ©

Mildenhall Treasure
Roman gods such as Neptune and Bacchus share space with early Christian symbols like the *chi-rho* (short for 'Christ') on the find's almost three dozen silver bowls, plates and spoons.

Buckingham Palace

The palace has been the Royal Family's London lodgings since 1837, when Queen Victoria moved in from Kensington Palace as St James's Palace was deemed too old-fashioned.

Great For...

☑ Don't Miss

Peering through the gates, a tour of the interior (in summer) or the Changing of the Guard.

The State Rooms are only open from mid-July to September, when Her Majesty is holidaying in Scotland. The Queen's Gallery and the Royal Mews are open year-round however.

State Rooms

The tour starts in the **Grand Hall** at the foot of the monumental **Grand Staircase**, commissioned by George IV in 1828. It takes in John Nash's Italianate **Green Drawing Room**, the **State Dining Room** (all red damask and Regency furnishings), the **Blue Drawing Room** (which has a gorgeous fluted ceiling by Nash) and the **White Drawing Room**, where foreign ambassadors are received.

The **Ballroom**, where official receptions and state banquets are held, was built between 1853 and 1855 and opened with

Changing of the Guard at Buckingham Palace

🛈 Need to Know

Map p274; 📞0303 123 7300; www.rct.uk/
visit/the-state-rooms-buckingham-palace;
Buckingham Palace Rd, SW1; adult/child/
under 5yr £25/14/free, incl Royal Mews &
Queen's Gallery £45/24.50/free; ⏱9.30am–
7pm mid-Jul–Aug, to 6pm Sep; Ⓤ Green Park
or St James's Park

✕ Take a Break

Enjoy delicious Italian fare at Cafe
Murano (p168).

★ Top Tip

Come early for front-row views of the
Changing of the Guard.

Changing of the Guard

Weather permitting, the old guard (Foot
Guards of the Household Regiment) comes
off duty to be replaced by the new guard on
the forecourt of Buckingham Palace with a
display of full-on **pageantry** (Map p274; www.
royal.uk/changing-guard; Buckingham Palace,
Buckingham Palace Rd, SW1; ⏱11am Sun, Mon,
Wed, Fri Aug–May, 11am daily Jun & Jul; Ⓤ St
James's Park or Green Park) **FREE**.

Crowds come to watch the carefully
choreographed marching and shouting of
the guards in their bright-red uniforms and
bearskin hats. It lasts about 45 minutes and
is very popular, so arrive early if you want to
get a good spot.

Queen's Gallery

Since the reign of Charles I, the Royal
Family has amassed a priceless collection of
paintings, sculpture, ceramics, furniture and
jewellery. The splendid **Queen's Gallery** (Map

a ball a year later to celebrate the end of
the Crimean War. The **Throne Room** is
rather anticlimactic, with his-and-hers pink
chairs initialled 'ER' and 'P', sitting under a
curtained theatre arch.

Picture Gallery & Garden

The most interesting part of the tour is
the 47m-long Picture Gallery, featuring
splendid works by such artists as Van Dyck,
Rembrandt, Canaletto, Poussin, Claude
Lorrain, Rubens, Canova and Vermeer.

Wandering the 18 hectares of gardens
is another highlight – as well as admiring
some of the 350 or so species of flowers and
plants and listening to the many birds, you'll
get beautiful views of the palace and a peek
of its famous lake.

p274; www.rct.uk/visit/the-queens-gallery-buckingham-palace; South Wing, Buckingham Palace, Buckingham Gate, SW1; adult/child £12/6, incl Royal Mews £20.70/11.20; ⊙10am-5.30pm, from 9.30am mid-Jul–Sep; Ⓤ St James's Park or Green Park) showcases some of the palace's treasures on a rotating basis.

The gallery was originally designed as a conservatory by John Nash. It was converted into a chapel for Queen Victoria in 1843, destroyed in a 1940 air raid and reopened as a gallery in 1962. A £20-million renovation for Elizabeth II's Golden Jubilee in 2002 added three times as much display space.

Royal Mews

Southwest of the palace, the **Royal Mews** (Map p274; www.rct.uk/visit/royalmews; Buckingham Palace Rd, SW1; adult/child £12/6.80, with Queen's Gallery £20.70/11.20; ⊙10am-5pm Apr-Oct, to 4pm Mon-Sat Feb, Mar & Nov; Ⓤ Victoria) started life as a falconry, but is now a working stable looking after the royals' three-dozen immaculately groomed horses, along with the opulent vehicles – motorised and horse-driven – the monarch uses for transport. The Queen is well known for her passion for horses; she names every horse that resides at the mews.

Nash's 1820 stables are stunning. Highlights of the collection include the enormous and opulent Gold State Coach of 1762, which has been used for every coronation since that of George III; the 1911 Glass Coach used for royal weddings and the Diamond Jubilee in 2012; Queen Alexandra's State Coach (1893), used to transport the Imperial State Crown to the official opening of Parliament; and a Rolls-Royce Phantom VI from the royal fleet.

The Gold State Coach

What's Nearby?

St James's Park   Park

(Map p274; www.royalparks.org.uk/parks/st-jamess-park; The Mall, SW1; ☺5am-midnight; [U]St James's Park or Green Park) At 23 hectares, St James's is the second-smallest of the eight royal parks after **Green Park** (Map p274; www.royalparks.org.uk/parks/green-park; ☺5am-midnight; [U]Green Park). But what it lacks in size it makes up for in grooming, as it is the most manicured green space in London. It has brilliant views of the London Eye, Westminster, St James's Palace, Carlton House Terrace and Horse Guards Parade; the picture-perfect sight of Buckingham Palace

---

★ **Did You Know?**
The State Rooms represent a mere 19 of the palace's 775 rooms.

DAVE GOODMAN/SHUTTERSTOCK ©

---

from the **Blue Bridge** spanning the central lake is the best you'll find.

Royal Academy of Arts   Gallery

(Map p274; ☎020-7300 8000; www.royalacademy.org.uk; Burlington House, Piccadilly, W1; ☺10am-6pm Sat-Thu, to 10pm Fri; [U]Green Park) **FREE** Britain's oldest society devoted to fine arts was founded in 1768 and moved here to Burlington House a century later. For its 250th birthday in 2018, the RA gave itself a £56-million makeover, opening up 70% more public space. It also made it free to visit its historic collection, which includes drawings, paintings, architectural designs, photographs and sculptures by past and present Royal Academicians, such as Joshua Reynolds, John Constable, Thomas Gainsborough, JMW Turner, David Hockney and Norman Foster.

The famous **Summer Exhibition** (www.royalacademy.org.uk; Burlington House, Piccadilly, W1; adult/child £16/free; ☺10am-6pm mid-Jun–mid-Aug; [U]Green Park), which has showcased contemporary art for sale by unknown and established artists since 1769, is the RA's biggest annual event.

Horse Guards Parade   Historic Site

(Map p274; off Whitehall, SW1; [U]Westminster or Charing Cross) In a more accessible version of Buckingham Palace's Changing of the Guard (p49), the mounted troops of the Household Cavalry change guard here daily, at the official vehicular entrance to the royal palaces. A slightly less pomp-filled version takes place at 4pm when the unmounted guards are changed. On the Queen's official birthday in June, the Trooping of the Colour is staged here.

★ **Did You Know?**
At the centre of Royal Family life is the Music Room, where four royal babies – the Prince of Wales (Prince Charles), Princess Royal (Princess Anne), Duke of York (Prince Andrew) and Duke of Cambridge (Prince William) – have been christened with water from the River Jordan.

Houses of Parliament

PETR KOVALENKOV/SHUTTERSTOCK ©

Houses of Parliament

Both the House of Commons and the House of Lords sit in the sumptuous Palace of Westminster, a neo-Gothic confection dating from the mid-19th century.

Great For...

☑ Don't Miss

Westminster Hall's hammer-beam roof and the Palace's Gothic Revival interior.

Towers

The most famous feature of the Houses of Parliament is the Clock Tower, officially named Elizabeth Tower to mark the Queen's Diamond Jubilee in 2012, but commonly known as **Big Ben** (Map p274; www.parliament.uk/visiting/visiting-and-tours/tours-of-parliament/bigben; Bridge St; Ⓤ Westminster). Ben is actually the bell hanging inside and is named after Benjamin Hall, the over-6ft-tall commissioner of works when the tower was completed in 1858. Ben rang in the New Year from 1924; however, since August 2017 the bell ceased ringing until 2021 while renovations are underway.

At the base of the taller **Victoria Tower** at the southern end is the **Sovereign's Entrance**, which is used by the Queen.

Big Ben

SARA LYNCH/EYEEM/GETTY ©

ⓘ Need to Know

Map p274; ☎tours 020-7219 4114; www.parliament.uk; Parliament Sq, SW1; guided tour adult/child/under 5yr £28/12/free, audio-guide tour £20.50/8.50/free; Ⓤ Westminster

✕ Take a Break

If you're planning to cross to the South Bank, consider having lunch in the elegant Skylon (p165) in the Royal Festival Hall.

★ Top Tip

There is airport-style security to enter the Houses of Parliament.

Westminster Hall

One of the most stunning elements of the Palace of Westminster, seat of the English monarchy from the 11th to the early 16th centuries, is Westminster Hall. Originally built in 1099, it is the oldest surviving part of the complex; the awesome hammer-beam roof was added around 1400. It has been described as 'the greatest surviving achievement of medieval English carpentry'. The only other part of the original palace to survive a devastating 1834 fire is the **Jewel Tower** (Map p274; ☎020-7222 2219; www.english-heritage.org.uk/visit/places/jewel-tower; Abingdon St, SW1; adult/child £5.40/3.30; ⊙10am-6pm daily Apr-Sep, to 5pm daily Oct, to 4pm Sat & Sun Nov-Mar; Ⓤ Westminster), built in 1365 and used to store the monarch's valuables.

Westminster Hall was used for coronation banquets in medieval times, and also served as a courthouse until the 19th century. The trials of William Wallace (1305), Thomas More (1535), Guy Fawkes (1606) and Charles I (1649) all took place here. In the 20th century, monarchs and Winston Churchill lay in state here after their deaths.

House of Commons

The House of Commons is where Members of Parliament (MPs) meet to propose and discuss new legislation and to grill the prime minister and other ministers.

The layout of the Commons Chamber is based on St Stephen's Chapel in the original Palace of Westminster. The chamber, designed by Giles Gilbert Scott, replaced the one destroyed by a 1941 bomb.

Although the Commons is a national assembly of 650 MPs, the chamber has seating for only 437. Government members sit to the right of the Speaker and Opposition members to the left.

House of Lords

The House of Lords is visited via the amusingly named Strangers' Gallery. The intricate 'Tudor Gothic' interior led its architect, Augustus Pugin (1812–52), to an early death from overwork and nervous strain.

Most of the 793 members of the House of Lords are life peers (appointed for their lifetime by the monarch); there is also a small number – 90 at the time of writing – of hereditary peers and a group of 'crossbench' members (numbering 186, not affiliated to the main political parties), and 26 bishops.

Tours

On Saturdays year-round and on most weekdays during Parliamentary recesses, including Easter, summer and Christmas, visitors can join a 90-minute guided tour, conducted by qualified Blue Badge Tourist Guides in seven languages, of both chambers, Westminster Hall and other historic buildings. A self-guided audio tour is also available.

What's Nearby?

Tate Britain   Gallery

(☏020-7887 8888; www.tate.org.uk/visit/tate-britain; Millbank, SW1; ⊘10am-6pm; ⓤPimlico) **FREE** On the site of the former Millbank Penitentiary, the older and more venerable of the two Tate siblings opened in 1892 and celebrates British art from 1500 to the present, including pieces from William Blake, William Hogarth, Thomas Gainsborough and John Constable, as well as vibrant modern and contemporary

No 10 Downing Street

pieces from Lucian Freud, Barbara Hepworth, Francis Bacon and Henry Moore. The stars of the show are, undoubtedly, the light-infused visions of JMW Turner in the Clore Gallery.

The gallery hosts the prestigious and often controversial Turner Prize from October to early January every year (adult/child £13/free), plus a programme of ticketed exhibitions that changes every few months; consult the website for what's on.

Free 45-minute **themed guided tours** are held four times a day, and the 3pm slot is invariably on the work of JMW Turner.

★ Did You Know?

The House of Lords contains Lords Spiritual, linked with the established church, and Lords Temporal, who are both appointed and hereditary.

DZARZYCKA/GETTYIMAGES ©

Churchill War Rooms Museum

(Map p274; ☎020-7416 5000; www.iwm.org.uk/visits/churchill-war-rooms; Clive Steps, King Charles St, SW1; adult/child £21/10.50; ☻9.30am-6pm; Ⓤ Westminster) Former Prime Minister Winston Churchill helped coordinate the Allied resistance against Nazi Germany on a Bakelite telephone from this underground complex during WWII. The Cabinet War Rooms remain much as they were when the lights were switched off in 1945, capturing the drama and dogged spirit of the time, while the modern multimedia Churchill Museum affords intriguing insights into the life and times of the resolute, cigar-smoking wartime leader.

No 10 Downing Street Historic Building

(Map p274; www.number10.gov.uk; 10 Downing St, SW1; Ⓤ Westminster) The official office of British leaders since 1735, when King George II presented No 10 to 'First Lord of the Treasury' Robert Walpole, this has also been the prime minister's London residence since the late 19th century. For such a famous address, No 10 is a small-looking Georgian building on a plain-looking street, hardly warranting comparison with the White House, for example. Yet it is actually three houses joined into one and boasts roughly 100 rooms plus a 2000-sq-metre garden.

★ Top Tip

When Parliament is in session, visitors are welcome to attend the debates in both houses. Enter via Cromwell Green Entrance. Expect queues.

National Gallery

With some 2300 European paintings on display, this is one of the world's richest art collections, including works by Leonardo da Vinci, Michelangelo, Titian, Van Gogh and Renoir.

The National Gallery's collection spans seven centuries of European painting displayed in sumptuous, airy galleries. All are masterpieces, but some stand out for their iconic beauty and brilliance. Don't overlook the astonishing floor mosaics in the main vestibule inside the entrance to the gallery.

Sainsbury Wing

The modern Sainsbury Wing on the gallery's western side houses paintings from 1250 to 1500. Here you will find largely religious paintings commissioned for private devotion, such as the *Wilton Diptych*, as well more unusual masterpieces, such as Botticelli's *Venus & Mars* and Van Eyck's *Arnolfini Portrait*.

Great For...

☑ Don't Miss

Venus & Mars by Botticelli, *Sunflowers* by Van Gogh and *Rokeby Venus* by Velázquez.

ALBERTO ZAMORANO/GETTY IMAGES ©

ℹ Need to Know

Map p274; ☑020-7747 2885; www.
nationalgallery.org.uk; Trafalgar Sq, WC2;
⊙10am-6pm Sat-Thu, to 9pm Fri; ⓊCharing
Cross FREE

✕ Take a Break

Portrait (p169) at the National Portrait
Gallery has stunning food and views.

★ Top Tip

Take a free tour to learn the stories
behind the gallery's most iconic works.

West Wing & North Wing

Works from the High Renaissance (1500–
1600) embellish the West Wing where
Michelangelo, Titian, Raphael, Correggio,
El Greco and Bronzino hold court; Rubens,
Rembrandt and Caravaggio grace the North
Wing (1600–1700). Notable are two self-
portraits of Rembrandt (age 34 and 63) and
the beautiful *Rokeby Venus* by Velázquez.

East Wing

Many visitors flock to the East Wing (1700–
1900), where works by 18th-century British
artists such as Gainsborough, Constable
and Turner and seminal Impressionist and
post-Impressionist masterpieces by Van
Gogh, Renoir and Monet await.

Visiting

The comprehensive audio guides (£5)
are highly recommended, as are the free
one-hour taster tours that leave from the
information desk in the Sainsbury Wing at
2pm Monday to Friday.

What's Nearby?

National Portrait Gallery Gallery
(Map p274; ☑020-7306 0055; www.npg.org.
uk; St Martin's Pl, WC2; ⊙10am-6pm Sat-Thu, to
9pm Fri; ⓊCharing Cross or Leicester Sq) FREE
What makes the National Portrait Gallery
so compelling is its familiarity; in many
cases, you'll have heard of the subject
(royals, scientists, politicians, celebrities)
or the artist (Andy Warhol, Annie Leibovitz,
Lucian Freud) but not necessarily recognise
the face. Highlights include the famous
'Chandos portrait', thought to be of William
Shakespeare (room 4), the first artwork the
gallery acquired (in 1856), and a touching
sketch of novelist Jane Austen by her sister
(room 18).

Nelson's Column (p60), Trafalgar Square

Trafalgar Square

In many ways Trafalgar Sq is the centre of London, where tens of thousands congregate for anything from Christmas celebrations to political protests. The great square was neglected over many years, until a scheme was launched in 2000 to pedestrianise it and transform it into the kind of space John Nash had intended when he designed it in the 19th century.

Great For...

ⓘ Need to Know

Map p274; Ⓤ Charing Cross or Embankment

★ **Top Tip**

Check www.london.gov.uk for events happening in the square during your stay, from street artists to open-air screens.

The Square

The square commemorates the 1805 victory of the British navy at the Battle of Trafalgar against the French and Spanish navies during the Napoleonic wars. The main square contains two beautiful fountains, which are dramatically lit at night. At each corner of the square is a plinth, three topped with statues of military leaders and the fourth, in the northeast corner, now an art space called the Fourth Plinth.

Note the much overlooked, if not entirely ignored, 19th-century brass plaques recording the precise length of imperial units – including the yard, the perch, pole, chain and link – set into the stonework and steps below the National Gallery (p57).

Nelson's Column

Standing in the centre of the square since 1843, the 52m-high Dartmoor granite Nelson's Column honours Admiral Lord Horatio Nelson, who led the fleet's heroic victory over Napoleon. The good (sandstone) admiral gazes down Whitehall towards the Houses of Parliament, his column flanked by four enormous bronze statues of lions sculpted by Edwin Landseer and only added in 1867. The battle plaques at the base of the column were cast with seized Spanish and French cannons.

The Fourth Plinth

Three of the four plinths at Trafalgar Sq's corners are occupied by notables: King George IV on horseback, and military men

The Invisible Enemy Should Not Exist on the Fourth Plinth, 2018

General Charles Napier and Major General Henry Havelock. The fourth, originally intended for a statue of William IV, has remained vacant for the past 150 years (although some say it is reserved for an effigy of Queen Elizabeth II, on her death).

In 1999 the Royal Society of Arts created the unimaginatively titled Fourth Plinth Project, to use the empty space for works by contemporary artists. They commissioned three works: *Ecce Homo* by Mark Wallinger (1999), a life-size statue of Jesus, which appeared tiny in contrast to the enormous plinth; Bill Woodrow's *Regardless of History*

> ### ☑ Don't Miss
> Every year, Norway gives London a huge Christmas tree, which is displayed on Trafalgar Sq, to commemorate Britain's help during WWII.

(2000); and Rachel Whiteread's *Monument* (2001), a resin copy of the plinth, turned upside down.

The mayor's office has since taken over what's now called the Fourth Plinth Commission, continuing with the contemporary-art theme. In 2018 the plinth was occupied by *The Invisible Enemy Should Not Exist*, by Michael Rakowitz, a re-creation of a sculpture destroyed by Isis. In 2020, it will be replaced by Heather Phillipson's *THE END*.

Admiralty Arch

To the southwest of Trafalgar Sq stands Admiralty Arch, from where the ceremonial Mall leads to Buckingham Palace. It is a grand Edwardian monument, a triple-arched stone entrance designed by Aston Webb in honour of Queen Victoria in 1910 and earmarked for transformation into a five-star hotel. The large central gate is opened only for royal processions and state visits.

What's Nearby?
St Martin-in-the-Fields   Church

(Map p274; ☎020-7766 1100; www.stmartin-in-the-fields.org; Trafalgar Sq, WC2; ⊙8.30am-6pm Mon-Fri, 9am-6pm Sat & Sun; Ⓤ Charing Cross) This parish church to the Royal Family is a delightful fusion of neoclassical and baroque styles. It was designed by architect James Gibbs, completed in 1726 and served as a model for many wooden churches in New England, USA. The church is well known for its excellent classical-music concerts, many by candlelight (£9 to £32), and its links to the Chinese community (with services in English, Mandarin and Cantonese).

> ### ✗ Take a Break
> Gordon's Wine Bar (p205) has a wonderful selection of wines, and serves great platters of cheese and cold meats.

Covent Garden

London's first planned square is now mostly the preserve of visitors, who flock here to shop among the quaint old arcades, enjoy the many street artists' performances or visit some of the excellent nearby sights.

Great For...

ℹ Need to Know

Map p274; ☏020-7420 5856; www.covent garden.london; Ⓤ Covent Garden

★ **Top Tip**

Covent Garden tube station gets unpleasantly busy at weekends – walk to Leicester Sq instead.

Whittard

History

Covent Garden was originally pastureland that belonged to a 'convent' associated with Westminster Abbey in the 13th century. The site was converted in the 17th century by architect Inigo Jones, who designed the elegant Italian-style piazza, which was dominated by a fruit and vegetable market. The market remained here until 1974 when it moved to South London.

The Piazza

Covent Garden seems to heave whatever the time of day or night. The arcades are chock-a-block with boutiques, market stalls, cafes, ice-cream parlours and restaurants. They're a magnet for street artists too.

The streets around the piazza are full of top-end boutiques, including famous British designers. Covent Garden is also home to the Royal Opera House and a number of theatres.

Sights

London Transport Museum
Museum

(Map p274; ☏020-7379 6344; www.ltmuseum. co.uk; Covent Garden Piazza, WC2; adult/child £17.50/free; ⏱10am-6pm; 🚸; Ⓤ Covent Garden) Housed in Covent Garden's former flower-market building, this captivating museum looks at how London developed as a result of better transport. It's stuffed full of horse-drawn omnibuses, vintage Underground carriages with heritage maps and double-decker buses, some of which you can clamber through, making this something of

London Transport Museum

a kids' playground. Take home an imaginative London souvenir from the gift shop: a historical Underground poster, tube socks or pillows made from the same fabric as the train seats will take you right back.

Bond In Motion
Museum

(London Film Museum; Map p274; ☑020-7836 4913; www.londonfilmmuseum.com; 45 Wellington St, WC2; adult/child £14.50/9.50; ☺10am-6pm; ⓤCovent Garden) Get shaken *and* stirred at the largest official collection of 007 vehicles, with more than two dozen on display, including James Bond's submersible Lotus Esprit (from *The Spy Who Loved Me*), the iconic Aston Martin DB5, Goldfinger's Rolls Royce Phantom III and Timothy Dalton's Aston Martin V8 (from *The Living Daylights*). Other exhibits display more personal curios, such as Bond's various passports. Film clips play in the background so you can relive your favourite scenes.

Royal Opera House
Opera

(Map p274; ☑020-7304 4000; www.roh.org. uk; Bow St, WC2; ☺gift shop & cafe from 10am; ⓤCovent Garden) If you want a peek behind the curtain, sign up for a guided tour (adult/child under 16 £15/11.50). The Velvet, Gilt and Glamour Tour is a general, 45-minute twirl around the auditorium; more distinctive is the 1¼-hour Backstage Tour taking you through the venue. The latter is a much better way to experience the preparation, excitement and histrionics before a performance. Photography is not allowed.

What's Nearby?

Somerset House
Historic Building

(Map p280; ☑020-7845 4600; www.somerset house.org.uk; Strand, WC2; ☺courtyard 7.30am-11pm; ⓤTemple) Designed in 1775 for government departments and royal societies – perhaps the world's first office block – Somerset House now contains galleries, restaurants and cafes that encircle a lovely open courtyard and extend to an elevated sun-trap terrace. The **Embankment Galleries** are devoted to temporary exhibitions (usually related to photography, design or fashion). In summer, the grand courtyard hosts open-air live performances, dancing fountains for kids to cool off in and the **Film4 Summer Screen** (☑0333 320 2836; tickets from £19.75; ☺Aug); there is an atmospheric ice-skating rink in winter.

> ☑ **Don't Miss**
>
> Clambering over old tramways at the London Transport Museum, and street artist performances.

NATALIIA ZHEKOVA/SHUTTERSTOCK ©

> ✕ **Take a Break**
>
> Join the queue at Dishoom (p167) for exquisite Indian street fare.

Traitors' Gate (p71), the Tower of London

KURLIN CAFE/SHUTTERSTOCK ©

ENTRY TO THE TRAITORS GATE

Tower of London

With a history as bleak as it is fascinating, the Tower of London is now one of the city's top attractions, thanks in part to the Crown Jewels.

Begun during the reign of William the Conqueror (1066–87), the Tower is in fact a castle containing 22 towers.

Tower Green

The buildings to the west and the south of this verdant patch have always accommodated Tower officials. Indeed, the current constable has a flat in Queen's House built in 1540. But what looks at first glance like a peaceful, almost village-like slice of the Tower's inner ward is actually one of its bloodiest.

Scaffold Site & Beauchamp Tower

Those 'lucky' enough to meet their fate here (rather than suffering the embarrassment of execution on Tower Hill, observed by tens of thousands of jeering and cheering onlookers) numbered but a handful and

Great For...

☑ **Don't Miss**

Colourful Yeoman Warders, spectacular Crown Jewels, famous ravens, and armour fit for a king.

oden Bridge, the Tower of London

ANDREY ALDONIN/SHUTTERSTOCK ©

ℹ️ Need to Know

Map p280; ☎020-3166 6000; www.hrp.org.
uk/tower-of-london; Petty Wales, EC3; adult/
child £26.80/12.70, audio guide £4; ⏰9am-
4.30pm Tue-Sat, from 10am Sun & Mon;
Ⓤ Tower Hill

✗ Take a Break

Opposite the Tower, Wine Library (p163)
is great for lunch.

★ Top Tip

Book online for cheaper tickets.

included two of Henry VIII's wives (and
alleged adulterers), Anne Boleyn and Catherine Howard; 16-year-old Lady Jane Grey,
who fell foul of Henry's daughter Mary I by
attempting to have herself crowned queen;
and Robert Devereux, Earl of Essex, once a
favourite of Elizabeth I.

Just west of the scaffold site is
brick-faced Beauchamp Tower, where
high-ranking prisoners left behind unhappy
inscriptions and other graffiti.

Chapel Royal of St Peter ad Vincula

Just north of the scaffold site is the
16th-century Chapel Royal of St Peter ad
Vincula (St Peter in Chains), a rare example
of ecclesiastical Tudor architecture. The
church can be visited on a Yeoman Warder
tour, or during the first and last hour of
normal opening times.

Crown Jewels

To the east of the chapel and north of the
White Tower is **Waterloo Barracks**, the
home of the Crown Jewels, said to be worth
up to £20 billion, but in a very real sense
priceless. Here, you file past film clips of the
jewels and their role through history, and
of Queen Elizabeth II's coronation in 1953,
before you reach the vault itself.

Once inside you'll be greeted by lavishly
bejewelled sceptres, church plate, orbs
and, naturally, crowns. A moving walkway
takes you past the dozen or so crowns
and other coronation regalia, including the
platinum crown of the late Queen Mother,
Elizabeth, which is set with the 106-carat
Koh-i-Noor (Mountain of Light) diamond,
and the State Sceptre with Cross topped
with the 530-carat First Star of Africa
(or Cullinan I) diamond. A bit further on,
exhibited on its own, is the centrepiece:
the Imperial State Crown, set with 2868
diamonds (including the 317-carat Second
Star of Africa, or Cullinan II), sapphires,
emeralds, rubies and pearls. It's worn by

Tower of London

TACKLING THE TOWER

Although it's usually less busy in the late afternoon, don't leave your assault on the Tower until too late in the day. You could easily spend hours here and not see it all. Start by getting your bearings on one of the Yeoman Warder (Beefeater) tours; they are included in the cost of admission, entertaining and the easiest way to access the ❶ **Chapel Royal of St Peter ad Vincula**, which is where they finish up.

When you leave the chapel, the ❷ **Scaffold Site** is directly in front. The building immediately to your left is Waterloo Barracks, where the ❸ **Crown Jewels** are housed. These are the absolute highlight of a Tower visit, so keep an eye on the entrance and pick a time to visit when it looks relatively quiet. Once inside, take things at your own pace. Slow-moving travelators shunt you past the dozen or so crowns that are the treasury's centrepieces, but feel free to double-back for a second or even third pass.

Allow plenty of time for the ❹ **White Tower**, the core of the whole complex, starting with the exhibition of royal armour. As you continue onto the 1st floor, keep an eye out for ❺ **St John's Chapel**.

The famous ❻ **ravens** can be seen in the courtyard south of the White Tower. Next, visit the ❼ **Bloody Tower** and the torture displays in the dungeon of the Wakefield Tower. Head next through the towers that formed the ❽ **Medieval Palace**, then take the ❾ **East Wall Walk** to get a feel for the castle's mighty battlements. Spend the rest of your time poking around the many other fascinating nooks and crannies of the Tower complex.

BEAT THE QUEUES

➜ Buy tickets online, avoid weekends and aim to be at the Tower first thing in the morning, when queues are shortest.

➜ The London Pass (www.london-pass.com) allows you to jump the queues and visit the Tower (plus some other 80 attractions) as often as you like.

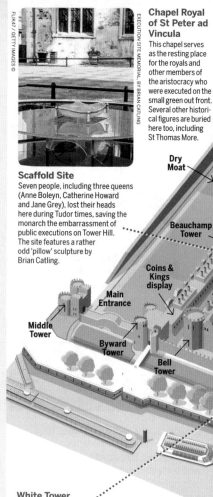

Chapel Royal of St Peter ad Vincula
This chapel serves as the resting place for the royals and other members of the aristocracy who were executed on the small green out front. Several other historical figures are buried here too, including St Thomas More.

Scaffold Site
Seven people, including three queens (Anne Boleyn, Catherine Howard and Jane Grey), lost their heads here during Tudor times, saving the monarch the embarrassment of public executions on Tower Hill. The site features a rather odd 'pillow' sculpture by Brian Catling.

Dry Moat

Beauchamp Tower

Coins & Kings display

Main Entrance

Middle Tower

Byward Tower

Bell Tower

FLIK47 / GETTY IMAGES ©

EXECUTION SITE MEMORIAL, BY BRIAN CATLING

White Tower
Much of the White Tower is taken up with an exhibition on 500 years of royal armour. Look for the virtually cuboid suit made to match Henry VIII's bloated 49-year-old body, complete with an oversized armoured codpiece to protect, ahem, the crown jewels.

CHRISDORNEY / SHUTTERSTOCK ©

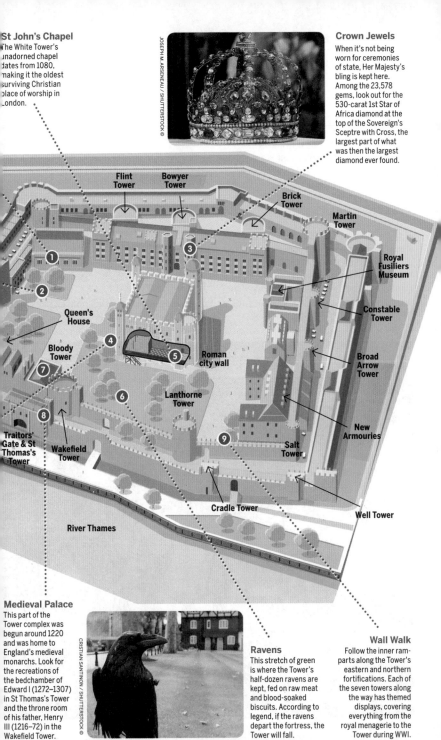

St John's Chapel
The White Tower's unadorned chapel dates from 1080, making it the oldest surviving Christian place of worship in London.

Crown Jewels
When it's not being worn for ceremonies of state, Her Majesty's bling is kept here. Among the 23,578 gems, look out for the 530-carat 1st Star of Africa diamond at the top of the Sovereign's Sceptre with Cross, the largest part of what was then the largest diamond ever found.

JOSEPH M. ARSENEAU / SHUTTERSTOCK ©

Flint Tower

Bowyer Tower

Brick Tower

Martin Tower

① ②

Queen's House

③

Royal Fusiliers Museum

Constable Tower

④ ⑤

Roman city wall

Bloody Tower

⑦

Broad Arrow Tower

⑥

Lanthorne Tower

⑧

Traitors' Gate & St Thomas's Tower

Wakefield Tower

New Armouries

⑨

Salt Tower

Cradle Tower

Well Tower

River Thames

Medieval Palace
This part of the Tower complex was begun around 1220 and was home to England's medieval monarchs. Look for the recreations of the bedchamber of Edward I (1272–1307) in St Thomas's Tower and the throne room of his father, Henry III (1216–72) in the Wakefield Tower.

CRISTIAN SANTINON / SHUTTERSTOCK ©

Ravens
This stretch of green is where the Tower's half-dozen ravens are kept, fed on raw meat and blood-soaked biscuits. According to legend, if the ravens depart the fortress, the Tower will fall.

Wall Walk
Follow the inner ramparts along the Tower's eastern and northern fortifications. Each of the seven towers along the way has themed displays, covering everything from the royal menagerie to the Tower during WWI.

the Queen at the State Opening of Parliament in May/June.

White Tower

Built in stone as a fortress in 1078, this was the original 'Tower' of London – its name arose after Henry III had it whitewashed in the 13th century. Standing just 30m high, it's not exactly a skyscraper by modern standards, but in the Middle Ages it would have dwarfed the wooden huts surrounding the castle walls and intimidated the peasantry.

Most of its interior is given over to a **Royal Armouries** collection of cannon, guns, and suits of mail and armour for men and horses. Among the most remarkable exhibits on the entrance floor are Henry VIII's two suits of armour, one made for him when he was a dashing 24-year-old and the other when he was a bloated 50-year-old with a waist measuring 129cm. You won't miss the oversize codpiece. Also here is the fabulous **Line of Kings**, a late-17th-century parade of carved wooden horses and heads of historic kings. On the 1st floor, check out the 2m suit of armour once thought to have been made for the giantlike John of Gaunt and, alongside it, a tiny child's suit of armour designed for James I's young son, the future Charles I. Up on the 2nd floor you'll find the block and axe used to execute Simon Fraser at the last public execution on Tower Hill in 1747.

Medieval Palace & the Bloody Tower

The Medieval Palace is composed of three towers: St Thomas's, Wakefield and

Royal Armouries collection

Langthorn. Inside **St Thomas's Tower** (1279) you can look at what the hall and bedchamber of Edward I might once have been like. Here, archaeologists have peeled back the layers of newer buildings to find what went before. Opposite St Thomas's Tower is **Wakefield Tower**, built by Edward's father, Henry III, between 1220 and 1240. Its upper floor is entered from St Thomas's Tower and has been even more enticingly furnished with a replica throne and other decor to give an impression of how, as an anteroom in

a medieval palace, it might have looked. During the 15th-century Wars of the Roses between the Houses of York and Lancaster, King Henry VI was murdered as (it is said) he knelt in prayer in this tower. A plaque on the chapel floor commemorates this Lancastrian king. The **Langthorn Tower**, residence of medieval queens, is to the east.

Below St Thomas's Tower along Water Lane is the famous **Traitors' Gate**, the portal through which prisoners transported by boat entered the Tower. Opposite Traitors' Gate is the huge portcullis of the Bloody Tower, taking its nickname from the 'princes in the Tower' – Edward V and his younger brother, Richard – who were held here 'for their own safety' and later murdered to annul their claims to the throne. An exhibition inside looks at the life and times of Elizabethan adventurer Walter Raleigh, who was imprisoned here three times by the capricious Elizabeth I and her successor James I.

East Wall Walk

The huge inner wall of the Tower was added to the fortress in 1220 by Henry III to improve the castle's defences. It is 36m wide and is dotted with towers along its length. The East Wall Walk allows you to climb up and tour its eastern edge, beginning in the 13th-century **Salt Tower**, probably used to store saltpetre for gunpowder. The walk also takes in **Broad Arrow Tower** and **Constable Tower**, each containing small exhibits. It ends at the **Martin Tower**, which houses an exhibition about the original coronation regalia. Here you can see some of the older crowns, with their precious stones removed. It was from this tower that Colonel Thomas Blood attempted to steal the Crown Jewels in 1671 disguised as a clergyman. He

KHUNMEE/SHUTTERSTOCK ©

> ★ **Did You Know?**
>
> Those beheaded on the scaffold outside the Chapel Royal of St Peter ad Vincula – notably Anne Boleyn, Catherine Howard and Lady Jane Grey – were reburied in the chapel in the 19th century.

> ★ **Did You Know?**
>
> Over the years, the tower has served as a palace, an observatory, an armoury, a mint and even a zoo.

was caught but – surprisingly – Charles II gave him a full pardon.

Yeoman Warders

True icons of the Tower, the Yeoman Warders have been guarding the fortress since at least the early 16th century. There can be up to 40 and, in order to qualify for the job, they must have served a minimum of 22 years in any branch of the British Armed Forces. They all live within the Tower walls and are known affectionately as 'Beefeaters', a nickname they dislike.

Currently there are two female Yeoman Warders, Moira Cameron, who in 2007 became the first woman to be given the post, and Amanda Clarke, appointed in 2017. While officially they guard the Tower and Crown Jewels at night, their main role is as tour guides. Free 45-minute-long tours leave from the bridge near the main entrance every 30 minutes until 3.30pm (2.30pm in winter).

What's Nearby?

All Hallows by the Tower   Church

(Map p280; ☏020-7481 2928; www.ahbtt.org. uk; Byward St, EC3; ☺10am-5pm; ⓤTower Hill) The oldest church in the City, All Hallows (meaning 'all saints') has been a place of worship since AD 675. Those executed at Tower Hill would often be buried here temporarily, including Thomas More (beheaded in 1535). It was virtually unscathed by the Great Fire (Samuel Pepys watched it briefly from the church tower), while destruction by German bombs in 1940 revealed the Saxon archway at the west end of the nave. Don't miss the 2nd-century Roman tile pavement in the undercroft (crypt).

Monument   Monument

(Map p280; ☏020-7621 0285; www.the monument.org.uk; Fish St Hill, EC3; adult/child £5/2.50, incl Tower Bridge Exhibition £12/5.50; ☺9.30am-5.30pm Apr-Sep, to 5pm Oct-Mar; ⓤMonument) Christopher Wren's 1677 column, known simply as the Monument, is a memorial to the Great Fire of London

of 1666, whose impact on the city's history cannot be overstated. An immense Doric column made of Portland stone, the Monument is 4.5m wide and 60.6m tall – the exact distance it stands from the bakery in Pudding Lane where the fire is thought to have started.

Although Lilliputian by today's standards, the Monument towered over London when it was built. Climbing up the column's 311 spiral steps still rewards you with great views, due to its central location as much as to its height.

Leadenhall Market   Market

(Map p280; www.leadenhallmarket.co.uk; Whittington Ave, EC3; ☺public areas 24hr; ⓤBank) The Romans had their Forum on this site, but this covered shopping strip off Gracechurch St harks back to the Victorian

Leadenhall Market

era, with cobblestones underfoot and late-19th-century ironwork linking its shops and bars. The market appears as Diagon Alley in *Harry Potter and the Philosopher's Stone*, while the optician's shop with a blue door on Bull's Head Passage was used as the entrance to the Leaky Cauldron in *Harry Potter and the Goblet of Fire*.

30 St Mary Axe   Notable Building

(Map p280; www.thegherkinlondon.com; 30 St Mary Axe, EC3; Ⓤ Aldgate) Nicknamed 'the Gherkin' for its distinctive shape and emerald hue, 30 St Mary Axe remains the City's most intriguing skyscraper, despite the best efforts of the engineering individualism that now surrounds it. It was built in 2003 by award-winning architect Norman Foster, with a futuristic exterior that has become an emblem of modern

London – as recognisable as Big Ben. While the building is generally only open to those working in it, **HELIX**, a 39th-floor restaurant with panoramic views, is open to everyone (booking essential).

★ **Local Knowledge**

Common ravens, which once feasted on the corpses of beheaded traitors, have been here for centuries. Nowadays, they feed on raw beef and biscuits.

★ **Did You Know?**

Yeoman Warders are nicknamed Beefeaters. It's thought to be due to the rations of beef – then a luxury food – given to them in the past.

PHILIP BIRD LRPS CPAGB/SHUTTERSTOCK ©

Columbia Road Flower Market

ELENA DIJOUR/SHUTTERSTOCK ©

A Sunday in the East End

The East End has a colourful, multicultural history. Waves of migrants (French Protestants, Jews, Bangladeshis) have left their mark on the area; add in Cockney heritage and 21st-century hipsters for an incredibly vibrant neighbourhood.

Great For...

☑ **Don't Miss**

The area's food offering is as diverse as its population, from curry houses to modern British cuisine.

On Sundays, this whole area feels like one giant, sprawling market. It is brilliant fun, but pretty exhausting, so pace yourself – there are plenty of cafes and restaurants where you can sit down, relax and take in the atmosphere.

Columbia Road Flower Market

A wonderful explosion of colour and life, this weekly **market** (Map p282; www.columbiaroad.info; Columbia Rd, E2; ⊗8am-3pm Sun; ⓊHoxton) sells a beautiful array of flowers, pot plants, bulbs, seeds and everything you might need for the garden. It's a lot of fun and the best place to hear proper Cockney barrow-boy banter ('We got flowers cheap enough for ya muvver-in-law's grave' etc).

Brick Lane Market

PAOLO PARADISO/SHUTTERSTOCK ©

Brick Lane's Famous Bagels

A relic of the Jewish East End, **Beigel Bake** (Map p282; ✆071 729 0616; 159 Brick Lane, E1; filled bagels £1.20-4.30; ⏰24hr; Ⓤ Shoreditch High St) on Brick Lane still makes a brisk trade serving dirt-cheap home-made bagels (filled with salmon, cream cheese and/or salt beef).

Old Spitalfields Market

Traders have been hawking their wares here since 1638 and it's still one of London's best markets. Today's covered **market** (Map p282; www.oldspitalfieldsmarket. com; Commercial St, E1; ⏰10am-8pm Mon-Fri, to 6pm Sat, to 5pm Sun; Ⓤ Liverpool St, Shoreditch High St or Aldgate East) was built in the late 19th century, with the more modern development added in 2006. Sundays are the biggest and best days, but Thursdays are good for antiques and Fridays for independent fashion. There are plenty of food stalls, too.

Brick Lane Markets

Head south towards **Brick Lane Market** (Map p282; ✆020-7364 1717; www.visitbrick lane.org; Brick Lane, E1; ⏰10am-5pm Sun; Ⓤ Shoreditch High St), which spills out into the surrounding streets with everything from household goods to bric-a-brac, second-hand clothes, cheap fashion and ethnic food. The best range and quality of products are to be found in the beautiful Old Truman Brewery's markets: **Sunday Upmarket** (Map p282; ✆020-7770 6028; www. sundayupmarket.co.uk; ⏰11am-6pm Sat, 10am-5pm Sun) and **Backyard Market** (Map p282; ✆020-7770 6028; www.backyardmarket.co.uk; ⏰11am-6pm Sat, 10am-5pm Sun), where young designers sell their creations, along with arts-and-crafts and cracking food stalls.

Brick Lane Great Mosque

After lunch, walk over to this fascinating **mosque** (No 59 Brick Lane). No building symbolises the different waves of immigration to Spitalfields quite as well as this one. Built in 1743 as the New French Church for the Huguenots, it was a Methodist chapel from 1819 until it was transformed into the Great Synagogue for Jewish refugees from Russia and Central Europe in 1898. In 1976 it changed faiths yet again, becoming the Great Mosque. Look for the sundial, high up on the Fournier St frontage.

Whitechapel Gallery

From Brick Lane Mosque, continue on to **Whitechapel Gallery** (Map p280; 020-7522 7888; www.whitechapelgallery.org; 77-82 Whitechapel High St, E1; 11am-6pm Tue-Sun; Aldgate East) FREE. A firm favourite of art students and the avant-garde cognoscenti, this groundbreaking gallery doesn't have a permanent collection, but is devoted to hosting edgy exhibitions of contemporary art. It made its name by staging exhibitions by both established and emerging artists, including the first UK shows by Pablo Picasso, Jackson Pollock, Mark Rothko and Frida Kahlo.

What's Nearby?

Geffrye Museum   Museum

(Map p282; 020-7739 9893; www.geffrye-museum.org.uk; 136 Kingsland Rd, E2; adult/child £5/free; almshouse tours on selected Tue, Wed, Sat; Hoxton) These beautiful ivy-clad brick almshouses were built in 1714 as a home for poor pensioners. Most are closed until spring 2020 for renovations, but one remains open a few days a week as part of a 30-minute guided tour. Two rooms have been furnished to show how residents lived in the 1770s and 1880s, atmospherically lit by candles and the original gas lamps. The attention to detail is impressive, down to the vintage newspaper left open on the breakfast table.

Dennis Severs' House

Dennis Severs' House   Historic Building

(Map p282; ☎020-7247 4013; www.dennissevers house.co.uk; 18 Folgate St, E1; day/night £10/15; ⊘noon-2pm & 5-9pm Mon, 5-9pm Wed & Fri, noon-4pm Sun; ⓤLiverpool St) This extraordinary Georgian house is set up as if its occupants – a family of Huguenot silk weavers – have just walked out the door. Each of the 10 rooms is stuffed with the minutiae of everyday life from centuries past: half-drunk cups of tea, emptied but gleaming wet oyster shells and, in perhaps unnecessary attention to detail, a used chamber pot by the bed. It's more an immersive experience than a traditional museum; explorations of the house are conducted in silence.

Old Truman Brewery   Historic Building

(Map p282; ☎020-7770 6000; www.truman brewery.com; Brick Lane, E1; ⓤShoreditch High St) Founded here in the 17th century, Truman's Black Eagle Brewery was, by the 1850s, the largest brewery in the world. Spread over a series of brick buildings and yards on both sides of Brick Lane, the complex is now completely given over to edgy markets, pop-up fashion stores, vintage clothes shops, cafes and bars – it's at its busy best when market stalls are set up on Sundays. Beer may not be brewed here any more, but it certainly is consumed.

After decades of decline, Truman's Brewery finally shut up shop in 1989 – temporarily as it turned out, with the brand subsequently resurrected in 2010 in new premises a bit further northeast in the neighbourhood of Hackney Wick.

Several of the brewery buildings are heritage listed, including the Director's House at 91 Brick Lane (built in the 1740s), the old Vat House directly opposite (c 1800) and the Engineer's House at 150 Brick Lane (dating from the 1830s).

✕ Take a Break

In the evening, check out Discount Suit Company (p194) on Brick Lane for splendid speakeasy cocktails.

ARCAID IMAGES/ALAMY STOCK PHOTO ©

★ Local Knowledge

There is plenty of graffiti to admire in the area but if you'd like to see a famous Banksy artwork, make a small detour to Cargo (p139).

Borough Market

Overflowing with food lovers, inveterate gastronomes, wide-eyed visitors and Londoners in search of inspiration for their next dinner party, this fantastic market has become a sight in its own right.

Great For...

Need to Know

Map p280; www.boroughmarket.org.uk; 8 Southwark St, SE1; full market 10am-5pm Wed & Thu, 10am-6pm Fri, 8am-5pm Sat; London Bridge

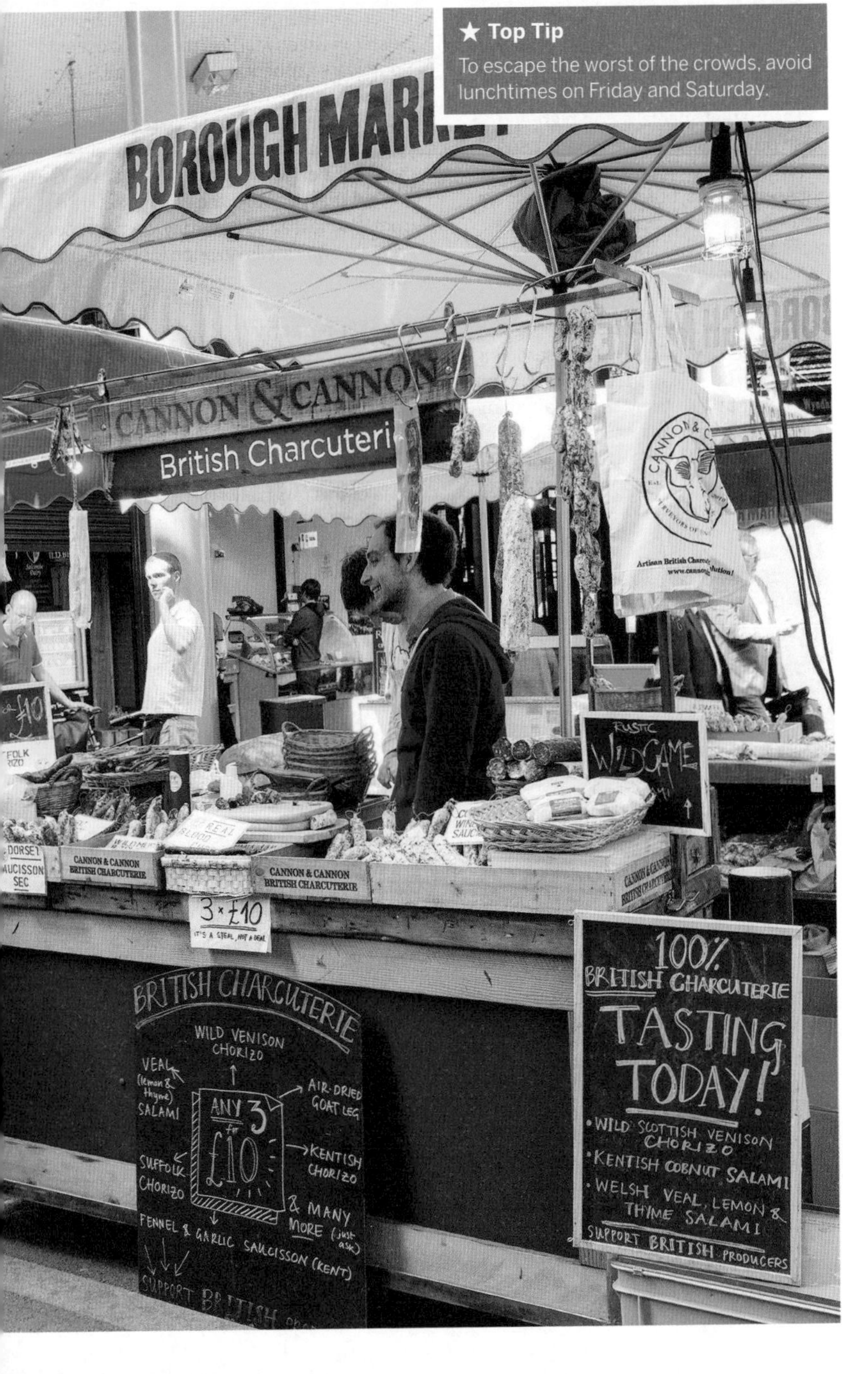

BOROUGH MARKET

CANNON & CANNON
British Charcuterie

RUSTIC
WILD GAME

3 × £10
IT'S A STEAL, NOT A DEAL

BRITISH CHARCUTERIE

WILD VENISON
CHORIZO

VEAL
(Lemon &
Thyme)
SALAMI

AIR-DRIED
GOAT LEG

ANY 3
for
£10

KENTISH
CHORIZO

SUFFOLK
CHORIZO

& MANY
MORE (just
ask)

FENNEL & GARLIC SAUCISSON (KENT)

SUPPORT BRITISH PR...

100%
BRITISH CHARCUTERIE
TASTING
TODAY!

• WILD SCOTTISH VENISON
CHORIZO
• KENTISH COBNUT SALAMI
• WELSH VEAL, LEMON &
THYME SALAMI
SUPPORT BRITISH PRODUCERS

Located here in some form or another since the 13th century, 'London's Larder' has enjoyed an astonishing renaissance in the past 20 years.

The market specialises in high-end fresh products, so you'll find the usual assortment of fruit and vegetable stalls, cheesemongers, butchers, fishmongers, bakeries and delis, as well as gourmet stalls selling spices, nuts, preserves and condiments. Prices tend to be high, but many traders offer free samples, a great perk for visitors and locals alike.

Food window-shopping (and sampling) over, you'll be able to grab lunch from one of the myriad takeaway stalls – anything from sizzling gourmet sausages to chorizo sandwiches and falafel wraps. There also seems to be an unreasonable number of cake stalls – walking out without a treat

will be a challenge! Many of the lunch stalls cluster in Green Market (the area closest to Southwark Cathedral). Allow £6 to £9 for a takeaway dish.

If you'd like some elbow space to enjoy your takeaway, walk five minutes in either direction along the Thames for river views.

Note that although the full market runs from Wednesday to Saturday, some traders and takeaway stalls do open Mondays and Tuesdays.

What's Nearby?
Southwark Cathedral   Church
(Map p280; ☏020-7367 6700; www.cathedral. southwark.anglican.org; Montague Cl, SE1; ⊙7.30am-6pm Mon-Fri, 9.30am-6pm Sat; ⓤLondon Bridge) The earliest surviving parts of this relatively small cathedral are the retrochoir at the eastern end, which

HMS Belfast at Tower Bridge

contains four chapels and was part of the 13th-century Priory of St Mary Overie, some ancient arcading by the southwest door and an arch that dates to the original Norman church. But most of the cathedral is Victorian. Inside there are monuments galore, including a Shakespeare memorial. Visiting may be restricted due to events, so check the website for details.

The Shard
Notable Building

(Map p280; www.theviewfromtheshard.com; 32 London Bridge St, SE1; adult/child £30.95/24.95; ☺10am-10pm; Ⓤ London Bridge) Puncturing the skies above London, the dramatic splinter-like form of the Shard has rapidly become an icon of London. The viewing platforms on floors 69 and 72 are open to the public and the views are, as you'd expect from a 244m vantage point, sweeping, but they come at a hefty price – book online at least a day in advance for a big saving.

HMS Belfast
Ship

(Map p280; www.iwm.org.uk/visits/hms-belfast; Queen's Walk, SE1; adult/child £17/8.50; ☺10am-6pm Mar-Oct, to 5pm Nov-Feb; Ⓤ London Bridge) *HMS Belfast* is a magnet for kids of all ages. This large, light cruiser – launched in 1938 – served in WWII, helping to sink the German battleship *Scharnhorst,* shelling the Normandy coast on D-Day and later participating in the Korean War. Its 6in guns could bombard a target 14 land miles distant. Displays offer a great insight into what life on board was like, in peacetime and during military engagements.

Golden Hinde
Ship

(Map p280; ☎020-7403 0123; www.golden hinde.co.uk; St Mary Overie Dock, Cathedral St, SE1; £5, small additional charge for events; ☺10am-6pm Apr-Oct, to 5pm Nov-Mar; ⓓ; Ⓤ London Bridge) Step aboard this replica of privateer Francis Drake's *Golden Hinde*, the warship that circumnavigated the globe in 1577–1580. Kids will love exploring all the decks and cabins, but mind your heads adults (the average crew member was just 1.6m tall). It's hard to believe that approximately 60 crew members would have been crammed in such a tiny space.

> ☑ **Don't Miss**
> Grazing on the free samples from the Borough Market or eating takeaway by the river.

NIGEL JARVIS/SHUTTERSTOCK ©

> ✕ **Take a Break**
> Arabica Bar & Kitchen (p165) serves up contemporary Middle Eastern fare.

A pond at Hampstead Heath

Hampstead Heath

With its rolling woodlands and meadows, sprawling Hampstead Heath feels a million miles away from the City of London – despite being approximately four.

Great For

☑ **Don't Miss**

Views from Parliament Hill, strolling in the woodlands, Kenwood House.

The Heath

Hampstead Heath is big: 320 hectares, most of it woods, hills and meadows. It is home to about 180 bird species, 23 species of butterfly, grass snakes, bats and a rich array of flora.

Unsurprisingly, it is very popular with Londoners, who treasure this little slice of wilderness. It's a wonderful place for a ramble, especially to the top of **Parliament Hill** (Ⓤ Hampstead Heath, Gospel Oak), which offers expansive views across the city and is popular to fly a kite. Alternatively head up the hill to **Kenwood**, with its landscaped gardens, or lose yourself in the **West Heath**. Signage is limited, but getting a little lost is part of the experience.

If walking is too pedestrian for you, the bathing ponds are another major attraction. There are separate ones for men and

TEDZ DURAN/500PX ©

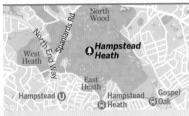

❶ Need to Know

www.cityoflondon.gov.uk; Ⓤ Hampstead
Heath, Gospel Oak

✕ Take a Break

The **Garden Gate** (www.thegardengate
hampstead.co.uk; 14 South End Rd, NW3;
⊙ noon-11pm Sun-Fri, 10am-11.30pm Sat;
🛜 🐾; Ⓤ Hampstead Heath) has an atmospheric beer garden for summer tipples.

★ Top Tip

Plan your itinerary carefully: the Heath
is huge and transport options vary.

In the garden, you'll find sculptures by
Henry Moore and Barbara Hepworth on
the lawn.

What's Nearby?

Highgate Cemetery   Historic Building
(www.highgatecemetery.org; Swain's Lane, N6;
East Cemetery adult/child £4/free; ⊙ 10am-
5pm Mar-Oct, 10am-4pm Nov-Feb; Ⓤ Archway)
A Gothic wonderland of shrouded urns,
obelisks, broken columns, sleeping angels,
Egyptian-style tombs and overgrown
graves, Highgate is a Victorian Valhalla
spread over 20 wonderfully wild and
atmospheric hectares. On the eastern side,
you can pay your respects to the graves
of Karl Marx and Mary Ann Evans (better
known as novelist George Eliot). The real
highlight, however, is the overgrown **West
Cemetery**, which can only be visited on a
guided tour (adult/child £12/6; ⊙ every 30min
10.30am-3pm Nov-Feb, to 4pm Mar-Oct, pre-
booking required Mon-Fri, no booking Sat & Sun;
Ⓤ Archway).

women and a slightly less secluded mixed
pond (p225).

Kenwood House

This magnificent neoclassical **mansion** (EH;
www.english-heritage.org.uk; Hampstead Lane,
NW3; ⊙ 10am-4pm; 👶; 🚌 210) FREE stands at
the northern end of Hampstead Heath in
a glorious sweep of landscaped gardens
that lead down to a picturesque lake. The
17th-century house was substantially
remodelled in the 1760s and rescued from
developers by Edward Cecil Guinness,
1st Earl of Iveagh, who donated it and the
wonderful collection of art it contains to
the nation in 1927. Among its treasures are
paintings by Rembrandt (one of his many
self-portraits), Constable, Gainsborough
and Vermeer.

Tower Bridge

One of London's most familiar sights, Tower Bridge doesn't disappoint up close. There's something about its neo-Gothic towers and blue suspension struts that makes it enthralling.

Great For...

☑ **Don't Miss**

The bridge lifting and the view from the top (as well as down through the new glass floor).

History & Mechanics

Built in 1894 by Horace Jones (who designed many of London's markets) as a much-needed crossing point in the east, Tower Bridge was equipped with a then-revolutionary bascule (see-saw) mechanism that could clear the way for oncoming ships in just three minutes. Although London's days as a thriving port are long over, the bridge still does its stuff, lifting largely for pleasure craft around 1000 times a year.

Tower Bridge Exhibition

Housed within is the **Tower Bridge Exhibition** (Map p280; ☎020-7403 3761; www. towerbridge.org.uk; Tower Bridge, SE1; adult/ child £9.80/4.20, incl the Monument £12/5.50; ⊙10am-5.30pm Apr-Sep, 9.30am-5pm Oct-Mar; Ⓤ Tower Hill), which explains the nuts and

R CLASSEN/SHUTTERSTOCK ©

ℹ Need to Know

Map p280; ☎020-7403 3761; www.tower bridge.org.uk; Tower Bridge, SE1; ⊗24hr; Ⓤ Tower Hill

✕ Take a Break

The Watch House (p164), on the South Bank, sells fabulous sandwiches and cakes from local bakers. It does great coffee too.

★ Top Tip

For the best views of the bridge, pop over to the southern bank of the river.

bolts of it all. If you're not technically minded, it's still fascinating to get inside the bridge and look along the Thames from its two walkways. A lift takes you to the top of the structure, 42m above the river, from where you can walk along the east- and west-facing walkways, lined with information boards.

The 11m-long glass floor, made of a dozen see-through panels, is stunning – acrophobes can take solace in knowing that each weighs a load-bearing 530kg. There are a couple of stops on the way down before you exit and continue on to the **Victorian Engine Rooms**, which house the beautifully maintained steam engines that powered the bridge lifts, as well as some excellent interactive exhibits and a couple of short films.

What's Nearby?

White Cube Bermondsey Gallery

(Map p280; www.whitecube.com; 144-152 Bermondsey St, SE1; ⊗10am-6pm Tue-Sat, noon-6pm Sun; Ⓤ London Bridge) **FREE** The newest and largest of the White Cube galleries, this spot impresses with its large exhibition spaces, which lend themselves to monumental pieces or expansive installations using several mediums. White Cube is the brainchild of Jay Jopling, dealer to the stars of the Brit Art movement. He made his reputation in the 1990s by exhibiting then-unknown artists such as Damien Hirst and Antony Gormley.

Tate Modern

This phenomenally successful gallery combines stupendous architecture and a seminal collection of 20th-century modern art. The huge extension, opened in 2016, dramatically increased its display space.

Great For...

ⓘ Need to Know

Map p280; 📞020-7887 8888; www.tate.org.uk; Bankside, SE1; ⏰10am-6pm Sun-Thu, to 10pm Fri & Sat; 🚆; Ⓤ Blackfriars, Southwark or London Bridge **FREE**

AND OPEN TO ALL

★ **Top Tip**

Take the **Tate Boat** (Map p280; www.tate. org.uk/visit/tate-boat; one-way adult/child £8.40/4.20) shuttle between Tate Britain (p54) and Tate Modern.

CARLOS NETO/SHUTTERSTOCK ©

Boiler House

The original gallery lies in what was once Bankside Power Station. Now called Boiler House, it is an imposing sight: a 200m-long building, made of 4.2 million bricks. Its conversion into an art gallery was a masterstroke of design.

Turbine Hall

The first thing to greet you as you pour down the ramp off Holland St (the main entrance) is the astounding 3300-sq-metre Turbine Hall. Originally housing the power station's humongous electricity generators, this vast space has become the commanding venue for large-scale installation art and temporary exhibitions.

Blavatnik Building

The Tate Modern extension that opened in 2016 echoes its sister building in appearance: it is also constructed of brick, although here these are slightly lighter and have been artistically laid out in a lattice to let light in (and out – the building looks stunning after dark).

The Tanks

The three huge subterranean tanks once stored fuel for the power station. These unusual circular spaces are now dedicated to showing live art, performance, installation and film, or 'new art' as the Tate calls it.

Viewing Gallery: Level 10

The views from level 10 are, as you would expect, sweeping. The river views are

Performance at Shakespeare's Globe

perhaps not quite as iconic as the full-frontal St Paul's view you get from Boiler House, but you get to see Boiler House itself, and a lot more in every direction. The views of the Shard looking east are especially good. And best of all, they are free.

Permanent Collection

Tate Modern's permanent collection is arranged on levels 2 and 4 of Boiler House and levels 0, 2, 3 and 4 of Blavatnik Building, which focuses on art from the 1960s onwards.

☑ Don't Miss

Turbine Hall, special exhibitions, the view of St Paul's from the Level 3 balconies of Boiler House and the Viewing Gallery on Level 10 of Switch House.

More than 60,000 works are on constant rotation. The curators have at their disposal paintings by Georges Braque, Henri Matisse, Piet Mondrian, Andy Warhol, Mark Rothko and Jackson Pollock, as well as pieces by Joseph Beuys, Damien Hirst, Rebecca Horn, Claes Oldenburg and Auguste Rodin.

A great place to start is the **Start Display** on level 2 of Boiler House: this small, specially curated 'taster' exhibit features some of the best-loved works in the collection and gives useful pointers for how to tackle unfamiliar (and an overwhelming amount of) art.

Special Exhibitions

Special exhibitions are found on level 3 of Boiler House and level 2 of Blavatnik Building (£13 to £18.50, children free). Past special exhibitions have included retrospectives on Henri Matisse, Frida Kahlo, Roy Lichtenstein, Nazism and 'Degenerate' Art, and Joan Miró.

What's Nearby?
Shakespeare's
Globe   Historic Building
(Map p280; ☏020-7902 1500; www.shakespearesglobe.com; 21 New Globe Walk, SE1; adult/child £17/10; ⊗9am-5pm; ♿; ⓤBlackfriars or London Bridge) The new Globe was designed to resemble the original as closely as possible, which means having the arena open to the fickle London skies, leaving the 700 'groundlings' (standing spectators) to weather London's spectacular downpours. Visits to the Globe include tours of the theatre (half-hourly) as well as access to the exhibition space, which has fascinating exhibits on Shakespeare, life in Bankside and theatre in the 17th century.

PADMAYOGINI/SHUTTERSTOCK ©

✗ Take a Break
Enjoy a taste of Eastern Europe at exquisite Baltic (p165).

St Paul's Cathedral

St Paul's Cathedral is one of the most majestic buildings in London. Despite the far higher skyscrapers of the Square Mile, it still manages to gloriously dominate the skyline.

Great For...

🛈 Need to Know

Map p280; ☎020-7246 8357; www.stpauls.co.uk; St Paul's Churchyard, EC4; adult/child £18/8; ⊗8.30am-4.30pm Mon-Sat; Ⓤ St Paul's

★ Top Tip

A visit to the church's hallowed ground must be made to fully appreciate its sublime architecture.

There has been a place of Christian worship on this site for over 1400 years. St Paul's Cathedral as we know it is the fifth Christian church to be erected here; it was completed in 1711 and sports the largest church dome in the capital.

Dome

Despite the cathedral's rich history and impressive (and uniform) English baroque interior, many visitors are more interested in climbing the dome for one of the best views of London. The dome actually consists of three parts: a plastered brick inner dome, a nonstructural lead outer dome visible on the skyline and a brick cone between them holding it all together, one inside the other. This unique structure, the first triple dome ever built and second only in size to St Peter's in the Vatican, made the cathedral

Christopher Wren's tour de force. It all weighs 59,000 tonnes.

Some 528 stairs take you to the top, but it's a three-stage journey. Through a door on the western side of the southern transept, and some 30m and 257 steps above, you reach the interior walkway around the dome's base. This is the **Whispering Gallery**, so called because if you talk close to the wall it carries your words around to the opposite side, 32m away. Climbing even more steps (another 119) you reach the **Stone Gallery**, an exterior viewing platform 53m above the ground, obscured by pillars and other suicide-preventing measures. The remaining 152 iron steps to the **Golden Gallery** are steeper and narrower than below, but are really worth the effort. From here, 85m above London,

Interior of St Paul's Cathedral

you can enjoy superb 360-degree views of the city.

Interior

Just beneath the dome is an **epitaph** written for Wren by his son: *Lector, si monumentum requiris, circumspice* (Reader, if you seek his monument, look around you). In the north aisle you'll find the grandiose **Duke of Wellington Memorial** (1912), which took 54 years to complete – the Iron Duke's horse Copenhagen originally faced the other way, but it was deemed unfitting that a horse's rear end should face the altar.

> ☑ **Don't Miss**
>
> Climbing the dome, witnessing the quire ceiling mosaics and visiting the tombs of Admiral Nelson and the Duke of Wellington.

KOTSOVOLOS PANAGIOTIS/SHUTTERSTOCK ©

In the north transept chapel is William Holman Hunt's celebrated painting **The Light of the World**, which depicts Christ knocking at a weed-covered door that, symbolically, can only be opened from within. Beyond, in the cathedral's heart, you'll find the spectacular **quire** (or chancel) – its ceilings and arches dazzling with green, blue, red and gold mosaics telling the story of Creation – and the **high altar**. The ornately carved choir stalls by Dutch–British sculptor Grinling Gibbons on either side of the quire are exquisite, as are the ornamental wrought-iron gates, separating the aisles from the altar, by Huguenot Jean Tijou (both men also worked on Hampton Court Palace).

Walk around the altar, with its massive gilded oak **baldachin** – a kind of canopy with barley-twist columns – to the **American Memorial Chapel**, commemorating the 28,000 Americans based in Britain who lost their lives during WWII. Note the Roll of Honour book turned daily, the state flags in the stained glass and American flora and fauna in the carved wood panelling.

In the south quire aisle, Bill Viola's new and very poignant **video installation** *Martyrs (Earth, Air, Fire, Water)* depicts four figures being overwhelmed by natural forces. A bit further on is an **effigy of John Donne** (1573–1631), metaphysical poet and one-time dean of Old St Paul's, that survived the Great Fire.

Crypt

On the eastern side of both the north and south transepts are stairs leading down to the crypt and the **OBE Chapel**, where services are held for members of the Order of the British Empire. The crypt has memorials to around 300 of the great and the good, including Florence Nightingale, TE Lawrence (of Arabia) and Winston Churchill, while both the **Duke of Wellington** and

> ✕ **Take a Break**
>
> Nearby Miyama (p162) serves near-celestial Japanese fare.

Admiral Nelson are actually buried here. On the surrounding walls are plaques in memory of those from the Commonwealth who died in various conflicts during the 20th century, including Gallipoli and the Falklands War.

Wren's tomb is also in the crypt, and many others, notably painters such as Joshua Reynolds, John Everett Millais, JMW Turner and William Holman Hunt, are remembered here, too.

The **Oculus**, in the former treasury, projects four short films onto its walls (you'll need the iPad audio tour to hear the sound). If you're not up to climbing the dome, experience it here audiovisually.

Exterior

Just outside the north transept, there's a simple **monument to the people of London**, honouring the 32,000 civilians killed (and another 50,000 seriously injured) in the city during WWII. Also to the north, at the entrance to Paternoster Sq, is **Temple Bar**, one of the original gateways to the City of London. This medieval stone archway once straddled Fleet St at a site marked by a silver dragon, but was removed to Middlesex in 1877. It was placed here in 2004.

Tours

The admission price includes a free audiovisual handset. Alternatively, there are free 1½-hour guided tours four times a day (10am, 11am, 1pm and 2pm) Monday to Saturday – head to the desk just past the entrance to check times and book a place.

What's Nearby?

Museum of London   Museum

(Map p280; ☎020-7001 9844; www.museumoflondon.org.uk; 150 London Wall, EC2; ☉10am-6pm; ⛛Barbican) **FREE** Set aside two hours to romp through 450,000 years of London history at this entertaining and educational museum, one of the capital's finest. Exhibiting everything from a mammoth's jaw found in Ilford to Oliver Cromwell's death mask via the desperate scrawls of convicts on a cell from Wellclose Prison, interactive displays

and reconstructed scenes transport visitors from Roman Londinium and Saxon Lundenwic right up to the 21st-century metropolis. Free themed tours are offered daily; times are displayed by the entrance.

Highlights include a video on the 1348 Black Death, a section of London's old Roman wall, the graffitied walls of a prison cell (1750), a glorious re-creation of a Victorian street, a 1908 taxi cab, a 1928 art-deco lift from Selfridges and a fascinating multimedia display on the suffragettes.

Sadly the much-asked-after 'fatberg' – a vast glob of waste pulled from the sewers beneath Whitechapel – can currently only be seen on the museum website.

Millennium Bridge   Bridge

(Map p280; ⛛St Paul's or Blackfriars) The elegant steel, aluminium and concrete

Crossing the Millennium Bridge

Millennium Bridge staples the south bank of the Thames, in front of Tate Modern, to the north bank, at the steps of Peter's Hill below St Paul's Cathedral. The low-slung frame designed by Norman Foster and Anthony Caro looks spectacular, particularly when lit up at night with fibre optics, and the view of St Paul's from the South Bank has become one of London's iconic images.

St Mary-le-Bow
Church

(Map p280; ☎020-7248 5139; www.stmaryle bow.co.uk; Cheapside, EC2; ☉7.30am-6pm Mon-Wed, to 4pm Thu & Fri; Ⓤ St Paul's or Bank) It's said that a true Cockney has to have been born within earshot of Bow Bells – and they ring out on the quarter of each hour from the delicate steeple at St Mary-le-Bow, one of Christopher Wren's great churches. Completed in 1710, the

church was badly damaged during WWII and didn't reopen until 1964, when the beautiful stained-glass windows were added. The lovely **Café Below** (Map p280; ☑020-7329 0789; www.cafebelow.co.uk; Cheapside, EC2; mains £10.50-16.50; ☉7.30-10am & 11.30am-2.30pm Mon-Fri; Ⓤ Mansion House) is in the crypt.

> ★ **Local Knowledge**
>
> The cathedral underwent a major clean-up in 2011. To see the difference, check the section of unrestored wall under glass by the Great West Door.

> ★ **Top Tip**
>
> Attending Evensong (5pm Monday to Saturday, 3.15pm Sunday) or the 11.30am Sunday Eucharist is free.

GEORGETHEFOURTH/SHUTTERSTOCK ©

The Southbank Centre

The South Bank

Ever since the London Eye came up in 2000, the South Bank has become a magnet for visitors and the area is always a buzz of activity. A roll call of riverside sights stretches along the Thames, commencing with the London Eye, running past the cultural enclave of the Southbank Centre and on to the Tate Modern.

Great For...

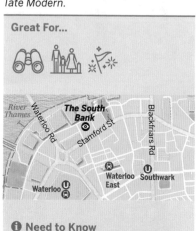

ⓘ Need to Know

Access the South Bank from Waterloo or Southwark stations.

★ Top Tip

Book online for the London Eye and London Dungeon to skip queues.

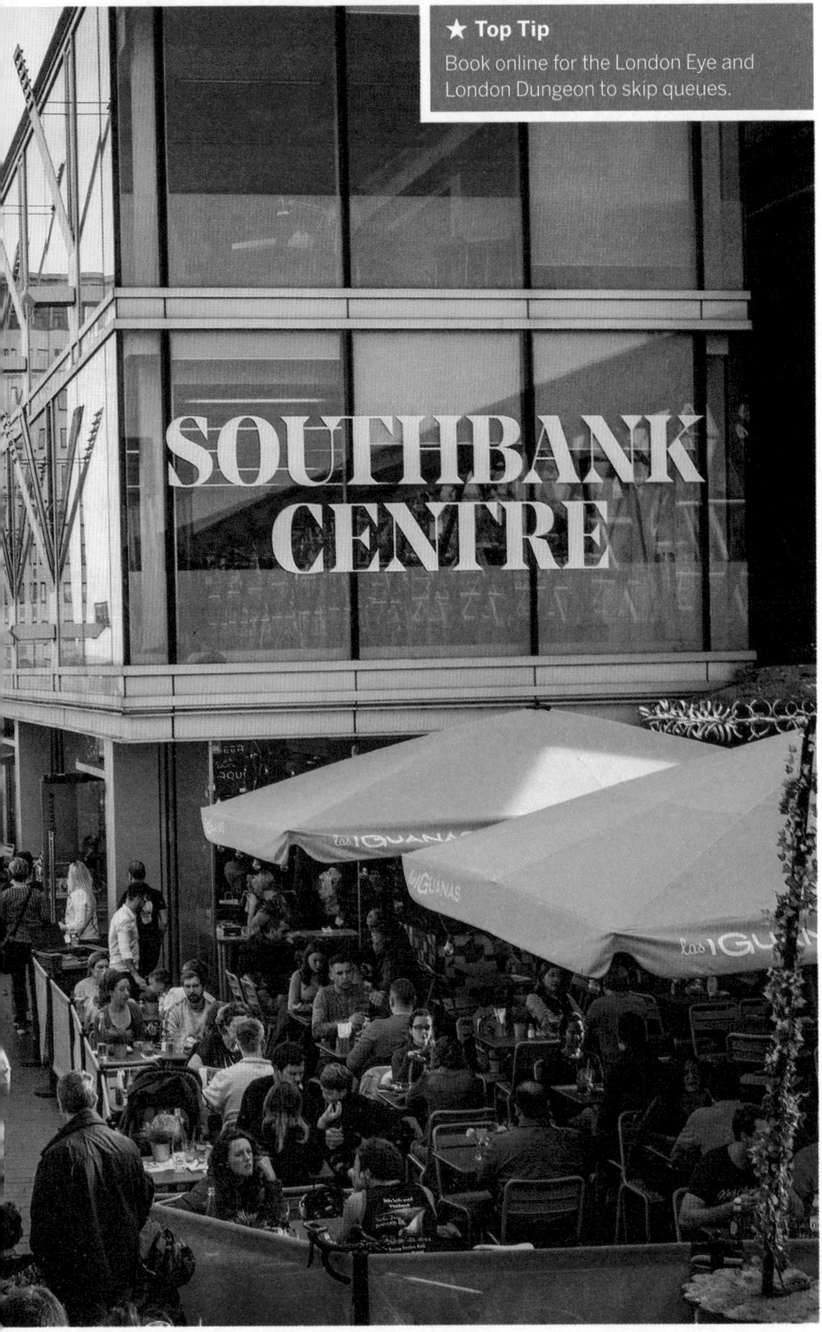

WILLY BARTON/SHUTTERSTOCK ©

The South Bank has a great vibe. As well as top attractions, there is plenty to take in while enjoying a stroll: views of the north bank of London (including great views of the Houses of Parliament and Big Ben), street artists, office workers on their lunchtime run, and boats toing and froing along the Thames.

South Bank Sights

London Eye   Viewpoint

(Map p280; www.londoneye.com; nr County Hall; adult/child £28/23; ⊙11am-6pm Sep-May, 10am-8.30pm Jun-Aug; Ⓤ Waterloo or Westminster) Standing 135m high in a fairly flat city, the London Eye affords views 25 miles in every direction, weather permitting. Interactive tablets provide great information (in six languages) about landmarks as they appear in the skyline. Each rotation – or 'flight' – takes a gracefully slow 30 minutes. At peak times (July, August and school holidays) it can feel like you'll spend more time in the queue than in the capsule; book premium fast-track tickets to jump the line.

Southbank Centre   Arts Centre

(Map p280; ☑020-3879 9555; www.southbank centre.co.uk; Belvedere Rd, SE1; ⊙10am-11pm; 🚻; Ⓤ Waterloo or Embankment) Southbank Centre is made up of several brutalist buildings on the riverfront, all dedicated to the arts. With cafes, restaurants, shops and bars, this is a hub of activity, somewhere to linger and people-watch. Look for the dancers rehearsing on the lower level of the Royal Festival Hall (p217), and hop in the 'singing lift' for a musical ride. Skateboarders practise in the graffiti-decorated hang-out under **Queen Elizabeth Hall**. Try street food and cocktails at the food market (Friday to Sunday).

London Eye on the River Thames

Hayward Gallery · Gallery

(Map p280; ☏020-3879 9555; www.southbank centre.co.uk/venues/hayward-gallery; Belvedere Rd, SE1; £14-16.50; ☺11am-7pm Mon, Wed, Sat & Sun, to 9pm Thu; Ⓤ Waterloo) Part of the Southbank Centre, the Hayward hosts a changing roster of contemporary art (video, photography, sculpture, painting etc) in a 1960s brutalist building. It puts on three to four exhibitions a year, either the work of individual or several artists with a connecting theme. Free exhibitions are occasionally held in the HENI Project Space.

London Dungeon · Amusement Park

(Map p280; www.thedungeons.com/london; County Hall, Westminster Bridge Rd, SE1; adult/ child £31/25; ☺10am-5pm Mon-Wed, Fri & Sun, 11am-5pm Thu, 10am-6pm Sat; Ⓤ Waterloo or Westminster) A scary tour of London's gruesome history awaits. Expect darkness, sudden loud noises, flashing lights, squirts of unspecified liquid and lots of unpleasant smells as you shuffle through themed rooms where actors, often covered in fake blood, tell creepy stories and goad visitors. It's interactive, it's spooky, and it's a lot of fun. Queues are long, even for those with pre-booked tickets. It takes around 1½ hours to work your way through the gory dungeon. Not suitable for young children.

What's Nearby?

Roupell St · Street

(Map p280; Roupell St, SE1; Ⓤ Waterloo) Wander the backstreets of Waterloo's transport hub and you'll find some amazing architecture. Roupell St is an astonishingly pretty row of workers' cottages, all dark bricks and coloured doors, dating back to the 1820s. The street is so uniform it looks like a film set.

Imperial War Museum · Museum

(☏020-7416 5000; www.iwm.org.uk; Lambeth Rd, SE1; ☺10am-6pm; Ⓤ Lambeth North) **FREE** Fronted by a pair of intimidating 15in naval guns and a piece of the Berlin Wall, this riveting museum is housed in what was the Bethlem Royal Hospital, a psychiatric hospital also known as Bedlam. Although the museum's focus is on military action involving British or Commonwealth troops largely during the 20th century, it covers war in the wider sense. Must-see exhibits include the state-of-the-art **First World War Galleries** and **Witnesses to War** in the forecourt and atrium above.

The museum is a short tube or bus ride from the South Bank and well worth the effort for anyone interested in WWI or WWII.

☑ **Don't Miss**

The astounding views from the London Eye.

RICHIE CHAN/SHUTTERSTOCK ©

✕ **Take a Break**

Enjoy a drink at the King's Arms (p203), one of London's most atmospheric pubs.

Hyde Park

London's largest royal park spreads itself over 142 hectares of neat gardens, wild grasses and glorious trees. As well as being a fantastic green space in the middle of London, it is home to a handful of fascinating sights.

Great For...

☑ **Don't Miss**

The opulence of Apsley House, the Albert Memorial, Royal Albert Hall and Kensington Palace.

Henry VIII expropriated Hyde Park from the church in 1536, after which it emerged as a hunting ground for kings and aristocrats; later it became a popular venue for duels, executions and horse racing. It was the first royal park to open to the public in the early 17th century, the famous venue of the Great Exhibition in 1851, and during WWII it became a vast potato bed. These days, as well as being an exquisite park, it is an occasional concert and music-festival venue.

Green Spaces

The eastern half of the park is covered with expansive lawns, which become one vast picnic-and-frolic area on sunny days. The western half is more untamed, with plenty of trees and areas of wild grass.

Kensington Palace (p103)

CHRISDORNEY/SHUTTERSTOCK ©

Speakers' Corner

Frequented by Karl Marx, Vladimir Lenin, George Orwell and William Morris, **Speakers' Corner** (Map p278; Park Lane; Ⓤ Marble Arch) in the northeastern corner of Hyde Park is traditionally the spot for oratorical acrobatics and soapbox ranting.

It's the only place in Britain where demonstrators can assemble without police permission, a concession granted in 1872 after serious riots 17 years before when 150,000 people gathered to demonstrate against the Sunday Trading Bill before Parliament, only to be unexpectedly ambushed by police concealed within Marble Arch.

The Serpentine & Galleries

Hyde Park is separated from Kensington Gardens by the L-shaped **Serpentine** (Map

ⓘ Need to Know

Map p278; www.royalparks.org.uk/parks/ hyde-park; ⏰ 5am–midnight; Ⓤ Marble Arch, Hyde Park Corner, Knightsbridge or Queensway

Take Break

For good Italian fare in spectacular setting, eat at Chucs (p160), in the Serpentine Sackler Gallery.

★ Top Tip

Hyde Park is an ideal picnic stop between sights.

p278; ☎ 020-7262 1330; Ⓤ Lancaster Gate or Knightsbridge), a small lake.

Straddling the Serpentine Lake, the Serpentine Galleries may look like quaint historical buildings, but they are one of London's most important contemporary-art galleries. Damien Hirst, Andreas Gursky, Louise Bourgeois, Gabriel Orozco, Tomoko Takahashi and Jeff Koons have all exhibited here.

The original exhibition space, **Serpentine Gallery** (Map p278; ☎ 020-7402 6075; www.serpentinegalleries.org; Kensington Gardens, W2; ⏰ 10am–6pm Tue–Sun; Ⓤ Lancaster Gate or Knightsbridge) FREE, is the 1930s former tea pavilion located in Kensington Gardens. In 2013 the **Serpentine Sackler Gallery** (West Carriage Dr, W2) FREE opened within the Magazine, a former gunpowder depot across the Serpentine Bridge in Hyde Park. Built in 1805, it has been augmented with a daring, undulating extension designed by Pritzker Prize–winning architect Zaha Hadid.

Diana, Princess of Wales Memorial Fountain

This **memorial fountain** (Map p278; off West Carriage Dr; ⊙10am-8pm Apr-Aug, to 7pm Sep, to 6pm Mar & Oct, to 4pm Nov-Feb; Ⓤ Knightsbridge or Lancaster Gate) is dedicated to the late Princess of Wales. Designed by Kathryn Gustafson as a 'moat without a castle', the circular double stream is composed of 545 pieces of Cornish granite, its waters drawn from a chalk aquifer more than 100m below ground. Unusually, visitors are actively encouraged to splash about, to the delight of children.

Gun Salutes

Royal Gun Salutes are fired in Hyde Park on 10 June for the Duke of Edinburgh's birthday and on 14 November for the Prince of Wales' birthday. The salutes are fired at midday and include 41 rounds (21 is standard, but being a royal park, Hyde Park gets a bonus 20 rounds).

What's Nearby?

Kensington Gardens   Park

(Map p278; ☎0300 061 2000; www.royal parks.org.uk/parks/kensington-gardens; ⊙6am-dusk; Ⓤ Queensway or Lancaster Gate) A gorgeous collection of manicured lawns, tree-shaded avenues and basins immediately west of Hyde Park, the pic-turesque expanse of Kensington Gardens is technically part of Kensington Palace, located in the far west of the gardens. The large **Round Pond** in front of the palace is enjoyable to amble around, and also worth a look are the lovely fountains in the **Italian Gardens**, believed to be a gift from

Rose Garden in Hyde Park

Prince Albert to Queen Victoria; they are now the venue of a cafe.

Kensington Palace
Palace

(Map p278; www.hrp.org.uk/kensington-palace; Kensington Gardens, W8; adult/child £19.50/9.70, cheaper weekdays after 2pm; ⊙10am-6pm Mar-Oct, to 4pm Nov-Feb; Ⓤ High St Kensington) Built in 1605, Kensington Palace became the favourite royal residence under William and Mary of Orange in 1689, remaining so until George III (r 1760-1820) became king and moved out. Today, it's still a royal residence, with the likes of Prince William and Catherine and Prince

> ### ☑ Don't Miss
> Each year an architect who has never built in the UK is commissioned to build a 'Summer Pavilion' (June to October) for the Serpentine Galleries.

Harry and Meghan living there. A large part of the palace is open to the public, however, including the King's and Queen's State Apartments.

Apsley House
Historic Building

(Map p277; ☎020-7493 8401; www.english-heritage.org.uk/visit/places/apsley-house; 149 Piccadilly, Hyde Park Corner, W1; adult/child £10/6, with Wellington Arch £12.70/7.60; ⊙11am-5pm Wed-Sun Apr-Oct, 10am-4pm Sat & Sun Nov-Mar; Ⓤ Hyde Park Corner) This stunning house, containing exhibits about the Duke of Wellington, who defeated Napoleon Bonaparte at Waterloo, was once the first building to appear when entering London from the west and was therefore known as 'No 1 London'. Wellington memorabilia, including the Duke's death mask, fills the basement **gallery**, while an astonishing collection of china and silver, and paintings by Velasquez, Rubens, Van Dyck, Brueghel, Murillo and Goya awaits in the 1st-floor Waterloo Gallery.

Albert Memorial
Monument

(Map p278; ☎tours 020-8969 0104; Kensington Gardens; tours adult/concession £9/8; ⊙tours 2pm & 3pm 1st Sun of month Mar-Dec; Ⓤ Knightsbridge or Gloucester Rd) This splendid Victorian confection on the southern edge of Kensington Gardens is as ostentatious as its subject wasn't. Queen Victoria's humble German husband Albert (1819–61) explicitly insisted he did not want a monument. Ignoring the good prince's wishes, the Lord Mayor instructed George Gilbert Scott to build the 53m-high, gaudy Gothic memorial – the 4.25m-tall gilded statue of the prince, surrounded by 187 figures representing the continents (Asia, Europe, Africa and America), the arts, industry and science, went up in 1876.

> ### ★ Top Tip
> Deckchairs are available for hire (one/four hours £1.60/4.60) throughout the park from March to October.

IRISPHOTO1/SHUTTERSTOCK ©

Cast Courts (p106) in the Victoria & Albert Museum

Victoria & Albert Museum

The Museum of Manufactures, as the V&A was known when it opened in 1852, was part of Prince Albert's legacy to the nation in the aftermath of the successful Great Exhibition of 1851. Its aims were the 'improvement of public taste in design' and 'applications of fine art to objects of utility'. It's done a fine job so far.

Great For...

ⓘ Need to Know

V&A; Map p278; ☏020-7942 2000; www.vam. ac.uk; Cromwell Rd, SW7; ⏱10am-5.45pm Sat-Thu, to 10pm Fri; Ⓤ South Kensington
`FREE`

★ Top Tip

The V&A's temporary exhibitions are reliably fantastic, so factor in some time to check them out.

Collection

Through 146 galleries, the museum houses the world's greatest collection of decorative arts, from ancient Chinese ceramics to modernist architectural drawings, Korean bronze and Japanese swords, cartoons by Raphael, gowns from the Elizabethan era, ancient jewellery, a Sony Walkman – and much, much more.

Tours

Free one-hour guided introductory tours leave the main reception area every day at 10.30am, 12.30pm, 1.30pm and 3.30pm. Check the website for details of other, more specific, tours.

Level 1

The street level is mostly devoted to art and design from India, China, Japan, Korea and Southeast Asia, as well as European art. One of the museum's highlights is the **Cast Courts** in rooms 46a and 46b, containing staggering plaster casts collected in the Victorian era, such as Michelangelo's *David*, acquired in 1858.

More European excellence is on display in room 48a in the form of the **Raphael Cartoons**. A series of huge preliminary 'sketches' of biblical scenes to be used to create equally huge tapestries, these are masterpieces in their own right and have a suitably grand space in which to appreciate them.

The **China Gallery** (rooms 44 and 47e) displays lovely pieces, including a beautifully lithe wooden statue of Guanyin seated in

Medieval and Renaissance Galleries, Victoria & Albert Museum

lalitasana pose from AD 1200; also check out a leaf from the *Twenty Views of the Yuanmingyuan Summer Palace* (1781–86), revealing the Haiyantang and the 12 animal heads of the fountain (now ruins) in Beijing. Within the subdued lighting of the **Japan Gallery** (room 45) stands a fearsome suit of armour in the Domaru style. More than 400 objects are within the **Islamic Middle East Gallery** (room 42), including ceramics, textiles, carpets, glass and woodwork from the 8th century up to the years before WWI. The exhibition's highlight is the gorgeous mid-16th-century **Ardabil Carpet**.

For fresh air, the landscaped **John Madejski Garden** is a lovely shaded inner courtyard. Cross it to reach the original **Refreshment Rooms** (Morris, Gamble and Poynter Rooms), dating from the 1860s and redesigned by McInnes Usher McKnight Architects (MUMA), who also renovated the **Medieval and Renaissance galleries** (1350–1600) to the right of the Grand Entrance.

Levels 2 & 4

The **British Galleries**, featuring every aspect of British design from 1500 to 1900, are divided between levels 2 (1500–1760) and 4 (1760–1900). The **Great Bed of Ware** is a highlight, so famous it was even mentioned by Shakespeare. Level 4 also boasts the **Architecture Gallery** (rooms 127 to 128a), which vividly describes architectural styles via models and videos, and the spectacular brightly illuminated **Contemporary Glass Gallery** (room 129).

Level 3

The **Jewellery Gallery** (rooms 91 to 93) is outstanding; the mezzanine level – accessed via the glass-and-perspex spiral staircase – glitters with jewel-encrusted swords, watches and gold boxes. The **Photography Centre** (rooms 100 and 101) is one of the nation's best, with access to over 500,000 images collected since the mid-19th century. **20th Century** (room 76) celebrates design classics from a 1985 Sony credit-card radio to a 1992 Nike 'Air Max' shoe, Peter Ghyczy's Garden Egg Chair from 1968 and the now-ubiquitous selfie stick.

Level 6

Among the pieces in the **Ceramics Gallery** (rooms 136 to 146) – the world's largest – are standout items from the Middle East and Asia. The **Dr Susan Weber Gallery** (rooms 133 to 135) celebrates furniture design over the past six centuries.

☑ **Don't Miss**

The temporary exhibitions, Photography Centre and Elizabethan gowns.

ANTON_IVANOV/SHUTTERSTOCK ©

✖ **Take a Break**

Stop for a coffee at the V&A Cafe (p159), if only to admire the magnificent Refreshment Rooms, which date from the 1860s.

Victoria & Albert Museum

HALF-DAY HIGHLIGHTS TOUR

The art- and design-packed V&A is vast: we have devised an easy-to-follow tour of the museum highlights to help cover some signature pieces while also allowing you to appreciate some of the grandeur of the museum architecture.

Enter the V&A by the main entrance off Cromwell Rd and immediately turn left to explore the Islamic Middle East Gallery and to discover the sumptuous silk-and-wool **❶ Ardabil Carpet**. Among the pieces from South Asia in the adjacent gallery is the terrifying automated **❷ Tipu's Tiger**. Continue to the outstanding **❸ Fashion Gallery** with its displays of clothing styles through the ages. The magnificent gallery opposite houses the **❹ Raphael Cartoons**, large paintings by Raphael used to weave tapestries for the Vatican. Take the stairs to level 2 and the Britain 1500–1760 Gallery; turn

Raphael Cartoons
These seven drawings by Raphael, depicting the acts of St Peter and St Paul, were the full-scale preparatory works for seven tapestries that were woven for the Sistine Chapel in the Vatican.

TRISTAN FEWINGS/ STRINGER / GETTY IMAGES ©

Fashion Gallery
With clothing from the 18th century to the present day, this circular and chronologically arranged gallery showcases evening wear, undergarments and iconic fashion milestones, such as 1960s dresses designed by Mary Quant.

The Great Bed of Ware
Created during the reign of Queen Elizabeth I, its headboard and bedposts are etched with ancient graffiti; the 16th-century oak Great Bed of Ware is famously name-dropped in Shakespeare's *Twelfth Night*.

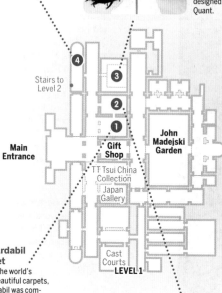

Britain 1500–1760 Gallery

Stairs to Level 2

Stairs from Level 1

❹ ❸ ❷ ❶ ❺ ❻

John Madejski Garden

Main Entrance

Gift Shop

TT Tsui China Collection

Japan Gallery

Stairs to Level 3

The Ardabil Carpet
One of the world's most beautiful carpets, the Ardabil was completed in 1540, one of a pair commissioned by Shah Tahmasp, ruler of Iran. The piece is most astonishing for the artistry of the detailing and the subtlety of design.

Cast Courts
LEVEL 1

LEVEL 2

Tipu's Tiger
This disquieting 18th-century wood-and-metal mechanical automaton depicts a European being savaged by a tiger. When a handle is turned, an organ hidden within the feline mimics the cries of the dying man, whose arm also rises.

Henry VIII's Writing Box
This exquisitely ornate walnut and oak 16th-century writing box has been added to over the centuries, but the original decorative motifs are superb, including Henry's coat of arms, flanked by Venus (holding Cupid) and Mars.

left in the gallery to find the **5 Great Bed of Ware**, beyond which rests the exquisitely crafted artistry of **6 Henry VIII's Writing Box**. Head up the stairs into the Ironwork Gallery on level 3 for the **7 Hereford Screen**. Continue through the Ironwork and Sculpture Galleries and through the Leighton Corridor to the glittering **8 Jewellery Gallery**. Exit through the Stained Glass gallery, at the end of which you'll find stairs back down to level 1.

LAPAS77 / SHUTTERSTOCK ©

TOP TIPS

➡ Museum attendants are always at hand along the route for information.

➡ Photography is allowed in most galleries, except the Jewellery Gallery, the Raphael Cartoons and in exhibitions.

➡ Avoid daytime crowds: visit the V&A in the evening, till 10pm on Fridays.

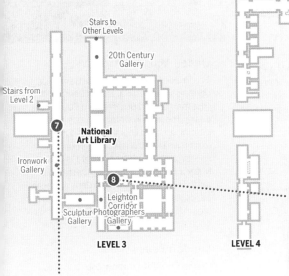

Stairs to Other Levels

20th Century Gallery

Stairs from Level 2

7

National Art Library

Ironwork Gallery

8

Leighton Corridor

Sculptur Photographers Gallery Gallery

LEVEL 3

LEVEL 4

Jewellery Gallery
The beautifully illuminated Jewellery Gallery has a stunning collection of items from ancient Greece to the modern day, including a dazzling gold Celtic breastplate, art nouveau jewellery and animals fashioned by Fabergé.

GAID KORNSILAPA / SHUTTERSTOCK ©

The Hereford Screen
Designed by George Gilbert Scott, this awe-inspiring choir screen is a labour of love, originally fashioned for Hereford Cathedral. It's an almighty conception of wood, iron, copper, brass and hardstone, and there were few parts of the V&A that could support its great mass.

Pond in Regent's Park

L-ANAD/SHUTTERSTOCK ©

Regent's Park

The most elaborate and formal of London's many parks, Regent's Park is one of the capital's loveliest green spaces. It's also home to London Zoo, one of the oldest zoos in the world.

Great For

☑ **Don't Miss**

Queen Mary's Gardens, London Zoo, views from Primrose Hill

Queen Mary's Gardens

The Prince Regent, the future George IV, commissioned star architect John Nash (the man behind Buckingham Palace) to design the park in what was once a royal hunting ground. There are broad avenues, expansive lawns, a lake, playgrounds and sports pitches but the highlight is **Queen Mary's Gardens**, at the southern end of the park. These landscaped gardens are beautiful, especially in June when the roses are in bloom. Performances take place here in an open-air theatre (p215) during summer.

London Zoo

Opened in 1828, **London Zoo** (Map p284; www.zsl.org/zsl-london-zoo; Outer Circle, Regent's Park, NW1; adult/child £25/22, discounts if booked in advance online; ◎10am-6pm Apr-Sep, to 5.30pm Mar & Oct, to 4pm Nov-Feb; ▥; ▣274)

Lemur in London Zoo

MARCELA NOVOTNA/SHUTTERSTOCK ©

is among the oldest in the world. The emphasis nowadays is firmly on conservation, breeding and education, with fewer animals and bigger enclosures. Highlights include **Land of the Lions**, **Gorilla Kingdom**, **Tiger Territory** and **Penguin Beach.** More interactive are the walk-through **In with the Lemurs**, where inquisitive ring-tailed lemurs usually come within touching distance, and **Butterfly Paradise**, where myriad butterflies and moths flutter from flower to flower.

The latter two are indoors and there is plenty more to guarantee some fun on a rainy day, including an **aquarium**, a **reptile house** and a building called **Bugs**, which is full of creepy-crawlies.

Regent's Canal

To escape the crowded streets and enjoy a picturesque, waterside side stretch of

North London, take to the **canals** (Map p284) that once played such a vital role in the transport of goods across the capital. The towpath of the Regent's Canal also makes an excellent shortcut across North London, either on foot or by bike. In full, the ribbon of water runs 9 miles from Little Venice (where it connects with the Grand Union Canal) to the Thames at Limehouse.

What's Nearby?

Primrose Hill   Park

(Map p284; Ⓤ Chalk Farm) On summer weekends, Primrose Hill park is absolutely packed with locals enjoying a picnic and the extraordinary views over the city skyline. Come weekdays, however, there are mostly just dog walkers and nannies. It's a lovely place to enjoy a quiet stroll or an al fresco sandwich.

Walking Tour: A Northern Point of View

This walk takes in North London's most interesting locales, including celebrity-infested Primrose Hill and chaotic Camden Town, home to loud guitar bands and the last of London's cartoon punks.

Start 🚇 Chalk Farm
Distance 2.5 miles
Duration Two hours

1 Affluent **Regent's Park Road** is home to many darlings of the women's mags, so keep your eyes open for famous faces.

Classic photo: London's skyline from atop Primrose Hill

2 In **Primrose Hill** (p111), walk to the top of the park, where you'll find a classic view of central London's skyline.

3 Walk downhill to Regent's Canal, where you'll pass the large aviary at **London Zoo** (p110), quaint boats, superb mansions and converted industrial buildings.

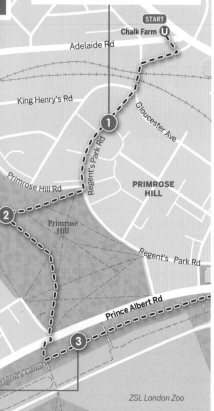

START
Chalk Farm 🚇

Adelaide Rd

King Henry's Rd

Gloucester Ave

Regent's Park Rd

Primrose Hill Rd

1

PRIMROSE HILL

2 Primrose Hill

Regent's Park Rd

Prince Albert Rd

3

Regent's Canal

ZSL London Zoo

4 At **Camden Lock** turn left into buzzing **Lock Market** (p182), with its original fashion, ethnic art and food stalls.

5 Exit onto **Camden High Street** and turn right onto bar-lined **Inverness Street**, which hosts its own little market.

6 At **Gloucester Crescent** turn left and walk past the glorious Georgian town houses.

Take a Break...
Food collective **KERB** (p162) offers an A to Z of world cuisine.

7 Head towards Delancey St and make a beeline for the **Edinboro Castle** (p200), where this walk ends with a well-deserved drink!

1 BJANKA KADIC/ALAMY STOCK PHOTO © 2 MIKADUN/SHUTTERSTOCK © 3 PCRUCIATTI/SHUTTERSTOCK ©

Blue Whale skeleton, Natural History Museum

ELROCE/SHUTTERSTOCK ©

Natural History Museum

This colossal building (a reason in itself to visit) is infused with the Victorian spirit of collecting, cataloguing and interpreting the natural world. Seasonal events and excellent temporary exhibitions make it one of the London's best museums, especially for families.

Great For...

☑ Don't Miss

The animatronic Tyrannosaurus rex, planet-earth displays in the Red Zone, the Darwin Centre and Gothic architecture.

Hintze Hall

Coming in through the museum's grand main entrance, this impressive central hall (part of the Green Zone) resembles a cathedral nave – quite fitting, as it was built in a time when the natural sciences were challenging the biblical tenets of Christian orthodoxy. Naturalist, first superintendent of the museum, and coiner of the word 'dinosaur' Richard Owen celebrated the building as a 'cathedral to nature'.

After 81 years in the Mammals Hall, in 2017 the blue whale skeleton was relocated to Hintze Hall, with the famous cast of a diplodocus skeleton (nicknamed Dippy) making way for the colossal marine mammal.

Blue Zone

Undoubtedly the museum's star attraction, the **Dinosaurs Gallery** takes you on an

Architectural details

Map p278; www.nhm.ac.uk; Cromwell Rd, SW7; ⊙10am-5.50pm; [♿]; [U]South Kensington FREE

🛈 Need to Know

✖ Take a Break

The Queen's Arms (p199) beckons with a cosy interior and a right royal selection of ales and ciders on tap.

★ Top Tip

Families can borrow an 'explorer backpack' or buy a themed discover trail (£1).

Equally rare and exceptional are the gems and rocks held in the **Vault**, including a Martian meteorite and the largest emerald ever found.

Take a moment to marvel at the trunk section of a 1300-year-old **giant sequoia tree** on the 2nd floor: its size is mind-boggling.

Back on the ground floor, the **Creepy Crawlies Gallery** is fantastic, delving into every aspect of insect life and whether they are our friends or foes (both!).

Red Zone

This zone explores the ever-changing nature of our planet and the forces shaping it. In the Volcanoes & Earthquakes Gallery, the **earthquake simulator**, which re-creates the 1995 Kobe earthquake in a grocery store (of which you can see footage) is a favourite, as is the **From the Beginning Gallery**, which retraces earth's history.

In **Earth's Treasury**, you can find out more about our planet's mineral riches and how they are used in our everyday lives, from jewellery to construction and electronics.

impressive overhead walkway, past a dromaeosaurus (a small and agile meat eater) before reaching a roaring animatronic T-rex and then winding its way through skeletons, fossils, casts and fascinating displays about how dinosaurs lived and died.

Another highlight of this zone is the **Mammals Gallery**, with its life-size blue-whale model and extensive displays on cetaceans.

Green Zone

While children love the Blue Zone, adults may prefer the Green Zone, especially the **Treasures in Cadogan Gallery**, on the 1st floor, which houses the museum's most prized possessions, each with a unique history. Exhibits include a chunk of moon rock, an emperor-penguin egg collected by Captain Scott's expedition and a 1st edition of Charles Darwin's *On the Origin of Species*.

Access to most of the galleries in the Red Zone is via **Earth Hall** and a very tall escalator that disappears into a large earth-metal sculpture. The most intact **stegosaurus fossil skeleton** ever found is displayed at the base.

Orange Zone

The **Darwin Centre** is the beating heart of the museum: this is where the museum's millions of specimens are kept and where its scientists work. The top two floors of the amazing 'cocoon' building are dedicated to explaining the kind of research the museum does (and how) – windows allow you to see the researchers at work.

If you'd like to find out more, pop into the **Attenborough studio** (named after famous naturalist and broadcaster David Attenborough) for one of the daily talks with the museum's scientists. The studio also shows films throughout the day.

Exhibitions

The museum hosts regular exhibitions (admission fees apply), some of them on a recurrent basis. **Wildlife Photographer of the Year** (adult/child £13.50/8, family £28-38; ☉Oct-Dec) has show-stopping images, and **Sensational Butterflies** (per person £5.85, family £19.80; ☉Apr-Sep), a tunnel tent on the East Lawn that swarms with what must originally have been called 'flutter-bys', has become a firm summer favourite. In winter, the same lawn turns into a very popular **ice-skating rink**.

Gardens

A slice of English countryside in SW7, the beautiful **Wildlife Garden** next to the West

Science Museum

Lawn encompasses a range of British lowland habitats, including a meadow with farm gates and a bee tree where a colony of honey bees fills the air.

What's Nearby?

Science Museum   Museum

(Map p278; ☎020-7942 4000; www.science museum.org.uk; Exhibition Rd, SW7; ⊙10am-6pm; ♿; ⓤSouth Kensington) FREE This scientifically spellbinding museum will mesmerise adults and children alike, with its interactive and educational exhibits covering everything from early technology to space travel. On the ground floor, a perennial favourite is **Exploring Space**, a gallery featuring genuine rockets and satellites and a full-size replica of the *Eagle*, the lander that took Neil Armstrong and Buzz Aldrin to the moon in 1969. The **Making the Modern World Gallery** next door is a visual feast of locomotives, planes, cars and other revolutionary inventions.

The 2nd-floor displays cover a host of subjects. The fantastic **Information Age Gallery** showcases how information and communication technologies – from the telegraph to smartphones – have transformed our lives since the 19th century. Standout displays include wireless messages sent by a sinking *Titanic*, the first BBC radio broadcast and a Soviet BESM 1965 supercomputer. **Mathematics: the Winton Gallery**, designed by Zaha Hadid Architects, is a riveting exploration of maths in the real world. The **Medicine Galleries**, opened in 2019, look at the medical world using objects from both the museum's collections and those of Henry Wellcome, pharmacist, entrepreneur, philanthropist and collector.

The 3rd floor's **Flight Gallery** (free tours 1pm most days) is a favourite place for children, with its gliders, hot-air balloons and aircraft. The rest of the floor is all about getting interactive, with top attractions including a **Red Arrows 3D flight-simulation theatre** (£5) and **Space Descent** (£7), a VR experience with (a digital) Tim Peake, British astronaut.

If you've got kids under the age of five, pop down to the basement and the **Garden**, where there's a fun-filled play zone, including a water-play area, besieged by tots in orange waterproof smocks.

★ **Top Tip**

As well as the obligatory dinosaur figurines and animal soft toys, the museum's shop has a fantastic collection of children's books.

GIANCARLO LIGUORI/SHUTTERSTOCK ©

★ **Did You Know?**

The entire museum and its gardens cover a huge 5.7 hectares; the museum contains 80 million specimens from across the natural world.

King's Cross

Formerly a dilapidated red-light district, King's Cross used to be a place better avoided. Fast-forward a couple of decades, though, and the area has metamorphosed, now boasting cool hang-outs and luxury hotels.

Great For...

☑ **Don't Miss**

The Sir John Ritblat Gallery at the British Library, Platform 9¾ sign and the fountains on Granary Square.

British Library Library

(Map p284; ☎0330-333 1144; www.bl.uk; 96 Euston Rd, NW1; ⏱galleries 9.30am-6pm Mon & Fri, to 8pm Tue-Thu, to 5pm Sat, 11am-5pm Sun; ⓤKing's Cross St Pancras) **FREE** Consisting of low-slung red-brick terraces and fronted by a large plaza featuring an oversized statue of Isaac Newton, Colin St John Wilson's British Library building is an architectural wonder. Completed in 1997, it's home to some of the greatest treasures of the written word, including the *Codex Sinaiticus* (the first complete text of the New Testament), Leonardo da Vinci's notebooks and a copy of the Magna Carta (1215).

The most precious manuscripts are held in the **Sir John Ritblat Gallery**, including the stunningly illustrated Jain sacred texts, explorer Captain Scott's final diary, Shakespeare's First Folio (1623), Gutenberg's

St Pancras Station

CAPTUREPB/SHUTTERSTOCK ©

❶ Need to Know

King's Cross St Pancras Station (p264)

✕ Take a Break

Lovely Real Food Market (p162) is open Wednesday to Friday.

★ Top Tip

Queues for the Platform 9¾ sign usually thin in the evening once the Harry Potter shop closes.

Bible of 1455, a copy of *The Diamond Sutra* in Chinese dating to 868 – the world's oldest block-printed book – as well as handwritten lyrics by the Beatles and the score to Handel's *Messiah*.

Book a one-hour guided library tour (£10 for non-members) for an eye-opening glimpse into the inner workings of the library. Tours can be arranged on the British Library website.

St Pancras Station
& Hotel   Historic Building

(Map p284; ☎020-8241 6921; www.stpancras london.com; Euston Rd, NW1; ⓤKing's Cross St Pancras) Looking at the jaw-dropping Gothic splendour of St Pancras, it's hard to believe that the 1873 Midland Grand Hotel languished empty for years and even faced near-demolition in the 1960s. Now home to a five-star hotel, 67 luxury

apartments and the Eurostar terminal, the entire complex has been returned to its former glory. Tours (£24; 10.30am, noon, 2pm and 3.30pm weekends) take you on a fascinating journey through the building's history, from its inception as the southern terminus for the Midland Railway line.

Harry Potter Shop
at Platform 9¾   Gifts & Souvenirs

(Map p284; www.harrypotterplatform934.com; King's Cross Station, N1; ⓧ8am-10pm Mon-Sat, 9am-9pm Sun; ⓤKing's Cross St Pancras) With Pottermania refusing to die down and Diagon Alley impossible to find, if you have junior witches and wizards seeking a wand of their own, take the family directly to King's Cross Station. This little wood-panelled store also stocks jumpers sporting the colours of Hogwarts' four houses (Gryffindor having pride of place) and assorted merchandise, including, of course, the books.

Expect long queues to pose for a trolley photo at Platform 9¾, and occasionally to enter the gift shop.

Granary Square · Square

(Map p284; www.kingscross.co.uk; Stable St, N1; U King's Cross St Pancras) Positioned on a sharp bend in the Regent's Canal north of King's Cross Station, Granary Sq is at the heart of a major redevelopment of a 27-hectare expanse once full of abandoned freight warehouses. Its most striking feature is the fountain made of 1080 individually lit water jets, which pulse and dance in sequence. On hot spring and summer days, it becomes a busy urban beach.

Coal Drops Yard · Area

(Map p284; www.coaldropsyard.com; Bagley Walk, N1C; ⊗varies by business; U King's Cross St Pancras) The latest part of post-industrial King's Cross to be regenerated is this double-level shopping and eating arcade, curving its way along the Regent's Canal, just west of Granary Square. Beautifully restored buildings that once housed Victorian coal stores (and, later, '80s raves) are now home to independent clothing outlets, a range of restaurants and bars, and changing art installations.

Gasholder Park · Park

(Map p284; U King's Cross St Pancras) Part of the impressive redevelopment of the King's Cross area, this urban green space right by Regent's Canal is a masterpiece of regeneration. The cast-iron structure used to be the frame of Gasholder No 8, the largest gas storage cylinder in the area (which was originally located across the canal). Carefully renovated, and with the addition of a central lawn, beautiful benches and a mirrored canopy, it has metamorphosed into a gorgeous pocket park.

Granary Square

House of Illustration
Gallery

(Map p284; www.houseofillustration.org.uk; 2 Granary Sq, N1C; adult/child £8.25/4.40; ⊙10am-6pm Tue-Sun; Ⓤ King's Cross St Pancras) This charity-run gallery founded by the legendary Quentin Blake (famed as the illustrator of Roald Dahl's books) is the UK's sole public gallery purely dedicated to illustration. It stages ever-changing exhibitions – everything from cartoons and book illustrations to advertisements and scientific drawings. The gift shop is, unsurprisingly, an excellent place to pick up original cards and books on illustration.

★ Local Knowledge
Walking along Regent's Canal is a lovely way to experience London's back alleys; allow 25-30 minutes from King's Cross to Camden.

RAVAN CROSS

RON ELLIS/SHUTTERSTOCK ©

What's Nearby?

Wellcome Collection
Museum

(www.wellcomecollection.org; 183 Euston Rd, NW1; ⊙10am-6pm Tue, Wed & Fri-Sun, to 10pm Thu; Ⓤ Euston Sq) **FREE** Focusing on the interface of art, science and medicine, this clever and resourceful museum is fascinating. The heart of the museum is Henry Wellcome's collection of medical curiosities (saws for amputation, forceps through the ages, sex aids and amulets etc), which illustrate the universal fascination with health and the body across civilisations. In the Medicine Now gallery, interactive displays and provocative artworks are designed to make you ponder about humanity and the human body.

London Canal Museum
Museum

(📞020-7713 0836; www.canalmuseum.org.uk; 12-13 New Wharf Rd, N1; adult/child £5/2.50; ⊙10am-4.30pm Tue-Sun & bank holidays; Ⓤ King's Cross St Pancras) This little museum traces the history of the Regent's Canal and explores what life was like for families living and working on Britain's impressively long and historic canal system. The exhibits in the stables upstairs are dedicated to the history of canal transport in Britain, including recent developments such as the clean-up of the Lea River for the 2012 Olympic Games. The museum is housed in a warehouse dating from 1858, where ice was once stored in two deep wells.

The ice trade was huge in Victorian London, with 35,000 tonnes imported from Norway in 1899 alone, arriving in the city at Regent's Canal Dock before being transported along the canal. You can access the wharf at the back of the museum where narrow boats are moored.

✕ Take a Break
Whatever the time of day, Caravan (p162) offers some of the most wonderful fusion cuisine.

Leicester Square

IR STONE/SHUTTERSTOCK ©

Leicester Square & Piccadilly Circus

This duo's buzz makes up for what they lack in cultural cachet. It's all flashing signs and crowds, yet no London visit would be complete without passing through these iconic places.

Great For...

☑ **Don't Miss**

Celebrity-spotting at film premieres on Leicester Sq.

Piccadilly Circus

John Nash had originally designed Regent St and Piccadilly in the 1820s to be the two most elegant streets in town but, curbed by city planners, couldn't realise his dream to the full. He may be disappointed, but suitably astonished, with Piccadilly Circus today: a traffic maelstrom, deluged with visitors and flanked by flashing advertisement panels.

At the centre of the circus stands the famous aluminium statue of Anteros (twin brother of Eros) dedicated to the philanthropist and child-labour abolitionist Lord Shaftesbury. Through the years, the figure has been mistaken for Eros, the God of Love, and the misnomer has stuck (you'll even see signs for 'Eros' from the Underground).

Anteros in Piccadilly Circus

IR STONE/SHUTTERSTOCK ©

❶ Need to Know

Map p274; Ⓤ Leicester Sq

✕ Take a Break

For delicious Levantine food with attitude, head to Palomar (p167).

★ Top Tip

Tkts Leicester Sq (p210) has bargain tickets to West End performances.

Leicester Square

Although Leicester Sq was very fashionable in the 19th century, more recent decades won it associations with pickpocketing, outrageous cinema-ticket prices and the nickname 'Fester Sq' during the 1979 Winter of Discontent strikes, when it was filled with refuse. As part of the Diamond Jubilee and 2012 Olympics celebrations, the square was given an extensive £15.5-million makeover to turn it once again into a lively plaza. Today a sleek, open-plan design replaces the once-dingy little park.

It retains its many cinemas and nightclubs, and as a glamorous premiere venue it still attracts celebrities and their spotters.

Pickpocketing used to be rife around Leicester Sq; things have improved but do keep a very close eye on your belongings.

What's Nearby?

Chinatown Gate   Landmark

(Map p274; www.chinatown.co.uk; Wardour St; Ⓤ Leicester Sq) Northwest of Leicester Sq but a world away in atmosphere, this grand tile-roofed and red-pillared gate marks the entrance into Chinatown. Although not as big as Chinatowns in other world-class cities – it's just Lisle and Gerrard Sts really – London's version is a lively quarter with street signs in Chinese script, red lanterns strung up across the streets bobbing in the breeze, and restaurants, noodle shops and Asian supermarkets crammed in cheek by jowl.

The quality of food varies enormously, but there's a good choice of places for dim sum and other cuisines from across China and other parts of Asia.

There's a smaller, more 'Westernised' gate at the junction of Gerrard St and Newport Pl. To see the area at its effervescent best, time your visit for Lunar New Year in late January or early February. London's original Chinatown was at Limehouse in the East End but moved here after heavy bombardments in WWII.

Day Trip: Hampton Court Palace

London's most spectacular Tudor palace, this 16th-century icon concocts an imposing sense of history, from the huge kitchens and grand living quarters to the spectacular gardens, complete with a 300-year-old maze. Tag along with a themed tour led by a costumed historian or grab one of the audio tours to delve into Hampton Court and its residents' tumultuous history.

Great For...

❶ Need to Know

www.hrp.org.uk/hamptoncourtpalace; Hampton Court Palace, KT8; adult/child/ family £22.70/11.35/40.40; ⊙10am-4.30pm Nov-Mar, to 6pm Apr-Oct; ⛴Hampton Court Palace, ☒Hampton Court

★ **Top Tip**

Ask one of the red-tunic-garbed warders for anecdotes and information.

Hampton Court Palace was built by Cardinal Thomas Wolsey in 1515, but was coaxed from him by Henry VIII just before Wolsey (as chancellor) fell from favour. In the 17th century Christopher Wren was commissioned to build an extension on what was one of the most sophisticated European palaces. The result is a beautiful blend of Tudor and 'restrained baroque' architecture.

Entering the Palace

Passing through the magnificent main gate, you arrive in the **Base Court** and beyond that **Clock Court**, named for its 16th-century astronomical clock. The panelled rooms and arched doorways in the **Young Henry VIII's Story** upstairs from Base Court are a rewarding introduction: note the Tudor graffiti on the fireplace.

Henry VIII's Apartments

The stairs inside Anne Boleyn's Gateway lead up to Henry VIII's Apartments, including the stunning **Great Hall**. The **Horn Room**, hung with impressive antlers, leads to the **Great Watching Chamber**, where guards controlled access to the king. Henry VIII's dazzling gemstone-encrusted **crown** has been re-created – the original was melted down by Oliver Cromwell – and sits in the **Royal Pew** (open 10am to 4pm Monday to Saturday and 12.30pm to 1.30pm Sunday), which overlooks the beautiful **Chapel Royal** (still a place of worship after 450 years).

Tudor Kitchens

Also dating from Henry's day are the delightful Tudor kitchens, once used to

Tudor Kitchens, Hampton Court Palace

rustle up meals for a royal household of some 1200 people. Don't miss the **Great Wine Cellar**, which handled the 300 barrels each of ale and wine consumed here annually in the mid-16th century.

Cumberland Art Gallery

The restored **Cumberland Suite** off Clock Court is the venue for a staggering collection of art works from the Royal Collection, including Thomas Gainsborough's *Diana and Actaeon* (c 1785–8) and Andy Warhol's *Reigning Queens (Royal Edition): Queen Elizabeth II* (1985).

> ☑ **Don't Miss**
>
> The Great Hall, the Chapel Royal, William III's apartments, the gardens and maze, and Henry VIII's crown.

William III's & Mary II's Apartments

A tour of William III's Apartments, completed by Wren in 1702, takes you up the grand **King's Staircase**. Highlights include the **King's Presence Chamber**, dominated by a throne backed with scarlet hangings. Don't miss the sumptuous **King's Great Bedchamber** (its bed topped with ostrich plumes) and the **King's Closet** (where His Majesty's toilet has a velvet seat). Restored in 2014, the unique **Chocolate Kitchens** were built for William and Mary in around 1689.

William's wife Mary II had her own apartments, accessible via the fabulous **Queen's Staircase** (decorated by William Kent).

Georgian Private Apartments

The Georgian Rooms were used by George II and Queen Caroline on the court's last visit to the palace in 1737. Do not miss the fabulous Tudor **Wolsey Closet** with its early 16th-century ceiling and painted panels, commissioned by Henry VIII.

Garden & Maze

Beyond the palace are the stunning gardens; keep an eye out for the **Real Tennis Court**, dating from the 1620s. The **Kitchen Garden** is a magnificent re-creation of the original one designed for William and Mary.

Don't leave Hampton Court without getting lost in the 800m-long **maze** (adult/child/family £4.40/2.70/12.80; ⊙10am-5.15pm Apr-Oct, to 3.45pm Nov-Mar; 🚢Hampton Court Palace, 🚉Hampton Court), accessible to those not entering the palace.

> ★ **Top Tip**
>
> From April to September, **Thames River Boats** (Map p274; ☑020-7930 2062; www.wpsa.co.uk; Westminster Pier, Victoria Embankment, SW1; adult/child Kew one-way £15/7.50, return £22/11, Hampton Court one-way £19/9.50, return £27/13.50; ⊙10am-4pm Apr-Oct; Ⓤ Westminster) runs a boat service from here to Westminster. It can take up to four hours depending on the tide.

KIEV.VICTOR/SHUTTERSTOCK ©

Hampton Court Palace

A DAY AT THE PALACE

With so much to explore in the palace and seemingly infinite gardens, it can be tricky knowing where to begin. It helps to understand how the palace has grown over the centuries and how successive royal occupants embellished Hampton Court to suit their purposes and to reflect the style of the time.

As soon as he had his royal hands upon the palace from Cardinal Thomas Wolsey,

Henry VIII began expanding the **1 Tudor architecture**, adding the **2 Great Hall**, the exquisite **3 Chapel Royal**, the opulent Great Watching Chamber and the gigantic **4 Tudor kitchens**. By 1540 it had become one of the grandest and most sophisticated palaces in Europe. James I kept things ticking over, while Charles I added a new tennis court and did some serious art-collecting, including pieces that can be seen in the **5 Cumberland Art Gallery**.

PETER FIELDS / ALAMY STOCK PHOTO ©

7 The Maze

Around 150m north of the main building
Created from hornbeam and yew and planted in around 1700, the maze covers a third of an acre within the famous palace gardens. A must-see conclusion to Hampton Court, it takes the average visitor about 20 minutes to reach the centre.

OPEN FOR INSPECTION

The palace was opened to the public by Queen Victoria in 1838.

Tudor Kitchens

These vast kitchens were the engine room of the palace, and had a staff of 200 people. Six spit-rack-equipped fireplaces ensured roast meat was always on the menu (to the tune of 8200 sheep and 1240 oxen per year).

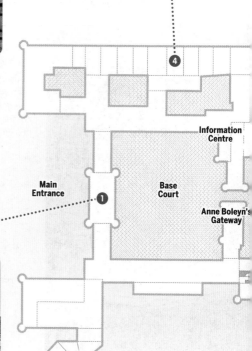

Information Centre

Main Entrance

Base Court

Anne Boleyn's Gateway

1

Tudor Architecture

Dating to 1515, the palace serves as one of the finest examples of Tudor architecture in the nation. Cardinal Thomas Wolsey was responsible for transforming what was originally a grand medieval manor house into a stunning Tudor palace.

KIEV.VICTOR / SHUTTERSTOCK ©

After the Civil War, puritanical Oliver Cromwell warmed to his own regal proclivities, spending weekends in the comfort of the former Queen's bedroom and selling off Charles I's art collection. In the late 17th century, William and Mary employed Christopher Wren for baroque extensions, chiefly the William III Apartments, reached by the **6 King's Staircase.** William III also commissioned the world-famous **7 maze.**

The Great Hall
This grand dining hall is the defining room of the palace, displaying what is considered England's finest hammer-beam roof, 16th-century Flemish tapestries that depict the story of Abraham, and some exquisite stained-glass windows.

Chapel Royal
The blue-and-gold vaulted ceiling was originally intended for Christ Church, Oxford, but was installed here instead; the 18th-century oak reredos was carved by Grinling Gibbons. Books on display include a 1611 1st edition of the King James Bible, printed by Robert Barker.

The King's Staircase
One of five rooms at the palace painted by Antonio Verrio and a suitably bombastic prelude to the King's Apartments, the overblown King's Staircase adulates William III by elevating him above a cohort of Roman emperors.

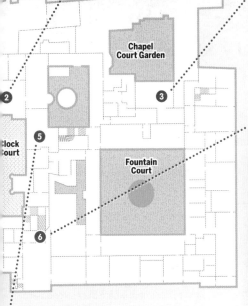

Chapel Court Garden

Fountain Court

Clock Court

2   **5**   **3**

6

Cumberland Art Gallery
The former Cumberland Suite, designed by William Kent, has been restored to accommodate a choice selection of some of the finest works from the Royal Collection.

GORDON BELL / SHUTTERSTOCK ©

Royal Observatory & Greenwich Park

The Royal Observatory, atop a hill within leafy, regal Greenwich Park, is where the study of the sea, the stars and time converge. The prime meridian charts its line through the grounds, dividing the globe into eastern and western hemispheres.

Great For...

☑ **Don't Miss**

Straddling hemispheres and time zones as you stand astride the actual meridian line in the Meridian Courtyard.

Royal Observatory

Unlike most attractions in Greenwich, the Royal Observatory contains free-access areas (Weller Astronomy Galleries, Great Equatorial Telescope) and ones you pay for (Meridian Line, Flamsteed House).

Flamsteed House & Meridian Courtyard

Charles II ordered construction of the Christopher Wren–designed Flamsteed House, the original observatory building, on the foundations of Greenwich Castle in 1675 after closing the observatory at the Tower of London. Today it contains the magnificent **Octagon Room** and the rather simple apartment where the Astronomer Royal, John Flamsteed, and his family lived. Here you'll also find the brilliant new **Time Galleries**, explaining how the longitude

The Time Ball at Flamsteed House

ⓘ Need to Know

Royal Observatory (Map p286; ✆020-8312 6565; www.rmg.co.uk/royal-observatory; Greenwich Park, Blackheath Ave, SE10; adult/child £10/6.50, incl Cutty Sark £20/11.50; ⊙10am-5pm Sep-Jun, to 6pm Jul & Aug; Ⓤ Greenwich or Cutty Sark)

✕ Take a Break

Enjoy a drink with river views on the side at the Cutty Sark Tavern (p197).

★ Top Tip

Get here before 1pm during the week to see the red Time Ball drop.

problem – how to accurately determine a ship's east-west location – was solved through astronomical means and the invention of the marine chronometer.

In the Meridian Courtyard, where the globe is decisively sliced into east and west, visitors can delightfully straddle both hemispheres, with one foot on either side of the meridian line. Every day the red **Time Ball** at the top of the Royal Observatory drops at 1pm, as it has done ever since 1833.

Astronomy Centre & Planetarium

The southern half of the observatory contains the highly informative (and free) **Weller Astronomy Galleries**, where you can touch the oldest object you will ever encounter: part of the Gibeon meteorite, a mere 4.5 billion years old. Other engaging exhibits include an orrery (a mechanical model of the solar system, minus the as-yet-undiscovered Uranus and Neptune) from 1780, astronomical documentaries, a first edition of Newton's *Principia Mathematica* and the opportunity to view the Milky Way in multiple wavelengths. To take star-gazing further, pick up a Skyhawk telescope from the shop.

The state-of-the-art **Peter Harrison Planetarium** (Map p286; ✆020-8312 6608; www.rmg.co.uk/whats-on/planetarium-shows; Greenwich Park, SE10; adult/child £8/5.35; ⊙10am-5pm Sep-Jun, to 6pm Jul & Aug; Ⓤ Greenwich or Cutty Sark) – London's only planetarium – can cast entire heavens onto the inside of its roof. It runs several informative shows a day. Bookings advised.

Greenwich Park

The **park** (Map p286; www.royalparks.org.uk; King George St, SE10; ⊙6am-around sunset; Ⓤ Greenwich, Maze Hill or Cutty Sark) is one of London's loveliest expanses of green, with a rose garden, picturesque walks,

Anglo-Saxon tumuli and astonishing views from the crown of the hill near the Royal Observatory towards Canary Wharf, the financial district across the Thames.

Covering 74 hectares, this is the oldest enclosed royal park and is partly the work of André Le Nôtre, the landscape architect who designed the palace gardens of Versailles.

Ranger's House

This elegant Georgian **villa** (Wernher Collection, EH; Map p286; ☏020-8294 2548; www.english-heritage.org.uk; Greenwich Park, Chesterfield Walk, SE10; adult/child £9/5.40; ⊙guided tours 11.30am & 2pm Sun-Wed late Mar-Sep; Ⓤ Greenwich or Cutty Sark), built in 1723, once housed the park's ranger and now contains a collection of 700 works of fine and applied art (medieval and Renaissance paintings, porcelain, silverware, tapestries) amassed by Julius Wernher (1850–1912), a German-born railway-engineer's son who struck it rich in the diamond fields of South Africa in the 19th century.

What's Nearby?

Old Royal Naval College
Historic Building

(Map p286; www.ornc.org; 2 Cutty Sark Gardens, SE10; ⊙10am-5pm, grounds 8am-11pm; Ⓤ Cutty Sark) **FREE** Christopher Wren's baroque masterpiece in Greenwich and indeed Britain's largest ensemble of baroque architecture, the Old Royal Naval College contains the neoclassical **Chapel of St Peter and St Paul** and the extraordinary **Painted Hall** (Map p286; ☏020-8269 4799 adult/child £12/free) **FREE**. The entire Old Royal Naval College, including the chapel,

Nelson's Ship in a Bottle by Yinka Shonibare, entrance to the National Maritime Museum

the **visitor centre** (Pepys Bldg, King William Walk), and the grounds, can be visited for free. Volunteers lead free 45-minute tours throughout the day from the visitor centre.

Cutty Sark   Museum
(Map p286; ☎020-8312 6608; www.rmg.co.uk/cuttysark; King William Walk, SE10; adult/child £13.50/7; ☺10am-5pm; Ⓤ Cutty Sark) The last of the great clipper ships to sail between China and England in the 19th century, the *Cutty Sark* endured massive fire damage in 2007 during a £25 million restoration. The exhibition in the hold of the fully restored ship tells its story as a tea clipper at the end of the 19th century. Launched in 1869

in Scotland, she made eight voyages to China in the 1870s, sailing out with a mixed cargo and coming back with tea.

Another fire took hold in 2014, but fire crews were quick to respond and extinguish the blaze. As you make your way up, there are films, interactive maps and plenty of illustrations and props to get an idea of what life on board was like. Book online for cheaper rates.

National Maritime Museum   Museum
(Map p286; ☎020-8312 6565; www.rmg.co.uk/national-maritime-museum; Romney Rd, SE10; ☺10am-5pm; Ⓤ Cutty Sark) **FREE** Narrating the long, briny and eventful history of seafaring Britain, this excellent museum's exhibits are arranged thematically, with highlights including *Miss Britain III* (the first boat to top 100mph on open water) from 1933, the 19m-long golden state barge built in 1732 for Frederick, Prince of Wales, the huge ship's propeller and the colourful figureheads installed on the ground floor. Families will love these, as well as the ship simulator and the 'All Hands' children's gallery on the 2nd floor.

Adults are likely to prefer the fantastic (and slightly more serene) galleries such as **Voyagers: Britons and the Sea** on the ground floor; the award-winning **Nelson, Navy, Nation 1688–1815,** which focuses on the history of the Royal Navy during the conflict-ridden 17th century; or the **Exploration Wing**, which contains four galleries – Pacific Exploration, Polar Worlds, Tudor and Stuart Seafarers, and Sea Things – devoted to the theme of exploration and human endeavour.

> ★ **Local Knowledge**
>
> In autumn Greenwich Park is one of the best places in London to collect chestnuts.

GOGA18128/SHUTTERSTOCK ©

> ✕ **Take a Break**
>
> The Buenos Aires Cafe (p158) does superb steaks and equally delicious pizzas.

Lily House (p136) at Kew Gardens

Day Trip: Kew Gardens

The 121-hectare gardens at Kew are the finest product of the British botanical imagination and really should not be missed. Don't worry if you don't know your quiver tree from your alang-alang, a visit to Kew is a journey of discovery for all.

Great For...

Syon Park · Kew Gardens · Mortlake Rd · Kew Rd · Kew Gardens · River Thames · Fulham Cemetery

❶ Need to Know

Royal Botanic Gardens, Kew; www.kew. org; Kew Rd, TW9; adult/child £13.50/4.50; ☺10am-6pm Sep, to 5pm Oct, to 3pm Nov-Jan, closes later Feb-Aug; ⛴Kew Pier, ₨Kew Bridge, ⓤKew Gardens

★ **Top Tip**

Kew is a big place so if you're pressed for time, or getting tired, take the Kew Explorer (p224), a hop-on/hop-off road train that takes in the main sights.

As well as being a public garden, Kew is a pre-eminent research centre, maintaining its reputation as the most exhaustive botanical collection in the world.

Conservatories

Assuming you travel by tube and enter via Victoria Gate, you'll come almost immediately to the enormous and elaborate 700-glass-paned **Palm House**, a domed hothouse of metal and curved sheets of glass dating from 1848, enveloping a splendid display of exotic tropical greenery; an aerial walkway offers a parrot's-eye view of the lush vegetation. Just northwest of the Palm House stands the tiny and irresistibly steamy **Waterlily House** (Kew Gardens, TW9; ⊗Mar-Dec; 🚲Kew Pier, 🚉Kew Bridge, Ⓤ Kew Gardens), sheltering the gigantic *Victoria cruziana* waterlily,

the vast pads of which can support the weight of a small adult.

In the southeast of Kew Gardens, **Temperate House** (built in 1860) is the world's largest surviving Victorian glasshouse, covering 4880 sq metres. It reopened in 2018 after five years of vital restoration work.

The angular **Princess of Wales Conservatory** houses plants in 10 different climatic zones – everything from a desert to a mangrove swamp. Look out for stone plants, which resemble pebbles (to deter grazing animals), carnivorous plants, gigantic waterlilies, cacti and a collection of tropical orchids.

Great Pagoda

Kew's 49.5m-tall eight-sided **pagoda** (Kew Gardens, TW9) (1762), designed by

Palm House at Kew Gardens

William Chambers (who designed Somerset House), is one of the Kew Gardens' architectural icons. During WWII the pagoda withstood the blast from a stick of Luftwaffe bombs exploding nearby, and was also secretly employed by the Ministry of Defence to test bomb trajectories (which involved cutting holes in each floor). Recently restored, the pagoda is a colourful explosion adorned with 80 gold-detailed, roaring dragons.

Kew Palace

Built in 1631 and the smallest of the royal palaces, adorable red-brick **Kew Palace**

☑ Don't Miss

The Palm House, Treetop Walkway, Chinese Pagoda, Temperate House and the numerous vistas.

KIEV.VICTOR/SHUTTERSTOCK ©

(www.hrp.org.uk/kewpalace; Kew Gardens, TW9; with admission to Kew Gardens; ⊙10.30am-5.30pm Apr-Sep; 🚢Kew Pier, 🚉Kew Bridge, Ⓤ Kew Gardens), in the northwest of the gardens, is a former royal residence once known as Dutch House. It was the favourite home of George III and his family; his wife, Queen Charlotte, died here in 1818 (you can see the very chair in which she expired). Don't miss the restored **Royal Kitchens** next door.

Treetop Walkway

In the **Arboretum,** this fascinating walkway first takes you underground and then 18m up in the air into the tree canopy (a big hit with kids).

Other Highlights

Several long vistas, **Cedar Vista**, **Syon Vista** and **Pagoda Vista**, are channelled by trees from vantage points within Kew Gardens. The idyllic, thatched **Queen Charlotte's Cottage** (Kew Gardens, TW9; ⊙11am-4pm Sat & Sun Apr-Sep; 🚢Kew Pier, 🚉Kew Bridge, Ⓤ Kew Gardens) in the southwest of the gardens was popular with 'mad' George III and his wife; the carpets of bluebells around here are a drawcard in spring. The **Marianne North Gallery** (Kew Gardens, TW9) displays the botanical paintings of Marianne North, an indomitable traveller who roamed the continents from 1871 to 1885, painting plants along the way.

✕ Take a Break

The aptly named Glasshouse (p162), with its Michelin star, is the perfect conclusion to a day exploring the gardens.

Cargo

DOUG MCKINLAY/LONELY PLANET ©

A Night Out in Shoreditch

Shoreditch has been at the vanguard of cool and edgy bars and clubs for a decade. If you're after good times, there is no better place to come to.

Great For...

☑ Don't Miss

Banksy's famous security guard and poodle graffiti in Cargo's courtyard (visible from the street).

Pre-dinner Drinks

Start your evening at **BrewDog** (☎020-7729 8476; www.brewdog.com/bars/uk/shoreditch; 51 Bethnal Green Rd, E1; ⊙noon-midnight Mon-Thu, to 2am Fri, 11am-2am Sat, 11am-midnight Sun; 🛜; Ⓤ Shoreditch High St). This small bar is a craft-beer paradise, with the likes of Punk IPA and Dead Pony Club on tap, plus some experimental suds and international guest beers. For something even more 'crafty', try **Mikkeller Bar London** (www.mikkeller.dk/location/mikkeller-bar-london; 2-4 Hackney Rd, E2; ⊙noon-11pm Mon-Thu, to midnight Fri & Sat, to 10.30pm Sun; Ⓤ Shoreditch High St or Old St), the Danish brewer's first London bar, the brainchild of its founder and musician Rick Astley.

Dinner

Having worked up an appetite, make a beeline for **Green Papaya** (Map p282;

Callooh Callay

TIM E WHITE/ALAMY STOCK PHOTO ©

Cub 🚫 · 🚇 Hoxton
Green 🚫
Papaya
Mikkeller Bar
London
City Rd
Callooh
Callay 🚫🚫 Cargo
BrewDog
Shoreditch
Old St 🚇 XOYO
Old St 🚇
Bethnal Green Rd 🚫
Cocktail Trading Co 🚫 Bake
Shoreditch High St 🚇

❶ Need to Know

🚇 Old Street, 🚇 Hoxton & Shoreditch High St.

✕ Take a Break

The 24-hour Beigel Bake (p75) on Brick Lane is a godsend for refuelling at any time of the day or night.

★ Top Tip

Not a night owl? No problem, the area is abuzz with eclectic markets on Sundays.

📞 020-7729 3657; www.green-papaya.com; 97 Kingsland Rd, E2; mains £6.95-10.95; ⏰ noon-11pm Tue-Sat, to 10.30pm Sun; 🚇 Hoxton), one of the best Vietnamese restaurants on the 'Pho Mile' (the area is home to a large Vietnamese community), which also serves dishes from Xi'an in China. The food is filling and inexpensive.

If you'd prefer a blow-out meal, try **Cub** (Map p282; 📞 020-3693 3202; www.lyancub.com; 153 Hoxton St, N1; set menu £67; ⏰ 6pm-midnight Wed-Sat; 🖋; 🚇 Hoxton) 🖋, a venture that's big on sustainability and quality.

Cocktail O'Clock

For all its edgy, don't-give-a-damn attitude, Shoreditch also knows how to put on classy act. Cue the exceptional **Cocktail Trading Co** (Map p282; 📞 020-7427 6097; www. thecocktailtradingco.co.uk; 68 Bethnal Green Rd,

E1; ⏰ 5-11.30pm Mon-Wed, to midnight Thu & Fri, 2pm-midnight Sat, 2-10.30pm Sun; 🚇 Shoreditch High St), which will wow you with its exquisite cocktails and Gentleman's Club decor.

The fabulous **Callooh Callay** (Map p282; 📞 020-7739 4781; www.calloohcallaybar.com; 65 Rivington St, EC2; ⏰ 6pm-1am; 🚇 Old St or Shoreditch High St) won't leave you wanting, with cocktails as exquisite as the dimly lit interior.

Clubbing

With the night in full swing, you'll have to fight your way through the throngs of punters at popular **Cargo** (Map p282; www. cargo-london.com; 83 Rivington St, EC2; ⏰ noon-1am Sun-Wed, to 3am Thu & Fri, to midnight Sat; 🚇 Shoreditch High St). Although perhaps past its heyday, it still draws a crowd. Alternatively, try the excellent **XOYO** (Map p282; 📞 020-7608 2878; www.xoyo.co.uk; 32-37 Cowper St, EC2; ⏰ 9.30pm-late Fri & Sat; 🚇 Old St): it hosts a rotating selection of resident DJs and a varied line-up of indie, hip-hop, electro, drum and bass and dubstep artists.

Expect queuing, and bring ID. Buy tickets online (up to the day before) – it's usually cheaper, and may save lining up.

Soho

London's original Bohemian quarter may have lost some of its edge to East London over the couple of decades, but it remains a vibrant neighbourhood with classic establishments and a proud gay community. There is also excellent shopping, with independent music stores and plenty of designer boutiques.

Great For...

ⓘ Need to Know

Oxford Circus, Piccadilly Circus and Leicester Square are the best tube stations for Soho.

★ **Top Tip**

Shops in the West End open until 9pm or even 10pm on Thursdays (they usually close around 8pm).

In a district that was once pastureland, the name Soho is thought to have evolved from a hunting cry. The neighbourhood definitely comes into its own in the evenings; during the day you'll be charmed by the area's bohemian side and its sheer vitality.

At Soho's northern end, leafy **Soho Square** is the area's back garden. It was laid out in 1681 and originally called King's Sq; a statue of Charles II stands in its northern half. In the centre is a tiny half-timbered mock-Tudor cottage built as a gardener's shed in the 1870s. The space below it was used as an underground bomb shelter during WWII.

South of the square is **Dean Street**, lined with bars and restaurants. No 28 was the home of Karl Marx and his family from 1851 to 1856; they lived here in extreme poverty

as Marx researched and wrote *Das Kapital* in the British Museum's Reading Room.

Old Compton Street is the epicentre of Soho's gay village. It's a street loved by all, gay or other, for its great bars, risqué shops and general good vibes.

Seducer and heart-breaker Casanova and opium-addicted writer Thomas de Quincey lived on nearby **Greek Street**, while the parallel **Frith Street** housed Mozart at No 20 for a year from 1764.

You'll find plenty of lovely boutiques in Soho but, with its long rock'n'roll tradition, it is particularly well-known for its thriving **independent music stores**.

The pedestrian **Carnaby Street** has become a magnet for shoppers, with top-end 'high street' brands and independent boutiques vying for your purse. The most high-profile – and most recognisable – store

The Spirit of Christmas by James Glancy Design, at Regent St

here is **Liberty** (Map p274; ☎020-7734 1234; www.libertylondon.com; Regent St, entrance on Great Marlborough St, W1; ⊙10am-8pm Mon-Sat, 11.30am-6pm Sun; 🛜; Ⓤ Oxford Circus) with its white-and-wood-beam Tudor Revival facade. A classic London gift or souvenir is a Liberty fabric print, especially in the form of a scarf.

What's Nearby?

The northern and western boundaries of Soho are Oxford St and Regent St, aka the shopping nerve centre of the West End.

Regent Street

The handsome border dividing the trainer-clad clubbers of Soho from the Gucci-heeled hedge-fund managers of Mayfair, Regent St was designed by John Nash as a ceremonial route linking Carlton House, the Prince Regent's long-demolished town residence, with the 'wilds' of Regent's Park. Nash had to downsize his plan and build the thoroughfare on a curve, but Regent St is today a well-subscribed shopping street lined with some lovely listed buildings.

Hamleys   Toys

(Map p274; ☎0371 704 1977; www.hamleys.com; 188-196 Regent St, W1; ⊙10am-9pm Mon-Fri, 9.30am-9pm Sat, noon-6pm Sun; 👪; Ⓤ Oxford Circus) The biggest and oldest toy emporium in the world, Hamleys houses six floors of fun for kids of all ages, from the basement's Star Wars and Harry Potter collections up to Lego World, a sweet shop and tiny cafe on the 5th floor. Staff on each level have opened the packaging and are playing with everything from boomerangs to bubbles.

Oxford Street

Oxford Street is all about chains, from Marks & Spencer to H&M, Topshop to Gap, with large branches of department stores, the most famous of which is Selfridges. The small lanes heading south to Mayfair are full of designer boutiques.

Selfridges   Department Store

(Map p278; ☎0800 123 400; www.selfridges. com; 400 Oxford St, W1; ⊙9am-10pm Mon-Sat, 11.30am-6pm Sun; Ⓤ Bond St) Set in a grandiose column-flanked Grade II–listed structure, Selfridges has been innovating since its doors opened in 1909. Its wacky, ever-changing window displays draw a crowd of its own, especially at Christmas. Inside, an unparalleled food hall, sprawling cosmetics stations and the usual department-store essentials are topped by a rooftop restaurant with delicious city views.

☑ **Don't Miss**

The Christmas lights in the area are spectacular, especially in Regent and Carnaby Sts.

4KCLIPS/SHUTTERSTOCK ©

✕ **Take a Break**

Yauatcha (p169) in Soho does the best dim-sum in town, hence the Michelin star. Booking is essential in the evening.

Design Museum

Since 2016 this slick museum has been in a stunning location by Holland Park. It's a crucial pit stop for anyone with an eye for modern and contemporary aesthetics.

Great For

☑ **Don't Miss**

The Designer Maker User gallery and the museum's architecture.

Collections & Exhibitions

Dedicated to popularising the importance and influence of design in everyday life, the Design Museum has a revolving programme of special exhibitions.

Most exhibitions are ticketed (from £14.50), as are talks in the auditorium (from £5), but the extensive, 2nd-floor **Designer Maker User** gallery is free. Exploring the iconography of design classics, the gallery contains almost 1000 objects that trace the history of modern design, from 1980s Apple computers to water bottles, typewriters, floppy discs and a huge advert for the timeless VW Beetle.

Iconic Building

Until 2016, the museum was housed in a former banana warehouse that had been given a 1930s modernist makeover

🛈 Need to Know

Map p278; 📞020-7940 8790; www.design museum.org; 224-238 Kensington High St, W8; ⏰10am-6pm, to 8pm 1st Fri of month; Ⓤ High St Kensington FREE

✕ Take a Break

For a delicious take on Greek cuisine, head to Mazi (p171).

★ Top Tip

Choose a sunny day to visit and wander around Holland Park afterwards.

by museum founder Terence Conran. The building, located by the Thames in Bermondsey, was a design success but it became too small for the museum's growing collection. For its new home, the museum chose another design jewel: the former Commonwealth Institute building, a listed 1960s beauty, which was given a 21st-century, £83-million facelift for the occasion.

What's Nearby?

Holland Park Park

(Map p278; Ilchester Pl; ⏰7.30am-dusk; Ⓤ High St Kensington or Holland Park) This hand-some park divides into dense woodland in the north, spacious and inviting lawns by Holland House, sports fields in the south, and some lovely gardens, including the restful Kyoto Garden. The park's splendid

peacocks are a gorgeous sight and a playground keeps kids occupied. Holland House – largely bombed to smithereens by the Luftwaffe in 1940 – is the venue of Opera Holland Park (p219) in summer.

Portobello Road Market Market

(Map p278; www.portobellomarket.org; Portobello Rd, W10; ⏰8am-6.30pm Mon-Wed, Fri & Sat, to 1pm Thu; Ⓤ Notting Hill Gate or Ladbroke Grove) Lovely on a warm summer's day, Portobello Road Market is an iconic London attraction with an eclectic mix of street food, fruit and veg, antiques, curios, collectables, fashion and trinkets. The shops along Portobello Rd open daily and the fruit and veg stalls (from Elgin Cres to Talbot Rd) only close on Sunday. But while some antique stalls operate on Friday, the busiest day by far is Saturday, when antique dealers set up shop (from Chepstow Villas to Elgin Cres).

Walking Tour: East End Eras

This route offers an insight into the old and new of East London. Wander through and soak up the unique character of its neighbourhoods.

Start Ⓤ Bethnal Green
Distance 3.6 miles
Duration 2½ hours

3 Just over Regent's Canal lies **Victoria Park**. Take the left path along the lake to the **Dogs of Alcibiades** howling on plinths.

2 On beautifully preserved **Cyprus Street** you'll get a taste of what Victorian Bethnal Green would have looked like.

1 The **Old Ford Road** area was bombed during WWII, and tower blocks were subsequently erected on the bomb sites.

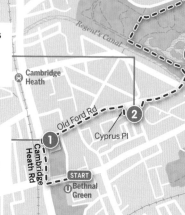

Mare St

Victoria Park Rd

Grove Rd

Regent's Canal

Cambridge Heath

Old Ford Rd

Cyprus Pl

Cambridge Heath Rd

START
Ⓤ Bethnal Green

Ⓝ 0 ___ 500 m
0 ___ 0.25 miles

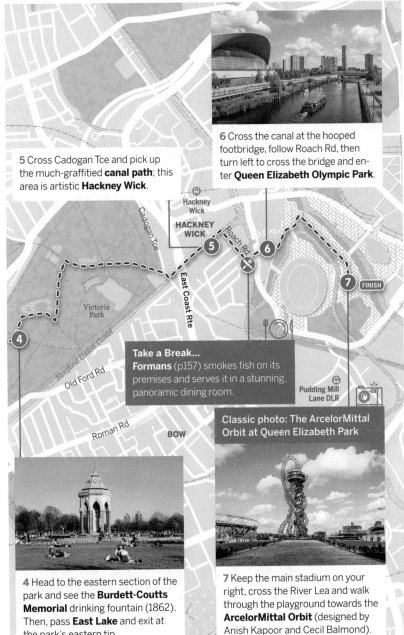

6 Cross the canal at the hooped footbridge, follow Roach Rd, then turn left to cross the bridge and enter **Queen Elizabeth Olympic Park**.

5 Cross Cadogan Tce and pick up the much-graffitied **canal path**; this area is artistic **Hackney Wick**.

Hackney Wick

HACKNEY WICK

5

Roach Rd

6

7 FINISH

Cadogan Tce

East Coast Rte

Victoria Park

4

Hertford Union Canal

Old Ford Rd

Take a Break...
Formans (p157) smokes fish on its premises and serves it in a stunning, panoramic dining room.

Pudding Mill Lane DLR

Roman Rd

BOW

Classic photo: The ArcelorMittal Orbit at Queen Elizabeth Park

4 Head to the eastern section of the park and see the **Burdett-Coutts Memorial** drinking fountain (1862). Then, pass **East Lake** and exit at the park's eastern tip.

7 Keep the main stadium on your right, cross the River Lea and walk through the playground towards the **ArcelorMittal Orbit** (designed by Anish Kapoor and Cecil Balmond).

3 LOOP IMAGES LTD/ALAMY STOCK PHOTO © 4 PAT TUSON/ALAMY STOCK PHOTO © 6 ESTHER BARRY/SHUTTERSTOCK © 7 ABS FOTOS/SHUTTERSTOCK ©

DINING OUT

Top-notch restaurants, gastropubs, afternoon tea and more

Dining Out

Once the butt of many a culinary joke, London has transformed itself over the last few decades and today is a global dining destination. World-famous chefs can be found at the helm of several top-tier restaurants, but it is the sheer diversity on offer that is head-spinning: from Afghan to Zambian, London delivers an A to Z of world cuisine.

In This Section

Price Ranges & Tipping

The following price ranges refer to a main course:

£ less than £12

££ £12–25

£££ more than £25

Most restaurants automatically tack a 'discretionary' service charge (usually 12.5%) onto the bill; this should be clearly advertised. If you feel the service wasn't adequate, you can ask for it to be removed. If there is no service charge on your bill and you would like to tip, 10% is about right.

North London
Myriad options, with
hidden delights (p161)

**Clerkenwell, Shoreditch
& Spitalfields**
Famous creative restaurants and
popular food markets (p154)

West London
Excellent, affordable and
varied choices (p171)

East London
Authentic ethnic
eateries, traditional
caffs, newer upmarket
restaurants
(p156)

The West End
Some of London's best restaurants,
great for Asian and fusion (p166)

The City
Geared towards the
business lunch (p162)

Kensington & Hyde Park
Chic, cosmopolitan and
often pricey (p158)

The South Bank
Chains on the river, more
authentic gems 'inland' (p164)

Richmond, Kew & Hampton Court
Excels in a variety of options,
particularly in Richmond (p162)
(9.5km)

River Thames

Greenwich & South London
A treat of fine dining and
eclectic market fare (p157)

Useful Websites

Time Out London (www.timeout.com/
london) Has the most up-to-date listings
of restaurants as well as information on
harder-to-track eateries and food trucks.

Open Table (www.opentable.co.uk)
Bookings for numerous restaurants,
as well as meal deals with excellent
discounts.

Wine Pages (www.wine-pages.com)
Keeps a useful directory of BYO
restaurants.

Must Try Dishes

Afternoon Tea An indulgent treat
consisting of finger sandwiches, a
selection of pastries, scones with
clotted cream and jam, and, of course,
tea. It's usually served after 3pm (skip
lunch and don't plan much for dinner
either!).

Pie & Mash A classic London com-
bination: traditional pies are filled
with minced meat but there are many
alternative fillings (including vegetarian), with a dollop or two of mashed
potatoes.

The Best...

Experience London's top restaurants and cafes

Budget Restaurants

Padella (p164) Handmade-pasta specialists in Borough Market.

Hook Camden Town (p161) Sustainable fish and chips with homemade sauces.

Towpath (p156) Sunny-day canalside cafe with tasty food and great coffee.

Asian Cuisine

Gymkhana (p169) Splendid club-style Raj environment and top cuisine.

Hoppers (p166; pictured above) A fabulous introduction to Sri Lankan food.

Gunpowder (p155) Punchy Indian cuisine in pocket-sized restaurant.

British Cuisine

Dinner by Heston Blumenthal (p160) Seriously good-looking Knightsbridge choice putting fresh spins on British culinary history (pictured above).

Rabbit (p159) Hop to King's Rd for seasonal British cuisine.

Rivington Grill (p157) Proudly British, with meat and fish taking pride of place.

St John (p154) Standard-bearer of head-to-tail cuisine.

Vegetarian

Gate (p154) Fusion vegetarian food with plenty of Indian and Middle Eastern influences.

Mildreds (p167) Soho stalwart with vegan dishes too.

Wulf & Lamb (p160) Vegan restaurant, with amazing desserts and wines.

Manna (p162) Catering to gourmet vegetarians and vegans long before this became trendy.

Vanilla Black (p163) One of the best restaurants in town – and it's vegetarian.

Gastropubs

Anchor & Hope (p165) Flying the gastropub flag on the South Bank for over a decade.

Empress (p157) Choice East End spot with an excellent modern British menu.

Afternoon Tea

Foyer & Reading Room at Claridge's (p169; pictured above) The last word in classic art-deco elegance.

Portrait (p169) The tea and accompaniments compete with the views.

Delaunay (p167) Viennese-style afternoon teas complete with *gugelhupfs* (fruit scones) and Sachertorte.

Views

City Social (p163) Wow-factor views from the City to the Shard and beyond.

Skylon (p165) Sweeping views from the South Bank to the City skyline.

Portrait (p169; pictured above) Classic views over Nelson's Column and down Whitehall to Big Ben.

Formans (p157) English fare with full-frontal views of the Queen Elizabeth Olympic Park.

★ Lonely Planet's Top Choices

Clove Club (p155) From Dalston supper club to stupendous Michelin-starred restaurant.

City Social (p163) The best of Modern British, with unforgettable views.

Glasshouse (p162) Kew stalwart serving exemplary contemporary European cuisine.

Breddos Tacos (p154) Once a food truck, now the best Mexican in town.

Smoking Goat (p154) Thai food at its best.

⊗ Clerkenwell, Shoreditch & Spitalfields

Breddos Tacos   Tacos £

(Map p282; ☎020-3535 8301; www.breddostacos. com; 82 Goswell Rd, EC1; tacos & tostadas £3.50-8.50; ⊙noon-11pm Mon-Fri, 1-11pm Sat; ☝; Ⓤ Old St or Farringdon) Started in an East London car park in 2011, Breddos found its first perma-nent home here in Clerkenwell, dishing out some of London's most authentic Mexican grub. Find a friend and order each of the seven or so tacos on the menu: the selection varies, but past favourites include the kung pao pork belly and the veggie-friendly mole, feta and organic egg.

MEATmission   Burgers £

(Map p282; ☎020-7739 8212; www.meatliquor. com/restaurant/meatmission; 15 Hoxton Market, N1; burgers £7.50-9.50; ⊙noon-midnight Mon-Sat, to 11pm Sun; Ⓤ Old St) Worship at this temple to the burger gods, somewhat sacrilegiously set in the former Hoxton Market Christian Mission and complete with stained-glass windows and a war memorial. Food is served on giant silver baking sheets below the watchful Masonic Eye of Providence painted on the ceiling. The Dead Hippie must be one of London's finest burgers.

Smoking Goat   Thai ££

(Map p282; www.smokinggoatbar.com; 64 Shore-ditch High St, E1; dishes £3.50-26; ⊙noon-3pm & 5.30-11pm Mon-Wed, noon-3.30pm & 5.30pm-1am Thu & Fri, 10am-4pm & 5pm-1am Sat, 10am-4pm & 5-11pm Sun; Ⓤ Shoreditch High St) Trotting in on one of London's fleeting flavours of the week, Smoking Goat's kick-arse modern Thai menu is top notch. The industrial-chic look of exposed brick, huge factory windows and original parquet floors surround the open kitchen. It's a tough place for the spice-shy; cool down with a cold one from the exquisite cocktail list. Don't miss the finger-licking chilli fish sauce wings.

Yuu Kitchen   Asian ££

(Map p280; ☎020-7377 0411; www.yuukitchen. com; 29 Commercial St, E1; dishes £4.50-8.50; ⊙5.30pm-late Mon & Tue, noon-2.30pm &

5.30pm-late Wed-Fri, noon-4pm & 5.30pm-late Sat & Sun; ☝; Ⓤ Aldgate East) Manga images pout on the walls and birdcages dangle from the ceiling at this fun, relaxed place. Dishes are either bite-sized or designed to be shared, and while the focus is mainly Asian, some dishes from further along the Pacific Rim pop up too. Hence Hawaiian *poke* (raw fish) sits alongside Vietnamese rolls and show-stopping *bao* (Taiwanese steamed buns).

St John   British ££

(Map p282; ☎020-7251 0848; www.stjohn restaurant.com; 26 St John St, EC1; mains £15.80-28; ⊙noon-3pm & 6-11pm Mon-Fri, 6-11pm Sat, 12.30-4pm Sun; Ⓤ Farringdon) Around the corner from London's last remaining meat market, St John is the standard-bearer for nose-to-tail cuisine, which makes use of every part of the animal. With whitewashed brick walls, high ceilings and simple wooden furniture, it's surely one of the most humble Michelin-starred restaurants. The menu changes daily but is likely to include the sig-nature roast bone marrow and parsley salad.

Som Saa   Thai ££

(Map p282; ☎020-7324 7790; www.somsaa. com; 43a Commercial St, E1; dishes £8-17.50; ⊙noon-2.30pm & 5-10.30pm Tue-Fri, noon-3pm & 5-10.30pm Sat, 5-10pm Mon; Ⓤ Aldgate East) So beloved is Som Saa that it successfully crowdfunded £700,000 to open its first permanent restaurant in this old fabric warehouse. The menu has expanded since its pop-up days but still has a laser-like focus on deliciously authentic curries, grilled meats, salads and stir-fries. Do as the other tables do and order the crowd favourite *nahm dtok pla thort* (whole deep-fried seabass).

The Gate   Vegetarian ££

(Map p282; ☎020-7278 5483; www.thegate restaurants.com; 370 St John St, EC1; mains £11-15; ⊙noon-10pm; ☝; Ⓤ Angel) The Gate can probably take a lot of credit for elevating vegetarian cuisine from uninspiring side dishes to starring in its own culinary right. Blending influences from India, the Middle East and Jewish traditions, the food is a riot

MEATmission

of flavours. The elegant dining room is in tune with its Islington surrounds: white walls and dark wooden tables and chairs.

Vegans are well catered for.

Gunpowder Indian ££

(Map p282; ☏020-7426 0542; www.gunpowder london.com; 11 White's Row, E1; dishes £3-16; ⊗noon-3pm & 5.30-10.30pm Mon-Sat; ☝; ⓤLiverpool St or Aldgate East) As you walk into this tiny Indian place, it's the smell that hits you: the delicious tang of spices and incense. The punchy food is inspired by family recipes and home cooking: plates are small and designed for sharing. The flavours of each dish are divine, though not always suitable for the heat-fearing.

Polpo Italian ££

(Map p282; ☏020-7250 0034; www.polpo.co.uk; 3 Cowcross St, EC1; dishes £4.80-13.50; ⊗11.30am-11pm Mon-Sat; ☝; ⓤFarringdon) London's take on a Venetian *bacàri* (small bar), Polpo dishes out sharing plates of pasta, meat and *pizzette* (petite pizzas), with excellent options for vegetarians. The succulent meatballs keep Londoners coming back; despite the

name, the octopus is best avoided. Portions are larger than *cicchetti* (bar snacks) found in Venice but smaller than a regular main, the perfect excuse to graze freely.

Moro Spanish ££

(Map p282; ☏020-7833 8336; www.moro.co.uk; 34-36 Exmouth Market, EC1; mains £16.50-24; ⊗noon-2.30pm & 6-10.30pm Mon-Sat, 12.30-2.45pm Sun; ⓤFarringdon) The Moorish cuisine on offer at this Exmouth Market institution straddles the Strait of Gibraltar, with influences from Spain, Portugal and North Africa – and a bit of Britain added to the mix. If the tables are full, you can often perch at the bar for some tapas, wine and dessert.

Clove Club Gastronomy £££

(Map p282; ☏020-7729 6496; www.thecloveclub. com; Shoreditch Town Hall, 380 Old St, EC1; lunch £65, dinner £95-145; ⊗noon-1.45pm Tue-Sat, 6-10.30pm Mon-Sat; ☝; ⓤOld St) From humble origins as a supper club in a London flat, the Clove Club has transformed into this impressive Michelin-starred restaurant, named one of the world's best in 2017. The menu is a mystery until dishes arrive at the

🍽 Vegetarians & Vegans

London has been one of the best places for vegetarians to dine out since the 1970s, initially due mostly to its many Indian restaurants, which have always catered for people who don't eat meat for religious reasons. It is also increasingly becoming a great spot for veganism, which has seen a boom in popularity. A number of dedicated vegetarian/vegan restaurants have since cropped up, offering imaginative, filling and truly delicious meals. Most nonvegetarian places generally offer a couple of veggie and vegan dishes, and some top-end places offer full vegetarian degustation menus.

Bhelpuri
SUBODHSATHE/GETTY IMAGES ©

table; expect intricately arranged plates with impeccably sourced ingredients from around the British Isles. Your wallet might feel empty, but you sure won't.

A vegetarian menu is available. Book far in advance.

Hawksmoor Spitalfields   Steak £££
(Map p282; ☏020-7426 4850; www.the hawksmoor.com; 157a Commercial St, E1; mains £20-50; ⊙noon-2.30pm Mon-Fri, to 3pm Sat, 5-10.30pm Mon-Sat, noon-9pm Sun; 🌐; ⑪Shoreditch High St) You could easily miss Hawksmoor, discreetly signed and clad in black brick, but dedicated carnivores will find it worth seeking out. The dark wood and velvet curtains make for a handsome setting in which to gorge yourself on the best of British beef.

The Sunday roasts (£21) are legendary, but it's *the* place in London to order a steak.

✪ East London

Towpath   Cafe £
(Map p282; ☏020-7254 7606; rear 42-44 De Beauvoir Cres, N1; mains £7-9.50; ⊙9am-5pm Tue & Wed, to 9.30pm Thu-Sun; ⑪Haggerston) Occupying four small units facing Regent's Canal towpath, this simple cafe is a super place to sit in the sun and watch the ducks and narrow boats glide by. The coffee and food are excellent, with delicious cookies and brownies on the counter and cooked dishes chalked up on the blackboard daily.

Berber & Q   North African ££
(Map p282; ☏020-7923 0829; www.berberandq. com; 338 Acton Mews, E8; mains £12-17; ⊙6-11pm Tue-Fri, 11am-3pm & 6-11pm Sat & Sun; ⑪Haggerston) A mouth-watering barbecue smell greets you as you enter nto this very cool Berber-style grill house. Smoked-aubergine mezze comes loaded with garlic, sumac and juicy bursts of pomegranate, and is served with charred pita. Lamb *shawarma* (kebab) is meltingly tender, while piquant treats include *biber salcasi* hot wings, sea bream in *chermoula*, and spiced beef *kofte*.

Corner Room   Modern British ££
(Map p285; ☏020-7871 0460; www.townhallhotel. com; Patriot Sq, E2; mains £13-14, 2-/3-course lunch £19/23; ⊙noon-4pm Mon-Fri, noon-2.30pm Sat & Sun, 6-9.45pm Mon-Wed, 6-10.15pm Thu-Sat; ⑪Bethnal Green) Tucked away on the 1st floor of the Town Hall Hotel, this relaxed industrial-chic restaurant serves expertly crafted dishes with complex yet delicate flavours, highlighting the best of British seasonal produce, with a French touch.

Brawn   European ££
(Map p282; ☏020-7729 5692; www.brawn.co; 49 Columbia Rd, E2; mains £14-19; ⊙noon-3pm Tue-Sat, 6-10.30pm Mon-Thu, to 11pm Fri & Sat, noon-4pm Sun; ⑪Hoxton) There's a French feel to this relaxed corner bistro, yet the menu wanders into Italian and Spanish territory as well, and even tackles the British Sunday

lunch (three courses £28). Dishes are seasonally driven and delicious, and there's an interesting selection of European wine on offer. Booking ahead is recommended.

Empress
Modern British ££

(Map p285; ☑020-8533 5123; www.empresse9. co.uk; 130 Lauriston Rd, E9; mains £13-27; ⊘6-10.15pm Mon, noon-3.30pm & 6-10.15pm Tue-Sat, 10am-9.30pm Sun; ☐277) This upmarket pub conversion belts out delicious Modern British cuisine in very pleasant surroundings. On Mondays there's a £10 main-plus-drink supper deal and on weekends it serves an excellent brunch.

Bistrotheque
Modern British ££

(Map p285; ☑020-8983 7900; www.bistrotheque. com; 23-27 Wadeson St, E2; mains £17-24, 3-course early dinner £25; ⊘6-10.30pm Mon-Fri, 11am-4pm & 6-10.30pm Sat & Sun; ⓤBethnal Green) This unmarked warehouse conversion ticks all the boxes of a contemporary upmarket London bistro. The food and service are uniformly excellent. One of the best weekend brunch spots in Hackney.

Formans
British ££

(Map p285; ☑020-8525 2365; www.formans. co.uk/restaurant; Stour Rd, E3; mains £15-20, brunch £6-10; ⊘7-11pm Thu & Fri, 10am-3pm & 7-11pm Sat, noon-5pm Sun; 🛜; ⓤHackney Wick) Curing fish since 1905, riverside Formans boasts prime views over the River Lea and the Olympic stadium and a contemporary art gallery overlooking its smokery. The menu includes a delectable choice of smoked salmon (including its signature 'London cure'), plenty of other seafood and a few nonfishy options. There's a great selection of British wines and spirits too.

⊗ Greenwich & South London

Paul Rhodes Bakery
Bakery £

(Map p286; 37 King William Walk, SE10; pastries/ sandwiches from £1.80/3.50; ⊘7am-6pm; ⓤCutty Sark) This handy corner bakery is a tip-top spot for a snack, baked goodies or a coffee.

¶◎¶ Pie & Mash

From the middle of the 19th century until just after WWII, the staple lunch for many Londoners was a spiced-eel pie (eels were once plentiful in the Thames) served with mashed potatoes and 'liquor' (a parsley sauce). Pies have been largely replaced by sandwiches nowadays, although they remain popular in the East End and can still be found in other parts of London. Try it at M Manze (p165) or Goddards.

PRISMA BY DUKAS/UIG VIA GETTY IMAGES ©

Delights include courgette, kale, hummus and tomato or chicken, bacon and avocado baguettes, marvellous lemon and chocolate tarts and vanilla cheesecake, served up by smiling staff. It's open early.

Goddards at Greenwich
British £

(Map p286; ☑020-8305 9612; www.goddardsat greenwich.co.uk; 22 King William Walk, SE10; pie and mash £4.30-7.50; ⊘10am-7.30pm Sun-Thu, to 8pm Fri & Sat; ⓤCutty Sark) If you're keen to try that archetypal English dish, pie and mash (minced beef, steak and kidney or even chicken in pastry, served with mashed potatoes and gravy), do so at this Greenwich institution, which always attracts a mixed crowd. Jellied eels, mushy peas and 'liquor' (a green sauce made from parsley and vinegar) are optional extras.

Rivington Grill
British ££

(Map p286; ☑020-8293 9270; www.rivington greenwich.co.uk; 178 Greenwich High Rd, SE10; mains £11.75-18.75; ⊘noon-10pm Mon-Fri, to 11pm Fri & Sat, from 10am Sat & Sun; ⓤGreenwich

🍴 English Cuisine

England might have given the world baked beans on toast, mushy peas and chip butties (french fries between slices of buttered white bread), but that's hardly the whole story. When well prepared – be it a Sunday lunch of roast beef and Yorkshire pudding (batter baked until fluffy, eaten with gravy) or a cornet of fish and chips sprinkled with salt and malt vinegar – English food can be excellent. And nothing quite beats a full English breakfast the morning after to soak up the excesses of a big night out.

Modern British food has become a cuisine in its own right, championing traditional (and sometimes underrated) ingredients such as root vegetables, smoked fish, shellfish, game, salt-marsh lamb, sausages, black pudding (a kind of sausage stuffed with oatmeal, spices and blood), offal, secondary cuts of meat and bone marrow.

Fish and chips
BEATS1/SHUTTERSTOCK ©

or Cutty Sark) This stylish restaurant has seating on two levels overlooking a lovely long bar. The seasonally adjusted menu is totally British, with chicken pie, lamb chops, suckling pig and luxury pies rubbing shoulders with grilled sardines, fish and chips and apple-and-rhubarb crumble. Warm and friendly welcome.

The full English breakfast (£12.50) at weekends is a gourmet treat.

Buenos Aires Cafe   Argentine ££

(Map p286; 🖉020-8858 9172; www.buenosaires cafe.co.uk/greenwich-restaurant; 15 Nelson Rd, SE10; 2-/3-course lunch £11.95/14.95, mains £8.95-32.95; ⊗10am-10.30pm Mon-Fri, 9am-10.30pm Sat & Sun; 🖲📶; Ⓤ Cutty Sark) Take a seat in the sunlight-filled orangery at the rear of this Argentine cafe or cosy up in the wood-interior front room. Dishes range from perfectly cooked steaks to pasta and pizza, and there's plenty of Argentine malbec to wash it down with. There's live Latin music on Tuesday and Thursday evenings. Advance booking is advised.

Vini Italiani   Italian ££

(Map p286; 🖉020-8465 5492; www.italianwines. com; 5 College Approach, SE10; mains £11-18; ⊗9am-11pm Mon-Sat, 10am-8pm Sun; Ⓤ Cutty Sark) This cosy Italian wine bar just outside Greenwich Market (p180) serves a small but well-formed menu of Italian dishes (try the 'gnoc'n'cheese') as well as charcuterie and cheese platters and salads. They also offer a traditional aperitivo hour, with free light bites when you buy a drink.

⊗ Kensington & Hyde Park

Pimlico Fresh   Cafe £

(🖉020-7932 0030; 86 Wilton Rd, SW1; mains from £4.50; ⊗7.30am-6pm Mon-Fri, 8.30am-6pm Sat & Sun; Ⓤ Victoria) This friendly two-room cafe will see you right, whether you need breakfast (French toast, bowls of porridge laced with honey or maple syrup), lunch (homemade quiches and soups, 'things' on toast) or just a good old latte and cake.

Comptoir Libanais   Lebanese £

(Map p278; 🖉020-7225 5006; www.comptoir libanais.com; 1-5 Exhibition Rd, SW7; mains from £8.50; ⊗8.30am-midnight Mon-Sat, to 10.30pm Sun; 🖲📶; Ⓤ South Kensington) If your battery's flat after touring the South Kensington museums, this colourful, good-looking and brisk restaurant just round the corner from the tube station is a moreish stop for Lebanese mezze, wraps, tagines (slow-cooked casseroles), *mana'esh* (flatbreads), salads and fine breakfasts. When the sun's shining, the outside tables quickly fill with munchers and people-watchers. No reservations – just turn up (elbows sharpened).

V&A Cafe
Cafe £

(Map p278; ☏020-7581 2159; www.vam.ac.uk/info/va-cafe; Victoria & Albert Museum, Cromwell Rd, SW7; mains £7.45-13.50; ☺10am-5.15pm Sat-Thu, to 9.30pm Fri; ☏; Ⓤ South Kensington) There is plenty of hot and cold food to choose from at the V&A Cafe, and although the quality is nothing to rave about, the setting most definitely is: the extraordinarily decorated Morris, Gamble and Poynter Rooms (1868) show Victorian Gothic style at its best. Plus there's often a piano accompaniment to your tea and cake.

Rabbit
Modern British ££

(Map p278; ☏020-3750 0172; www.rabbit-restaurant.com; 172 King's Rd, SW3; small plates £6-13, set lunch of 2/3 courses £14.50/19.50; ☺noon-midnight Tue-Sat, noon-6pm Sun, 6-11pm Mon; ☑; Ⓤ Sloane Sq) Three brothers grew up on a farm. One became a farmer, another a butcher, while the third worked in hospitality.

So they pooled their skills and came up with Rabbit, a breath of fresh air in upmarket Chelsea. The restaurant rocks the agri-chic look, and the creative, seasonal Modern British cuisine is fabulous.

Tom's Kitchen
Modern European ££

(Map p278; ☏020-7349 0202; www.toms kitchen.co.uk/chelsea; 27 Cale St, SW3; mains £16-28; ☺9am-2.30pm & 6-10.30pm Mon-Fri, 9.30am-3.30pm & 6-10.30pm Sat, 10am-9pm Sun; ☏☑; Ⓤ South Kensington) ✐ Recipe for success: mix one part relaxed and efficient staff, and one part light and airy decor to two parts divine food and voila: you have Tom's Kitchen. Classics such as grilled steaks, burgers, slow-cooked pork belly and chicken schnitzel are cooked to perfection, while seasonal choices such as the homemade ricotta or pan-fried scallops are sublime.

Kensington Palace Pavilion
British ££

(Map p278; ☏020-3166 6115; www.hrp.org.uk/kensington-palace/hire-a-venue/the-pavilion; Kensington Gardens, W8; afternoon tea £30;

Tom's Kitchen

⊘10am-4.45pm Mar-Oct, to 4pm Nov-Feb; 🖉; Ⓤ High St Kensington) Temporarily replacing the **Orangery restaurant** (Map p278; 🖉 020-3166 6113; www.orangerykensington palace.co.uk; ⊘10am-5pm) while it undergoes restoration until 2021; what the Kensington Palace Pavilion lacks in history, it makes up for with the same excellent menu of breakfasts, light lunches and, the standout, afternoon tea. The sandwiches, scones and cakes stacked high on their elegant tiers are just the thing for refuelling after a visit to Kensington Palace (p103) itself.

Wulf & Lamb — Vegan ££

(Map p278; 🖉 020-3948 5999; www.wulfand lamb.com; 243 Pavilion Rd, SW1; mains from £11.95; ⊘8am-10pm Mon-Sat, 9am-9pm Sun; 🖉; Ⓤ Sloane Sq) Picture-perfect Pavilion Rd, a side street tucked off Sloane Sq, has been redeveloped in recent years to create a village-like collection of independent, artisan retailers. Standing out amid the cheesemonger, butcher, coffee shop and many others is Wulf & Lamb, a vegan restaurant that offers an elegant setting for its animal-friendly menu.

Chucs — Italian ££

(Map p278; 🖉 020-7298 7552; www.chucs restaurants.com/serpentine; Serpentine Sackler Gallery, West Carriage Dr, W2; mains £12-27; ⊘9am-6.30pm Tue-Sat; 🛜🖉; Ⓤ Lancaster Gate or Knightsbridge) Located in the elegant extension of the Serpentine Sackler Gallery (p101), Chucs might be part of a small chain, but its setting is unique. The curving, cool, Zaha Hadid–designed building is a beautiful location for enjoying the high-quality Italian food (mainly pastas and pizza), and the outdoor terrace is a gardened suntrap with a view (across a busy road) of Hyde Park.

Dinner by Heston Blumenthal — Modern British £££

(Map p278; 🖉 020-7201 3833; www.dinnerby heston.com; Mandarin Oriental Hyde Park, 66 Knightsbridge, SW1; 3-course set lunch £45, mains £33-52; ⊘noon-2pm & 6-10.15pm Mon-Fri, noon-2.30pm & 6.30-10.30pm Sat & Sun; 🛜; Ⓤ Knightsbridge) Sumptuously presented Dinner is a gastronomic tour de force, taking diners on a journey through British culinary history (with inventive modern inflections).

Chin Chin Labs ice cream

WILL JONES/LONELY PLANET ©

Dishes carry historical dates to convey context, while the restaurant interior is a design triumph, from the glass-walled kitchen and its overhead clock mechanism to the large windows looking onto the park. Book ahead.

✖ North London

Ruby Violet   Ice Cream £

(Map p284; www.rubyviolet.co.uk; Midlands Goods Shed, 3 Wharf Rd, N1C; 1 scoop £3; ⊙11am-10pm Tue-Sat, to 7pm Sun & Mon; Ⓤ King's Cross St Pancras) 🍴 Ruby Violet takes ice cream to the next level: flavours are wonderfully original (masala chai, raspberry and sweet potato) and toppings and hot sauces are house-made. Plus, there's Pudding Club on Friday and Saturday nights, when you can dive into a mini baked Alaska or hot chocolate fondant. Eat in or sit by the fountain on Granary Sq (p120). No cash; cards only.

Hook Camden Town   Fish & Chips £

(Map p284; www.hookrestaurants.com; 63-65 Parkway, NW1; mains £8-12; ⊙hours vary, usually noon-3pm & 5.30-9pm/10pm most days; 👪; Ⓤ Camden Town) 🍴 In addition to working entirely with sustainable small fisheries and local suppliers, Hook makes all its sauces on-site and wraps its fish in recycled materials, supplying diners with extraordinarily fine-tasting morsels. Totally fresh, the fish arrives in panko breadcrumbs or tempura batter, with seaweed salted chips. Wash it down with craft beer, wines and cocktails.

Sauces go beyond the usual suspects, and range from ketchup and tartare to garlic truffle, chipotle, hot mango and lime, chimichurri and piri-piri. There's also a great kids' menu, free-range chicken and tacos.

Chin Chin Labs   Ice Cream £

(Map p284; www.chinchinlabs.com; 49-50 Camden Lock Pl, NW1; ice cream £4-5; ⊙noon-7pm; Ⓤ Camden Town) This is food chemistry at its absolute best. Chefs prepare the ice-cream mixture and freeze it on the spot by adding liquid nitrogen. Flavours change regularly and match the seasons (spiced hot cross bun, passionfruit and coconut, for instance).

🍽 Food Markets

The boom in London's eating scene has extended to its markets, which come in three categories: food stalls that are part of a broader market and appeal to visitors keen to soak up the atmosphere (Old Spitalfields, p75, and Camden, p180); specialist food and farmers markets, which sell pricey local and/or organic produce and artisanal products (Borough, p78, Broadway, p179; see www.lfm.org. uk for others); and the many colourful general markets, where the oranges and lemons come from who knows where and the barrow boys and girls speak with perfect Cockney or Caribbean accents (such as Portobello Road, p145).

Camden Market
PRICEM/SHUTTERSTOCK ©

Sauces and toppings are equally creative. Try the ice-cream sandwich if you can: ice cream wedged inside gorgeous brownies or cookies. Cash only.

It's directly opposite Shaka Zulu inside Camden Lock Market.

Waitrose
King's Cross   Supermarket £

(Map p284; www.waitrose.com; Midland Goods Shed, 1 Wharf Rd, N1C; ⊙8am-10pm Mon-Sat, noon-6pm Sun; Ⓤ King's Cross St Pancras) Perfect for grabbing ingredients for a picnic by the canal, this branch of the upmarket supermarket isn't your typical grocery shopping experience. Not only does it have an excellent takeaway section with lovely salads and deli fare, there's also a bakery, juice bar, coffee bar and wine bar, with occasional live music, as well as cookery classes on-site.

Real Food Market   Market £

(Map p284; www.realfoodfestival.co.uk; King's Cross Sq, N1; dishes £4-12; ☺noon-7pm Wed-Fri; ☑; Ⓤ King's Cross St Pancras) This vibrant market brings together two dozen gourmet food stalls three times a week. You can get anything from lovely cheeses, cured meats, smoked haddock and artisan bread to takeaway dishes such as wraps, curries and delicious cakes.

KERB Camden Market   Market £

(Map p284; www.kerbfood.com; Camden Lock Market; mains £6-10; ☺noon-late; ☑; Ⓤ Camden Town) From Argentine to Vietnamese, the KERB food-market collective is like an A–Z of world cuisines. Each stall looks more mouthwatering than the next, and there should be enough choice to keep even the fussiest of eaters happy. Eat at the big communal tables or find a spot somewhere along the canal.

Caravan   International ££

(Map p284; ☏020-7101 7661; www.caravan restaurants.co.uk; 1 Granary Sq, N1C; small plates £6-8, mains £15-19; ☺8am-10.30pm Mon-Fri, 10am-10.30pm Sat, 10am-4pm Sun; ☍☑; Ⓤ King's Cross St Pancras) Housed in the lofty Granary Building, Caravan is a vast industrial-chic destination for tasty fusion bites from around the world. You can opt for several small plates to share tapas-style, or stick to main-sized dishes. The outdoor seating area on Granary Sq is especially popular on warm days, and cocktails are popular regardless of the weather.

Manna   Vegetarian ££

(☏020-7722 8028; www.mannav.com; 4 Erskine Rd, NW3; mains £8-15; ☺noon-3pm & 6.30-10pm Tue-Sat, noon-7.30pm Sun; ☑; Ⓤ Chalk Farm) Tucked away on a side street, this upmarket little place does a brisk trade in inventive vegetarian and vegan cooking. The menu features mouthwatering, beautifully presented dishes incorporating elements of Californian, Mexican and Asian cuisine with nods to the raw-food trend. The cheesecake of the day is always a hit.

⊗ Richmond, Kew & Hampton Court

Glasshouse   Modern European ££

(☏020-8940 6777; www.glasshouserestaurant. co.uk; 14 Station Pde, TW9; 3-course lunch from £39.50, 3-course dinner from £57.50; ☺noon-12.30pm & 6.30-9.30pm Tue-Thu, noon-2.30pm & 6.30-10.30pm Fri & Sat, 12.30-4pm Sun; ☍☈; ☒ Kew Gardens, Ⓤ Kew Gardens) A day at Kew Gardens finds a perfect conclusion at this Michelin-starred gastronomic highlight. The glass-fronted exterior envelops a delicately lit, low-key interior, where the focus remains on divinely cooked food. Diners are rewarded with a seasonal, consistently accomplished menu from chef Greg Wellman that combines English mainstays with modern European innovation.

⊗ The City

Ask For Janice   British £

(Map p282; ☏020-7600 2255; www.askforjanice. co.uk; 50-52 Long Lane, EC1; sharing plates £5-9; ☺7.30am-midnight Mon-Fri, from 10.30am Sat; ☍; Ⓤ Barbican) It's all go behind the red neon sign of this all-day bar-restaurant: steam rises from the coffee machine; the bubbling rush of tonic water cracks the ice of a British gin and tonic. Expect seasonal sharing plates, foraged salads and hearty breakfasts such as easy-over eggs and black pudding atop generous portions of bubble and squeak.

Miyama   Japanese ££

(Map p280; ☏020-7489 1937; www.miyama-restaurant.co.uk; 17 Godliman St, EC4; mains from £13.50; ☺11.30am-2.30pm & 5.45-9.30pm Mon-Fri; Ⓤ St Paul's) There's the sense of a well-kept secret about this excellent Japanese restaurant, tucked away in a basement of a nondescript building (enter from Knightrider St). The menu runs from soba and udon noodles to sushi and bento boxes. Sit at the sushi or teppanyaki bar for culinary drama, or opt for the more discreet main restaurant.

Ask about the good-value set menu lunch – staff like to keep it a secret.

Fortnum & Mason   British ££

(Map p280; ☏020-7734 8040; www.fortnum andmason.com/stores/the-royal-exchange; Threadneedle St, EC3; mains £19-42; ⊗7am-11pm Mon-Fri, from 8am Sat; 🖋; Ⓤ Bank) The august **Royal Exchange** (Map p280; ☏020-7283 8935; www.theroyalexchange.co.uk) provides a fitting setting for the latest bar-restaurant from Fortnum & Mason (p183), London's poshest department store. Expect oysters and caviar from the pale green oval-shaped bar, while bygone British standards like chicken, eel and 'liquor' pie are served in the open dining area.

Kym's   Chinese ££

(Map p280; ☏020-7220 7088; www.kyms restaurant.com; 19 Bloombery Arcade, EC4; mains £12.50-30; ⊗noon-3pm & 5-11pm Mon-Sat, noon-6pm Sun; Ⓤ Cannon Street or Mansion House) Centred around the artificial cherry blossom that climbs the staircase, this highly stylised Andrew Wong restaurant, more informal than his Michelin-starred endeavours in Pimlico, is a celebration of Chinese roasting techniques. The Three Treasure dish assembles the best mains in one – crispy pork belly, Iberico *char siu* (pork in hoisin sauce) and soy chicken. Veggies book elsewhere.

Wine Library   Buffet ££

(Map p280; ☏020-7481 0415; www.winelibrary. co.uk; 43 Trinity Sq, EC3; buffet £18; ⊗buffet 11.30am-3pm Mon-Fri, 11am-5pm Sat, shop 10am-6pm Mon, to 8pm Tue-Fri, 11am-5pm Sat; Ⓤ Tower Hill) This distinguished cellar has a self-serve buffet on par with its storied wine selection. Ask owner Peter to help select a bottle from the vast collection (£9.50 corkage fee) and take it into the vaulted cellar to enjoy with an array of Loire Valley pâtés, strong farmhouse cheeses, thinly sliced Dorset ham, vegetarian mousses, soft bread and more.

Vanilla Black   Vegetarian £££

(Map p280; ☏020-7242 2622; www.vanillablack. co.uk; 17-18 Took's Ct; 3-/4-course £31/41.50;

🍽️ Desserts

England does a mean dessert, and establishments serving British cuisine revel in these indulgent treats. Favourites include bread-and-butter pudding, sticky toffee pudding (steamed pudding with dates, topped with a caramel sauce), the alarmingly named spotted dick (steamed suet pudding with currants and raisins), Eton mess (meringue, cream and strawberries mixed into a gooey mass), and seasonal musts such as Christmas pudding (a steamed pudding with candied fruit and brandy) and fruity crumbles.

Eton Mess
WESTEND61/GETTY IMAGES ©

⊗noon-2.30pm & 6-10pm Mon-Sat; 🖋; Ⓤ Chancery Lane) You'll need a reservation (and perhaps a compass) to dine at this vegetarian institution, located along an empty backstreet behind Chancery Lane. But your efforts will be rewarded with one of the finest dining experiences in the City. An ever-changing menu of imaginative, deconstructed dishes elevates vegetables from sideshow to superstar; think vanilla-roasted celeriac profiteroles with dill and raisins.

City Social   Modern British £££

(Map p280; ☏020-7877 7703; http://citysocial london.com; L24, 25 Old Broad St, EC2; mains £24-38; ⊗noon-2.30pm & 6-10.30pm Mon-Fri, 5-10.30pm Sat; Ⓤ Bank) The remarkable views from this low-lit glamour puss on the 24th floor of Tower 42 are as heady as the resulting dinner bill, but executive art-deco surrounds and delicate Michelin-starred

cuisine – think Lancashire rabbit and Romney Marsh lamb – make this a seriously impressive dining spot. Bookings essential; expect airport-style security at the door.

🚫 The South Bank

Padella — Italian £

(Map p280; www.padella.co; 6 Southwark St, SE1; dishes £4-11.50; ⊘noon-3.45pm & 5-10pm Mon-Sat, noon-3.45pm & 5-9pm Sun; 🖋; ⓤLondon Bridge) A fantastic part of the foodie enclave of Borough Market (p78), Padella is a small, energetic bistro specialising in hanmade pasta dishes, inspired by the owners' extensive culinary adventures in Italy. The portions are small, which means that, joy of joys, you can (and should!) have more than one dish. Outstanding, but be prepared to queue (no reservations taken).

Watch House — Cafe £

(Map p280; 🖉020-7407 6431; www.thewatch house.com; 199 Bermondsey St, SE1; mains from £4.95; ⊘7am-6pm Mon-Fri, 8am-6pm Sat & Sun; 🖋; ⓤBorough or London Bridge) Saying

that the Watch House nails the sandwich wouldn't really do justice to this tip-top cafe: the sandwiches really are delicious. There is also great coffee, and treats for the sweet-toothed. The small but lovely setting is a renovated 19th-century watch-house from where guards watched over the next-door cemetery. No bathroom.

Flat Iron Square — Food Hall £

(Map p280; www.flatironsquare.co.uk; Flat Iron Sq, btwn Union & Southwark Sts; mains from £8; ⊘noon-9pm Mon, to midnight Tue-Fri, 11am-midnight Sat, 10am-8pm Sun; 🖋; ⓤLondon Bridge) Weaving through several railway arches, this stylish twist on a food court has a great vibe. Traders and street-food vans serve gyoza, pizza, noodles, buttermilk chicken, salads, veggie dishes and much more. Grab your favourite and head to the indoor communal tables or outside to the cobbled courtyard. Also hosts events, including vintage markets and theme nights.

Maltby Street Market — Market £

(Map p280; www.maltby.st; Maltby St, SE1; dishes £5-10; ⊘10am-5pm Sat, 11am-4pm Sun; ⓤLondon

Bridge or Bermondsey) Tucked alongside and under railway arches, Maltby Street Market is a smaller alternative to sprawling Borough. Food stalls offer top-notch fare from all over the world. Grab a dish and find a seat at one of the few benches, or head for one of the restaurants or bars set up in the arches.

M Manze   British £

(www.manze.co.uk; 87 Tower Bridge Rd, SE1; mains £4.30; ⊙11am-2pm Mon, 10.30am-2pm Tue-Thu, 10am-2.15pm Fri, to 2.45pm Sat; ⓤBorough) Dating from 1902, M Manze started off as an ice-cream seller before moving on to selling its legendary staples: minced-beef pies. It's a classic operation, from the ageing tilework to the traditional workers' menu of pie and mash served with gravy or liquor (a parsley-based sauce). Try eels, a traditional East End dish, served jellied or stewed. Vegetarian pies available.

The Table Café   Cafe £

(Map p280; ☑020-7401 2760; www.thetablecafe .com; 83 Southwark St, SE1; Mains £10-15; ⊙7.30am-10.30pm Mon-Wed, to 11.30pm Thu & Fri, 8am-4pm Sat & Sun; ⓤSouthwark) This smart, independent café/restaurant/bar (depending what time you visit) has become something of an institution on the Southwark dining scene. The breakfasts, brunches and lunches are creative (the Breakfast Bruschetta is ridiculously good) and use top-quality, ethically-sourced ingredients. As evening draws in, the venue becomes popular with office folk pining for an after-work cocktail; the rum-based Dark & Stormy comes recommended.

Baltic   Eastern European ££

(Map p280; ☑020-7928 1111; www.baltic restaurant.co.uk; 74 Blackfriars Rd, SE1; mains £13.50-19, 2-course lunch menu £17.50; ⊙5.30-11.15pm Mon, noon-3pm & 5.30-11.15pm Tue-Sat, noon-4.30pm & 5.30-10.30pm Sun; ☑; ⓤSouthwark) In a bright and airy, high-ceilinged dining room with glass roof and wooden beams, Baltic is travel on a plate: dumplings and blini, pickle and smoke, rich stews and braised meat. From Polish to Georgian, the flavours are authentic and

the dishes beautifully presented. The wine and vodka lists are equally diverse.

Anchor & Hope   Gastropub ££

(Map p280; ☑020-7928 9898; www.anchorand hopepub.co.uk; 36 The Cut, SE1; mains £12-20; ⊙5-11pm Mon, 11am-11pm Tue-Sat, 12.30-3.15pm Sun; ⓤSouthwark) The Anchor & Hope is a quintessential gastropub: elegant but not formal, serving utterly delicious European fare with a British twist. The menu changes daily, but could include grilled sole served with spinach, or roast rabbit with green beans in a mustard and bacon sauce. Bookings taken for Sunday lunch only.

Bar Tozino   Tapas ££

(Map p280; www.tozino.co.uk; Rope Walk; tapas £6-15; ⊙5-10pm Wed & Thu, noon-10pm Fri & Sat, to 5pm Sun; ⓤLondon Bridge or Bermondsey) Superb tapas and wine bar in the ever-popular Maltby Street Market. Cava and a range of Spanish wines by the glass, wonderful plates of tapas and accommodating staff. Place your order at the bar, grab a nearby stool or squeeze in at one of the few tables. The hand-carved *jamón* is spectacular.

Arabica Bar & Kitchen   Middle Eastern £££

(Map p280; ☑020-3011 5151; www.arabicabarand kitchen.com; 3 Rochester Walk, Borough Market, SE1; dishes £6-14; ⊙noon-11pm Mon-Fri, 9am-11.30pm Sat, noon-9pm Sun; ☑; ⓤLondon Bridge) Lively, and often packed at dinner time, Arabica specialises in pan–Middle Eastern cuisine. Dishes are beautifully presented and absolutely delicious. Aim to have two to three small dishes per person, but remember that this tapas approach means the bill can add up quickly. Booking is recommended.

Skylon   Modern European £££

(Map p280; ☑020-7654 7800; www.skylon-restaurant.co.uk; 3rd fl, Royal Festival Hall, Southbank Centre, Belvedere Rd, SE1; 3-course menu grill/restaurant £25/30; ⊙grill noon-11pm Mon-Sat, to 10pm Sun, restaurant 12.30-2.30pm & 5-10.30pm Mon-Sat; ☑🖤; ⓤWaterloo) This excellent restaurant inside the Royal Festival Hall (p217) is divided into grill and fine-dining sections by a large bar. The decor is cutting-edge 1950s, with muted colours and period chairs (trendy then, trendier now), while floor-to-ceiling windows bathe you in magnificent views of the Thames and the city. Booking is advised.

Children under 10 eat free, except on Saturdays. Brunch on Sundays is available with bottomless Prosecco. The bar is open for drinks without a restaurant reservation.

The West End

Beijing Dumpling   Chinese £

(Map p274; ☑020-7287 6888; www.facebook. com/beijingdumpling; 23 Lisle St, WC2; mains £7-12.50; ☺noon-11.30pm Mon-Sat, 11.30am-10.30pm Sun; Ⓤ Leicester Sq) You can see the stars of the show before you even walk in, as tiny dough pockets ready to be made into *xiaolongbao* (soup dumplings) are kneaded at speed behind the steamy front window: do not leave without ordering a basket or three. Though the surroundings are no-frills, nearly every dish is top-notch. Service can be gruff but is always efficient.

Kanada-Ya   Ramen £

(Map p274; ☑020-7240 0232; www.kanada-ya. com; 64 St Giles High St, WC2; mains £7-14; ☺noon-3pm & 5-10.30pm Mon-Sat, to 8.30pm Sun; Ⓤ Tottenham Court Rd) In the eternal debate over London's best ramen, we're still voting for this one. With no reservations taken, queues can get impressive outside this tiny and enormously popular canteen, where ramen cooked in *tonkotsu* (pork-bone broth) draws in diners from near and far. The noodles arrive at just the right temperature and hardness, steeped in a delectable broth and rich flavours.

Hoppers   Sri Lankan £

(Map p274; www.hopperslondon.com; 49 Frith St, W1; dishes £5-21; ☺noon-2.30pm & 5.30-10.30pm Mon-Thu, noon-10.30pm Fri & Sat; Ⓤ Tottenham Court Rd or Leicester Sq) This enormously popular place specialises in the Sri Lankan national dish of hoppers: thin pancakes of rice flour and coconut milk with spices. Eat them (or dosas) with

Palomar

HUFTON+CROW-VIEW/ALAMY STOCK PHOTO ©

various types of *kari* (curry) or *kothu,* a dish of chopped flatbread with spices and meat, fish, crab or vegetables. The decor here is Old Ceylon, and the service swift but personable.

Counter at the Delaunay   Cafe £

(Map p280; ☎020-7499 8558; www.the delaunay.com/counter; 55 Aldwych, WC2; soups & sandwiches £4.75-9.50; ☺7am-8.30pm Mon-Fri, from 10.30am Sat, 11am-5.30pm Sun; Ⓤ Temple or Covent Garden) The more informal sibling of the Delaunay next door, the Counter goes full Vienna with *Sachertorte* (dark chocolate iced cake filled with apricot jam), *Wiener Kaffee* (a double espresso and whipped cream) and Stiegl Austrian beer. It's a great place for a pick-me-up after shopping with the crowds in Covent Garden.

Dishoom   Indian £

(Map p274; ☎020-7420 9320; www.dishoom. com; 12 Upper St Martin's Lane, WC2; mains £6.70-11.90; ☺8am-11pm Mon-Thu, to midnight Fri, 9am-midnight Sat, to 11pm Sun; ☏; Ⓤ Covent Garden) This branch of a highly successful mini-chain takes the fast-disappearing Iranian cafe culture of Mumbai and gives it new life. Distressed with a modern twist (ceiling fans, stained mirrors and sepia photos), here you'll find yummy favourites like *sheekh kabab* and spiced chicken ruby, okra fries and snack foods such as *bhel* (Bombay mix and puffed rice with pomegranate, onion, lime and mint).

Mildreds   Vegetarian £

(Map p274; ☎020-7484 1634; www.mildreds.co.uk; 45 Lexington St, W1; mains £7-12; ☺noon-11pm Mon-Sat; ☏☕; Ⓤ Oxford Circus or Piccadilly Circus) Central London's most inventive vegetarian restaurant, Mildreds is crammed at lunchtime so don't be shy about sharing a table in the sky-lit dining room. Expect the likes of Sri Lankan sweet-potato and cashew-nut curry, ricotta and truffle tortellini, Middle Eastern mezze, wonderfully exotic (and filling) salads and delicious stir-fries. There are also vegan and gluten-free options.

Palomar   Middle Eastern ££

(Map p274; ☎020-7439 8777; www.thepalomar. co.uk; 34 Rupert St, W1; dishes £7.50-26; ☺noon-2.30pm & 5.30-11pm Mon-Sat, 12.30-3.30pm & 6-9pm Sun; ☏; Ⓤ Piccadilly Circus) With a stack of 'restaurant of the year' awards, Palomar is a firm favourite, and the wait for one of the 16 bar stools or 40 seats is testament to that. It celebrates modern Jerusalem cuisine, with flavours stretching from the Levant to the Maghreb. *Kubaneh* (bread dipped in tomato and tahini), 'octo-hummus' and balsamic-glazed chicken livers are a few of the must-orders.

The Delaunay   European ££

(Map p280; ☎020-7499 8558; www.the delaunay.com; 55 Aldwych, WC2; mains £14.50-35; ☺7am-11pm Mon-Fri, from 8am Sat, 9am-10pm Sun; ☏☕; Ⓤ Temple or Covent Garden) This smart spot channels the majesty of the grand cafes of *Mitteleuropa* (Central Europe). Schnitzels and wieners take pride of place on the menu, which is rounded out with Alsatian *tarte flambée* (thin crust usually topped with *crème fraîche*, onions and bacon lardons) and a rotating *Tagesteller* (dish of the day). Its location in Theatreland makes it ideal for pre- or post-show eats.

Lina Stores   Italian ££

(Map p274; ☎020-3929 0068; www.linastores. co.uk/restaurant; 51 Greek St, W1; dishes £5.50-14; ☺noon-2.30pm & 5-11pm Mon-Sat; Ⓤ Tottenham Court Rd) Lina Stores has been operating a **deli** (Map p274; ☎020-7437 6482; 18 Brewer St, W1; ☺8.30am-7.30pm Mon & Tue, to 8.30pm Wed-Fri, 9am-7.30pm Sat, 11am-5pm Sun; Ⓤ Piccadilly Circus) on Soho's Brewer St since 1944, and they've finally started dishing up their perfect handmade pasta to drooling diners. Plates are small but satisfying. The creamy *pici alla norcina* with fat spaghetti-like pasta twirled around porcini mushrooms and Umbrian sausage is the most popular menu option, and it's not hard to taste why.

🍴 British Cheese

For a nation that has traditionally held its nose in response to strong flavours, it makes the exception for some particularly pungent blue cheeses. Stilton is the most famous, but look out for Stinking Bishop and the blues from Wensleydale, Derby, Dorset and Shropshire. The king of the crumbly hard cheeses is aged cheddar; Cheshire, Lancashire and Caerphilly all have their own distinctive varieties.

Great places to sample British cheeses include Rippon Cheese (p182) and Borough Market (p78).

Neal's Yard Dairy at Borough Market

MARK CHILVERS/LONELY PLANET ©

Mortimer House Kitchen
Mediterranean ££

(Map p274; ☎020-7139 4401; www.mortimer house.com/restaurant; 37-41 Mortimer St, W1; mains £12-28; ⊗7.30am-11.30pm Mon-Thu, to midnight Fri, 9am-midnight Sat, 9am-6pm Sun; Ⓤ Goodge St or Oxford Circus) Tranquil isn't a word ever applied to Soho, even in this slightly less trafficked part, but somehow this restaurant channels Great Gatsby–style zen and confidence in its art-deco–flavoured dining room. The Med meets the Middle East on its menu, hopscotching from charcoal cauliflower and shakshuka to buffalo ricotta ravioli and black truffle with delicious ease. Service is stellar.

Temper
Grill ££

(Map p274; ☎020-3879 3834; www.temper restaurant.com/temper-soho; 25 Broadwick St, W1; dishes £7.50-18; ⊗noon-10.30pm Mon-Wed, to 11pm Thu-Sat, to 9pm Sun; Ⓤ Oxford Circus or Piccadilly Circus) Temper doesn't do things by halves: this restaurant under a Soho street has a 6m-long fire pit running down the middle, and prides itself on being a 'whole meat barbecue', meaning all meat is butchered in-house and less is wasted. The menu is impossible to pin down, as it roves from tacos to meat-topped *parathas* (Indian flatbread) and Szechuan guacamole.

Kiln
Thai ££

(Map p274; www.kilnsoho.com; 58 Brewer St, W1; dishes £4.50-14; ⊗noon-3pm & 5-11pm Mon-Thu, noon-11pm Fri & Sat, to 9pm Sun; Ⓤ Piccadilly Circus) Crowned the UK's best restaurant in 2018, this tiny Thai grill cooks up a storm in its long, narrow kitchen, supervised by diners on stools opposite. The short menu rides the small-plates wave and works best with a few friends so you can order more. The rich, saucy beef neck curry is phenomenal, as are the signature glass noodles.

Cafe Murano
Italian ££

(Map p274; ☎020-3371 5559; www.cafe murano.co.uk; 33 St James's St, SW1; mains £16-24; ⊗noon-3pm & 5.30-11pm Mon-Sat, 11.30am-4pm Sun; Ⓤ Green Park) The setting may seem demure at this superb and busy restaurant from British Michelin-starred chef and Gordon Ramsay protégé Angela Hartnett, but with such a sublime northern Italian menu on offer, it sees no need to be flashy and of-the-moment. The set menu is excellent value (two/three courses £19/23), with the suggested wine costing nearly as much.

Barrafina
Spanish ££

(Map p274; ☎020-7440 1456; www.barrafina. co.uk; 26-27 Dean St, W1; tapas £7-18.80; ⊗noon-3pm & 5-11pm Mon-Sat, 1-3.30pm & 5.30-10pm Sun; Ⓤ Tottenham Court Rd) Tapas are always better value in Spain than in London, but the quality of the food at Barrafina justifies the extra expense. Along with *gambas al ajillo* (prawns in garlic), there are more unusual items, such as tuna tartar and grilled quail with aioli, plus a wonderful changing menu of specials.

Customers sit along the bar, so it's not a good choice for groups (and the maximum party size is four). No reservations, so prepare to queue.

Gymkhana · Indian ££

(Map p274; ✆020-3011 5900; www.gymkhana london.com; 42 Albemarle St, W1; mains £10-38, 4-course lunch/dinner £28.50/40; ⊗noon-2.30pm & 5.30-10.15pm Mon-Sat; ☎; ⓤGreen Park) The rather sombre setting is all British Raj – ceiling fans, oak ceiling, period cricket photos and hunting trophies – but the menu is lively, bright and inspiring. For lovers of variety, there is a six-course tasting meat/vegetarian menu (£70/65). The bar is open to 1am.

Foyer & Reading Room at Claridge's · British £££

(Map p278; ✆020-7107 8886; www.claridges. co.uk; Brook St, W1; afternoon tea £65, with champagne £75-85; ⊗afternoon tea 2.45-5.30pm; ☎; ⓤBond St) Extend that pinkie finger to partake in afternoon tea within the classic art-deco foyer and Reading Room of the landmark hotel **Claridge's** (✆020-7629 8860; r/ste from £450/780; P ❋ @ ☎ ❋; ⓤBond St), where the gentle clink of fine porcelain and champagne glasses could be a defining memory of your trip to London. The setting is gorgeous and the dress code is elegant, smart casual to befit the surroundings.

Portrait · Modern European £££

(Map p274; ✆020-7312 2490; www.npg.org.uk/ visit/shop-eat-drink/restaurant; 3rd fl, National Portrait Gallery, St Martin's Pl, WC2; mains £19.50-29.50; ⊗10am-4.30pm daily, 5.30-8.30pm Thu-Sat; ☎; ⓤCharing Cross or Leicester Sq) This stunningly located restaurant above the excellent National Portrait Gallery (p57) comes with dramatic views over Trafalgar Sq and down to the Houses of Parliament and London Eye. Prices are a bit steep, but it's a fine choice for tantalising food and the chance to relax after hours of picture-gazing at the gallery. It's best to book in advance.

Pollen Street Social · European £££

(Map p274; ✆020-7290 7600; www.pollenstreet social.com; 8-10 Pollen St, W1; mains £34.50-38; ⊗noon-2.30pm & 6-10.30pm Mon-Sat; ⓤOxford

🍽 Breakfast delights

The Brits have always been big on breakfast – and they even invented one, the Full English (p370).

Fashionable once again is porridge (oats boiled in water or milk, served hot), sweet or savoury. Top-end restaurants serving breakfast have played a big part in glamming up what was essentially poor folk's food. It's great with banana and honey, fruit compote or even plain with some chocolate powder.

Semolina porridge with banana and hazelnuts
FASCINADORA/SHUTTERSTOCK ©

Circus) Chef Jason Atherton's cathedral to haute cuisine (Michelin-starred within six months of opening) is a worthy splurge, and the excellent-value set lunch (£37 for three courses) makes it more accessible. The menu is playful, and the nine-course tasting menu (£98) showcases the best, from oyster ice cream to deer saddle, and starts with a savoury take on 'afternoon tea'.

Yauatcha · Chinese £££

(Map p274; ✆020-7494 8888; www.yauatcha. com; 15-17 Broadwick St, W1; dishes £6-48; ⊗noon-10.30pm Mon-Sat, to 10pm Sun; ⓤPiccadilly Circus or Oxford Circus) London's most glamorous dim-sum restaurant has a Michelin star and is divided into two: the ground-floor dining room offers a delightful oasis of calm from the chaos of Berwick Street Market, while downstairs has a smarter feel, with constellations of 'star' lights. The venison puffs are a must, and the dessert selection is to die for.

London on a Plate

Vegetables, ideally
roast tomatoes and
mushrooms

Bacon and sausages
(we insist on the 'and')

Hash browns and/
or toast – breakfast
needs carbs

Baked beans,
especially the sauce,
which just goes with
everything

Eggs, fried or
scrambled

NEIL LANGAN UK/GETTY IMAGES ©

The Full English

The Full English breakfast (also sometimes called a fry-up) is something of
a protein overload but there's nothing
quite like it to mop up the excesses of
a night on the tiles. You'll find countless
brightly lit, grotty caffs (cafes) – nicknamed 'greasy spoons' – serving these
monster plates. They're also a must
at gastropubs and in top-end British
restaurants.

ETORRES/SHUTTERSTOCK ©

★ Top Five For English Breakfast

Tom's Kitchen (p159) Divine food in a
pleasant setting.

Ask for Janice (p163) Expect hearty
breakfasts in this hectic bar-restaurant.

Fortnum & Mason (p163) The latest
bar-restaurant from London's poshest
department store.

Karpo (☎020-3096 9900; www.karpo.
co.uk; 23-27 Euston Rd, NW1; mains £11-19,
breakfast £7-10; ◷7am-10pm Mon-Sat,
8am-9pm Sun; Ⓤ King's Cross St Pancras)
Delicious, and in a great setting too.

Rivington Grill (p157) The real McCoy,
with top-notch ingredients.

⊗ West London

Lowry & Baker
Cafe **£**

(Map p278; ☎020-8960 8534; 339 Portobello Rd, W10; mains from £7.50; ⊗8am-4pm Mon-Sat, from 10am Sun; ☎; Ⓤ Ladbroke Grove or Westbourne Park) With its colourfully mixed-up cups and cutlery and snug interior, this appealing cafe has a jumble-sale charm. There's fine Monmouth coffee and tasty platters, and it's a great spot for breakfast (home-made granola, toasted brioche etc), brunch (such as avocado on toast with poached eggs), or just for putting your feet up after schlepping around Portobello Road Market.

Cockney's Pie and Mash
Pies **£**

(Map p278; ☎020-8960 9409; 314 Portobello Rd, W10; pies £3.50; ⊗11.30am-5pm Tue-Sat; Ⓤ Ladbroke Grove or Westbourne Park) For fine helpings of London's classic working-class staples: pie, mash and liquor (parsley sauce).

Acklam Village Market
Market **£**

(Map p278; www.acklamvillage.com; 4-8 Acklam Rd, W10; ⊗11am-7.30pm Sat Feb, Mar, Nov & Dec, 11am-7.30pm Sat & Sun Apr-Oct; Ⓤ Ladbroke Grove) Stuffed under the Westway, this lively and aromatic street-eats market at the north end of Portobello Rd serves snacks from all over the globe: take your pick from Palestinian, African, Peruvian, Chinese, Mexican, Greek, Moroccan, Polish, Portuguese or plain old British. There's craft beers, cocktails and live music to wash it down.

Taquería
Mexican **£**

(Map p278; ☎020-7229 4734; www.taqueria. co.uk; 139-143 Westbourne Grove; tacos £7.20-10.20; ⊗noon-11pm Mon-Thu, to 11.30pm Fri & Sat, to 10.30pm Sun; ☎; Ⓤ Notting Hill Gate) ✔ As you'd expect, the tacos are the thing here, and they're just as they should be: fresh, rich and comforting. Starting life as a stall on Portobello Rd, Taquería is a small, casual place with an appealing vibe, committed to environmental mores: the eggs, chicken and pork are free-range, the meat British, the fish MSC-certified, and the milk and cream organic.

Mazi
Greek **££**

(Map p278; ☎020-7229 3794; www.mazi.co.uk; 12-14 Hillgate St, W8; mains £11-25; ⊗noon-3pm Tue-Sun, 6.30-11pm Mon-Sat, 6.30-10pm Sun; ☎; Ⓤ Notting Hill Gate) Tucked away on pretty Hillgate St, Mazi offers a modern take on Greek cuisine, with a lively, seasonally updated menu that encourages sharing ('mazi' means 'together'). The interior is bright and neat, and there's a small back garden (open April to October) and an all-Greek wine list. It's small and popular, so reservations are important.

Geales
Seafood **££**

(Map p278; ☎020-7727 7528; www.geales.com; 2 Farmer St, W8; 2-course lunch £20, mains £14-36; ⊗noon-3pm Tue-Fri, 5.30-10pm Mon-Fri, noon-10pm Sat & Sun; ☎; Ⓤ Notting Hill Gate) Frying since 1939, Geales has endured with its quiet location on the corner of Farmer and Uxbridge Sts. The fish in crispy batter is a fine catch, but the fish pie and rich mushy peas are also worth angling for.

Ledbury
French **£££**

(Map p278; ☎020-7792 9090; www.theledbury. com; 127 Ledbury Rd, W11; 4-course set lunch £80, 4-course dinner £125; ⊗noon-2pm Wed-Sun & 6.30-9.45pm daily; ☎; Ⓤ Westbourne Park, Royal Oak or Notting Hill Gate) With two Michelin stars, Brett Graham's elegant French restaurant attracts well-heeled diners in jeans with designer jackets. Artful dishes such as veal tartare, steamed cuttlefish, warm bantam's egg with celeriac and dried ham, or Herdwick lamb with salt-baked turnips, celery cream and wild garlic are triumphs. Gastronomes have the Ledbury on speed dial, so reservations well in advance are crucial.

TREASURE HUNT

Begin your shopping adventure

London Evening News'

LONDON TRANSPORT

Treasure Hunt

From charity-shop finds to designer bags, there are thousands of ways to spend your hard-earned cash in London. Many of the big-name shopping attractions, such as Harrods, Hamleys, Camden Market and Old Spitalfields Market, have become must-sees in their own right. Chances are that with so many temptations, you'll give your wallet a full workout.

In This Section

Taxes & Refunds

○ In stores displaying a 'tax free' sign, visitors from non-EU countries are entitled to claim back the VAT on purchases.

○ The retailer should provide a VAT 407 form, which needs to be completed and presented at Customs when leaving the country, along with the receipt and goods. See www.gov.uk/tax-on-shopping/taxfree-shopping.

North London
It's all about market stalls and
secondhand clothes (p182)

**Clerkenwell, Shoreditch
& Spitalfields**
Vintage, vintage, vintage,
fashion and jewellery (p178)

West London
Famous market, vintage
stores and lovely
boutiques (p186)

The West End
Shopping galore, from
franchises to independent
music and book shops (p183)

The City
Good for suits but
little else (p183)

East London
Wonderful markets,
discounted fashion
(p179)

Kensington & Hyde Park
High fashion and
glamorous shopping
(p181)

The South Bank
Not known for its shopping;
some independent boutiques
and vintage markets (p183)

Greenwich & South London
Antiques, jewellery, handicrafts,
with fine boutiques and
small shops (p180)

River Thames

Opening Hours

○ Shops generally open from 9am
or 10am to 6pm or 7pm Monday to
Saturday.

○ Most stores in popular strips open on
Sunday, typically from noon to 6pm but
sometimes 10am to 4pm.

○ West End stores open to 9pm on
Thursday; those in Chelsea, Knights-
bridge and Kensington open late on
Wednesday.

Sales Seasons

Winter sales Run from Boxing Day (26
December) to the tail end of January.

Summer sales Usually start the last
week of June and run until the end of July.

The Best...

Experience London's best shopping

For Souvenirs

We Built This City (p184) Great London-themed souvenirs, minus tackiness.

Arty Globe (p181) Unusual fish-eye photographs of London.

Jo Loves (p182) Perfumes and candles devised by Jo Malone.

Fortnum & Mason (p183) Wide range of British treats, beautifully packaged.

Markets

Sunday Upmarket (p75) Load up on delicious food before tackling the designer stalls.

Camden Market (p180) From authentic antiques to tourist tat – and everything in between.

Portobello Road Market (p145) Classic Notting Hill sprawl, perfect for vintage everything.

Broadway Market (p179) Local market known for its food.

Old Spitalfields Market (p75; pictured above) One of London's best for young fashion designers.

Fashion Shops

Selfridges (p143; pictured above) Everything from streetwear to high fashion under one roof.

Collectif (p178) Spitalfields store taking inspiration from the 1940s and '50s.

Hackney Walk (p180) Big-brand outlet shopping at its very best.

Browns (p186) Great for up-and-coming designers.

For Vintage

Traid (p180) Dalston not-for-profit selling both top-notch vintage duds and new clothes made from offcuts.

Atika (p179) A massive selection of just about everything.

Beyond Retro (p180; pictured above) London vintage empire with a rock 'n' roll heart.

Bookshops

John Sandoe Books (p181) Gorgeous bookshop stuffed with gems.

Lutyens & Rubinstein (p186; pictured above) Curated selections of exceptional writing.

Foyles (p185) A brilliant selection covering most bases and incorporates the Grant & Cutler foreign-language bookshop.

Hatchards (p184) London's oldest bookshop, selling the good stuff since 1797.

Department Stores

Harrods (p181; pictured above) Enormous, overwhelming and indulgent, with a world-famous food hall.

Liberty (p143) Fabric, fashion and much, much more.

Selfridges (p143) Over 100 years of retail innovation.

★ **Lonely Planet's Top Choices**

Sunday Upmarket (p75) Up-and-coming designers, cool tees and terrific food.

Fortnum & Mason (p183) The world's most glamorous grocery store?

Stanfords (p184) A shop for travellers and curious minds.

Stables Market (p182) Nothing says London like Camden Market.

Conran Shop (p181) A treasure trove of cool things.

Music Shops

Rough Trade East (p179; pictured above) Excellent selection of vinyl and CDs, plus in-store gigs.

Casbah Records (p181) Classic vinyl and memorabilia.

Reckless Records (p186) Legendary establishment in Soho.

⓰ Clerkenwell, Shoreditch & Spitalfields

Collectif
Fashion & Accessories

(Map p282; ☑020-7650 7777; www.collectif. co.uk; 58 Commercial St, E1; ⊙10am-6pm; Ⓤ Aldgate East) If you love the looks of the 1940s and '50s, you will swoon over Collectif's vintage-inspired dresses, shirts, coats and accessories, with racks upon racks of eye-popping polka dots and bright patterns.

InSpitalfields
Gifts & Souvenirs

(Map p282; ☑020-7247 2477; www.inspitalfields .co.uk; Old Spitalfields Market, 13 Lamb St, E1; ⊙10am-7pm; Ⓤ Aldgate East or Liverpool St) Here's the place to pick up that T-rex skull table centrepiece or avocado-print wrapping paper you never knew you needed. InSpitalfields is spellbinding, and every item is bound to make you chuckle or at least stop and stare in wonder.

Brick Lane Vintage Market
Vintage

(Map p282; ☑020-7770 6028; www.vintage-market.co.uk; Old Truman Brewery, 85 Brick Lane, E1; ⊙11am-6pm Mon-Sat, from 10am Sun; Ⓤ Shoreditch High St) This basement fashion emporium is a sprawling sea of vintage threads from the 1920s to the '90s, plus a few tucked-away stands of vinyl. Stalls are hired out and run individually, so be sure to pay before moving on to the next one. Shopping can get elbow-to-elbow busy at the weekend.

Tea Rooms
Market

(Map p282; ☑020-7770 6028; www.bricklane-tearooms.co.uk; Old Truman Brewery, 146 Brick Lane, E1; ⊙11am-6pm Sat, 10am-5pm Sun; Ⓤ Shoreditch High St) Whether you're after retro maps, air plants in science-class-beaker terrariums, vintage special-occasion glassware or taxidermied birdlife, this warren of stalls should see you right. Long & Short Coffee Roastery has a cosy cafe in the back if you need a pick-me-up after a long bout of Brick Lane browsing.

Boxpark
Shopping Centre

(Map p282; www.boxpark.co.uk/shoreditch; 2-10 Bethnal Green Rd, E1; ⊙8am-11pm Mon-Sat, 10am-10pm Sun; 🛜; Ⓤ Shoreditch High St) The world's

The Boiler House at Brick Lane Vintage Market

OLI SCARFF/GETTY IMAGES ©

first pop-up mall, Boxpark is a shopping and street-food enclave made from upcycled shipping containers. Fashion, design and gift shops populate the ground floor; head to the upper level for restaurants, bars and a terrace. Opening hours vary by trader; retail outlets are required to close up shop by 6pm on Sunday, but food and bar venues stay open later.

Rough Trade East   Music
(Map p282; ☑020-7392 7788; www.roughtrade. com; Old Truman Brewery, 91 Brick Lane, E1; ⊘9am-9pm Mon-Thu, to 8pm Fri, 10am-8pm Sat, 11am-7pm Sun; ⓤShoreditch High St) It's no longer directly associated with the legendary record label (home to the Smiths, the Libertines and the Strokes, among others), but this huge record shop is still tops for picking up indie, soul, electronica and alternative music. In addition to an impressive selection of CDs and vinyl, it also dispenses coffee and stages gigs and artist signings.

Tatty Devine   Jewellery
(Map p282; ☑020-7739 9191; www.tattydevine. com; 236 Brick Lane, E2; ⊘10am-6pm Mon-Fri, 11am-6pm Sat, 10am-5pm Sun; ⓤShoreditch High St) Harriet Vine and Rosie Wolfenden design the hip laser-cut acrylic jewellery on sale in this small space. Their creations feature flora- and fauna-inspired jewellery, as well as pieces sporting Day of the Dead–style skulls, gin bottles and glittery lightning bolts. Name necklaces (made to order in 30 minutes) are a treat. All pieces are handmade in the UK.

Magma   Books
(Map p282; ☑020-7242 9502; www.magmabooks. com; 117-119 Clerkenwell Rd, EC1; ⊘10am-7pm Mon-Fri, from 10.45am Sat; ⓤChancery Lane) This much-loved shop sells a quirky collection of coffee-table books, magazines, card games and stationery, most on the themes of typography, graphic design and architecture, in keeping with the surrounding buildings full of ad agencies and architecture studios. It has some lovely children's books and games too, including Bird Bingo, which was developed by one of the shop's founders.

 British Designers

London-based designers are well established in the fashion world and a visit to Stella McCartney, Vivienne Westwood, Paul Smith or Burberry is an experience in its own right. The fashion house started by the late Alexander McQueen is now under the creative direction of Sarah Burton, perhaps most famous as the designer of Princess Catherine's wedding dress. Other names to watch out for include Molly Goddard (Browns, p186), Christopher Kane and Mimi Wade (Selfridges, p143).

Vivienne Westwood bag
ANDERSPHOTO/SHUTTERSTOCK ©

Atika   Fashion & Accessories
(Map p282; ☑020-7377 0730; www.atikalondon. co.uk; 55-59 Hanbury St, E1; ⊘11am-7pm; ⓤAldgate East) One of the capital's biggest vintage clothing stores, Atika has more than 20,000 hand-selected items for men and women spanning around four decades since the 1970s. The eclectic selection includes anything from mainstream brands such as Nike to mid-century Japanese kimonos and American workwear like Carhartt. Up-and-coming labels also compete for space.

East London

Broadway Market   Market
(Map p285; www.broadwaymarket.co.uk; Broadway Market, E8; ⊘9am-5pm Sat; ⛴394) There's been a market down here since the late 19th century, but the focus these days is artisan food, handmade gifts and unique clothing.

London Markets

Perhaps the biggest draw for shoppers is the capital's famed markets. A treasure trove of small designers, unique jewellery pieces, original framed photographs and posters, colourful vintage pieces and bric-a-brac, they are the antidote to impersonal, carbon-copy shopping centres.

The most popular markets are **Camden** (Map p284; www.camdenmarket.com; Camden High St, NW1; ☺10am-late; Ⓤ Camden Town or Chalk Farm), Old Spitalfields (p75) and Portobello Road (p145), which operate most days, but there are dozens of others, such as Brick Lane's excellent Sunday Upmarket (p75), which only pop up on the weekend. Camden and Old Spitalfields are both mainly covered, but even the outdoor markets are busy, rain or shine.

Portobello Road
WILLIAM PERUGINI/SHUTTERSTOCK ©

Cafes along both sides of the street do a roaring trade with coffee-drinking shoppers. Stock up on edible treats then head to **London Fields** (Map p285; Richmond Rd, E8; Ⓤ London Fields) for a picnic.

Hackney Walk   Fashion & Accessories
(Map p285; www.hackneywalk.com; 163 Morning Lane, E9; ☺10am-6pm; Ⓤ Hackney Central) Tucked between Morning Lane and the train tracks, this new development has created a discount fashion precinct out of an area known for its Burberry and Pringle of Scotland outlet stores. Newcomers include big brands such as Joseph and Nike, with end-of-run stock at up to 70% off regular prices.

Pringle of Scotland Outlet Store   Clothing
(Map p285; ☏020-8533 1158; www.pringlescotland.com; 90 Morning Lane; ☺10am-6.30pm Mon-Sat, 12-5pm Sun; Ⓤ Hackney Central) There are proper bargains to be had at this excellent outlet store that stocks seconds and end-of-line items from the Pringle range. Expect high-quality merino, cashmere and lambswool knitwear for men and women.

Burberry Outlet Store   Clothing
(Map p285; www.burberry.com; 29-31 Chatham Pl, E9; ☺10am-7pm Mon-Sat, to 6pm Sun; Ⓤ Hackney Central) This backstreet outlet shop has excess international stock from the luxury British brand's current and last-season collections. Prices are around 30% lower than those in department stores; it's a detour worth the money.

Traid   Clothing
(Map p285; ☏020-7923 1396; www.traid.org.uk; 106-108 Kingsland High St, E8; ☺11am-7pm Mon-Sat, to 5pm Sun; Ⓤ Dalston Kingsland) Banish every preconception you have about charity shops, for Traid is nothing like the ones you've seen before: big and bright, with not a whiff of mothball. The offerings aren't necessarily vintage but rather quality, contemporary second-hand clothes for a fraction of the usual prices. It also sells its own creations made from offcuts.

Beyond Retro   Vintage
(Map p285; ☏020-7729 9001; www.beyondretro.com; 110-112 Cheshire St, E2; ☺10am-7pm Mon-Wed, Fri & Sat, to 8pm Thu, 11.30am-6pm Sun; Ⓤ Shoreditch High St) A huge selection of vintage clothes, including wigs, shoes, jackets and sunglasses, expertly slung together in a lofty warehouse.

🄐 Greenwich & South London

Greenwich Market   Market
(Map p286; www.greenwichmarketlondon.com; College Approach, SE10; ☺10am-5.30pm; Ⓤ Cutty Sark) Greenwich Market is one of London's

smaller and more atmospheric covered markets. On Tuesdays, Wednesdays, Fridays and weekends, stallholders tend to be small, independent artists selling original prints, beauty products, unique jewellery and fashion pieces. On Tuesdays, Thursdays and Fridays, you'll find vintage, antiques and collectables. Loads of street food, too.

Look out for the monthly 'Park it in the Market', when classic-car owners bring their vehicles to the market of a Thursday evening, and there's live music and food.

Casbah Records   Music

(Map p286; ☑020-8858 1964; www.casbah records.co.uk; 320-322 Creek Rd, SE10; ⊙11.30am-6pm Mon, 10.30am-6pm Tue-Fri, 10.30am-6.30pm Sat & Sun; Ⓤ Cutty Sark) This record store is a meeting ground of classic, vintage and rare vinyl (Bowie, Rolling Stones, soul, rock, blues, jazz, indie etc) – as well as DVDs and memorabilia. They originally traded at Greenwich Market before upgrading to this highly browsable shop.

Arty Globe   Gifts & Souvenirs

(Map p286; ☑020-7998 3144; www.artyglobe. com; 15 Greenwich Market, SE10; ⊙11am-6pm, closed Mon Jan-Apr; Ⓤ Cutty Sark) The unique fisheye-view drawings of various areas of London (and other cities) by architect Hartwig Braun are works of art and appear on the shopping bags, place mats, note-books, coasters, mugs and jigsaws available in this tiny shop in Greenwich Market.

ⓐ Kensington & Hyde Park

John Sandoe Books   Books

(Map p278; ☑020-7589 9473; www.johnsandoe .com; 10 Blacklands Tce, SW3; ⊙9.30am-6.30pm Mon-Sat, 11am-5pm Sun; Ⓤ Sloane Sq) The perfect antidote to impersonal book superstores, this atmospheric three-storey bookshop in 18th-century premises is a treasure trove of literary gems and hidden surprises. It's been in business for over six decades; loyal customers swear by it, and knowledgeable booksellers spill forth with well-read pointers and helpful advice.

Conran Shop   Design

(Map p278; ☑020-7589 7401; www.conranshop. co.uk; Michelin House, 81 Fulham Rd, SW3; ⊙10am-6pm Mon, Tue & Fri, to 7pm Wed & Thu, to 6.30pm Sat, noon-6pm Sun; Ⓤ South Kensington) The original design store (going strong since 1987), the Conran Shop is a treasure trove of beautiful things – from radios to sunglasses, kitchenware to children's toys and books, bathroom accessories to greeting cards. Browsing bliss. Spare some time to peruse the magnificent art-nouveau/deco **Michelin House** the shop is housed in.

Harrods   Department Store

(Map p278; ☑020-7730 1234; www.harrods.com; 87-135 Brompton Rd, SW1; ⊙10am-9pm Mon-Sat, 11.30am-6pm Sun; Ⓤ Knightsbridge) Garish and stylish in equal measure, perennially crowded Harrods is an obligatory stop for visitors, from the cash-strapped to the big spenders. The stock is astonishing, as are many of the price tags. High on kitsch, the 'Egyptian Elevator' resembles something out of an Indiana Jones epic, while the memorial fountain to Dodi and Di (lower ground floor) merely adds surrealism.

Many visitors don't make it past the ground floor, where designer bags, myriad scents from the perfume hall and the mouthwatering counters of the food hall provide plenty of entertainment. The food hall actually makes for an excellent and surprisingly affordable option for a picnic in nearby Hyde Park. It's browsing time only from 11.30am to noon on Sundays.

Pickett   Gifts & Souvenirs

(Map p278; ☑020-7823 5638; www.pickett. co.uk; cnr Sloane St & Sloane Tce, SW1; ⊙9.30am-6.30pm Mon, Tue, Thu & Fri, 10am-7pm Wed, to 6pm Sat; Ⓤ Sloane Sq) ✿ Walking into Pickett as an adult is a bit like walking into a sweet shop as a child: the exquisite leather goods are all so colourful and beautiful that you don't really know where to start. Choice items include the perfectly finished handbags, the exquisite roll-up backgammon sets and the men's grooming sets. All leather goods are made in Britain.

Jo Loves
Cosmetics

(Map p278; ☎020-7730 8611; www.joloves.com; 42 Elizabeth St, SW1; ⏰10am-6pm Mon-Wed, Fri & Sat, to 7pm Thu, noon-5pm Sun; ⓊVictoria) Famed British scent-maker Jo Malone opened this place in 2013 on a street where she once had a job as a young florist. It features the entrepreneur's signature candles, fragrances and bath products in a range of delicate scents – Pomelo is the most popular. All products come exquisitely wrapped in white boxes with red bows.

Rippon Cheese
Cheese

(☎020-7931 0628; www.ripponcheeselondon. com; 26 Upper Tachbrook St, SW1; ⏰8am-5.30pm Mon-Fri, 8.30am-5pm Sat; ⓊVictoria or Pimlico) A seductively inviting stink greets you as you near this cheesemonger, thanks to its 500 varieties of mostly British and French cheeses. Ask the knowledgeable staff for recommendations, and taste as you go, then stock up for a picnic in a London park.

British Red Cross
Vintage

(☎020-7376 7300; 69-71 Old Church St, SW3; ⏰10am-6pm Mon-Sat, noon-5pm Sun; ⓊSloane Sq) The motto 'One man's rubbish is another man's treasure' couldn't be truer in this part of London, where the 'rubbish' is made up of designer gowns, cashmere sweaters and first editions. Prices are a little higher than most charity shops, but it's still a bargain for the quality, and browsing is half the fun.

🔒 North London

Stables Market
Market

(Map p284; www.camdenmarket.com; Chalk Farm Rd, NW1; ⏰10am-late; ⓊChalk Farm) Connected to the Lock Market, the Stables overflows with antiques, Asian artefacts, rugs, retro furniture and clothing. As the name suggests, it used to be a stables, where up to 800 horses (who worked hauling barges on Regent's Canal) were housed. Follow the wall on the right as you enter to find the FEST Camden (p200) live-music venue.

Camden Lock Market
Market

(Map p284; www.camdenmarket.com; Camden Lock Pl, NW1; ⏰10am-late; ⓊCamden Town) Right next to the canal lock, this section of

Camden Market is the best place to go for diverse food stalls – at KERB (p162) – as well as for several nice bars with views of the canal. There are also shops selling crafts, ceramics and clothes.

🏢 The City

London Silver Vaults Arts & Crafts

(Map p280; ☎020-7242 3844; www.silvervaults london.com; 53-64 Chancery Lane, WC2; ☉9am-5.30pm Mon-Fri, to 1pm Sat; ⓤChancery Lane) The 30-odd shops that work out of these secure subterranean vaults make up the largest collection of silver under one roof in the world. Different businesses tend to specialise in particular types of silverware – from cutlery sets to picture frames, and lots of jewellery. The entrance is just south along Southampton Buildings.

🏢 The South Bank

Tin Lid Toys

(Map p280; ☎020-7407 5331; www.tinlidshop. com; 142 Bermondsey St; ☉10am-6pm Mon-Wed & Sat, 11am-7pm Thu & Fri, 10am-5pm Sun; ⓤLondon Bridge) Lovely boutique store packed with beautifully designed high-quality wooden toys, games and cuddlies for kids. Also stocks a range of women's clothes and accessories.

Lovely & British Gifts & Souvenirs

(Map p280; ☎020-7378 6570; 132a Bermondsey St, SE1; ☉10am-6pm Mon-Fri, to 7pm Sat, 11am-5pm Sun; ⓤLondon Bridge) As the name suggests, this gorgeous Bermondsey boutique prides itself on stocking prints, jewellery and London-themed pieces of home decor all created by British designers. It's an eclectic mix of items, with very reasonable prices, which make for lovely presents or souvenirs.

Southbank Centre Shop Gifts & Souvenirs

(Map p280; www.southbankcentre.co.uk/visit/shopping; Festival Tce, SE1; ☉10am-9pm Mon-Fri, to 8pm Sat, noon-8pm Sun; ⓤWaterloo) This eclectic shop stocks quirky London books,

Chain Stores

Many bemoan the fact that chains have taken over the main shopping centres, but since they're cheap, fashionable and always conveniently located, Londoners (and others) keep going back for more. As well as familiar overseas retailers, such as Gap, H&M and Zara, there are plenty of home-grown chains, including luxury womenswear brand **Karen Millen** (Map p183; ☎020-7836 5355; www.karenmillen.com; 2-3 James St, WC2; ☉10am-8pm Mon-Sat, 11am-6pm Sun; ⓤCovent Garden) and global giant **Topshop** (Map p183; ☎03448 487487; www.topshop.com; 214 Oxford St, W1; ☉9.30am-10pm Mon-Fri, 9am-10pm Sat, 11.30am-6pm Sun; ⓤOxford Circus).

Greenwich Market (p180)

1950s-inspired homewares, original prints, toys, cards, jewellery and creative gifts.

South Bank Book Market Market

(Map p280; Riverside Walk, SE1; ☉11am-7pm, shorter hours winter; ⓤWaterloo) The South Bank Book Market sells fresh and second-hand books under the arches of Waterloo Bridge. You'll find anything here, from fiction to children's books, and comics to classics.

🏢 The West End

Fortnum & Mason Department Store

(Map p274; ☎020-7734 8040; www.fortnum andmason.com; 181 Piccadilly, W1; ☉10am-9pm Mon-Sat, 11.30am-6pm Sun; ⓤGreen Park or

Piccadilly Circus) With its classic eau-de-Nil (pale green) colour scheme, the 'Queen's grocery store' established in 1707 refuses to yield to modern times. Its staff – men and women – still wear old-fashioned tailcoats, and its glamorous food hall is supplied with hampers, marmalade and speciality teas. Stop for a spot of afternoon tea at the Diamond Jubilee Tea Salon, visited by Queen Elizabeth II in 2012.

We Built This City Gifts & Souvenirs

(Map p274; ☏020-3642 9650; www.webuilt-this city.com; 56b Carnaby St, W1; ☻10am-7pm Mon-Wed, to 8pm Thu-Sat, 11am-6.30pm Sun; Ⓤ Oxford Circus or Piccadilly Circus) Taking a commendable stand against tacky souvenirs, We Built This City sells locally themed merch that the recipient might actually want – most of which Londoners would happily put in their own homes, too. Gorgeous framed prints line the walls and celebrate London's neighbourhoods and the city's creativity.

Stanfords Books

(Map p274; ☏020-7836 1321; www.stanfords. co.uk; 7 Mercer Walk, WC2; ☻9am-8pm Mon-Sat,

11.30am-6pm Sun; Ⓤ Leicester Sq or Covent Garden) Trading since 1853, this grandaddy of travel bookshops and seasoned seller of maps, guides and globes is a destination in its own right. Explorer Ernest Shackleton, Victorian missionary David Livingstone and Michael Palin have all shopped here. In 2019 Stanfords left the iconic Long Acre building it had been housed in since 1901 and moved round the corner to its new address.

Hatchards Books

(Map p274; ☏020-7439 9921; www.hatchards. co.uk; 187 Piccadilly, W1; ☻9.30am-8pm Mon-Sat, noon-6.30pm Sun; Ⓤ Green Park or Piccadilly Circus) The UK's oldest bookshop dates back to 1797, and has been holed up in this Georgian building for more than 200 years. Holding three royal warrants, Hatchards has a solid supply of signed editions, and a strong selection of first editions takes up shelf space on the ground floor.

Cambridge Satchel Company Fashion & Accessories

(Map p274; ☏020-3077 1100; www.cambridge satchel.com; 31 James St, WC2; ☻10am-8pm

Mon-Fri, to 7pm Sat, 11am-6pm Sun; [U]Covent Garden) Colourful Cambridge Satchel Company is the perfect place to pick up a British-made leather bag, passport holder or steamer trunk for your next adventure. Items can be personally embossed in-store, which takes just 15 minutes.

Foyles
Books

(Map p274; [J]020-7434 1574; www.foyles.co.uk; 107 Charing Cross Rd, WC2; ⊙9.30am-9pm Mon-Sat, 11.30am-6pm Sun; [U]Tottenham Court Rd) This is London's most legendary bookshop, where you can bet on finding even the most obscure of titles. Once synonymous with chaos, Foyles got its act together and in 2014 moved just down the road into the spacious former home of Central St Martins art school. Thoroughly redesigned, its stunning new home is a joy to explore.

The cafe is on the 5th floor, where you can also find the Gallery at Foyles for art exhibitions. **Grant & Cutler** ([J]020-7440 3248; www.grantandcutler.com; ⊙9.30am-9pm Mon-Sat, 11.30am-6pm Sun), the UK's largest foreign-language bookseller, is on the 4th floor, while **Ray's Jazz** ([J]020-7440 3205; ⊙9.30am-9pm Mon-Sat, 11.30am-6pm Sun) is on the 2nd floor.

James Smith & Sons Umbrellas
Fashion & Accessories

(Map p274; [J]020-7836 4731; www.james-smith. co.uk; 53 New Oxford St, WC1; ⊙10am-5.45pm Mon, Tue, Thu & Fri, 10.30am-5.45pm Wed, 10am-5.15pm Sat; [U]Tottenham Court Rd) Nobody makes and stocks such elegant umbrellas (not to mention walking sticks and canes) as this place. It's been fighting the British weather from the same address since 1857, and London's ever-present drizzle means they're bound to be here for years to come. Prices are high but so is the quality.

Even if you're not interested in buying, the beautiful signage is worth a photo.

Molton Brown
Cosmetics

(Map p274; [J]020-7240 8383; www.molton brown.co.uk; 18 Russell St, WC2; ⊙10am-7pm Mon-Sat, 11am-6pm Sun; [U]Covent Garden) Made in England with rare, exotic ingredients

 Vintage Fashion

The realm of vintage apparel has moved from being sought out by those looking for something offbeat and original, to an all-out mainstream shopping habit. Vintage designer garments and odd bits and pieces from the 1920s to the 1980s are all gracing the rails in some surprisingly upmarket boutique vintage shops.

The less self-conscious charity shops – especially those in areas such as Chelsea and Kensington – are your best bets for real bargains on designer wear (usually, the richer the area, the better the second-hand shops).

Greenwich Market (p180)

from around the globe, fabulously fragrant natural-beauty brand Molton Brown is *the* toiletries choice for boutique hotels, posh restaurants and first-class airline bathrooms. No matter where you're going on your trip, its 'London Via the World' range of soaps, lotions and perfumes is bound to take your travels even further.

Milroy's of Soho
Alcohol

(Map p274; [J]020-7734 2277; https://shop. milroys.co.uk; 3 Greek St, W1; ⊙10am-midnight Tue-Sat, to 7pm Mon; [U]Tottenham Court Rd) A whiskey shop that has achieved iconic status over the half-century it's been around. Every bottle is handpicked by the passionate staff, with prices ranging from £20 to £2000. The range will make you as giddy as the alcohol. There are regular tasting sessions (£25) and even a secret bar in the cellar, accessible via a fake bookcase door.

Agent Provocateur   Clothing

(Map p274; 020-7439 0229; www.agent
provocateur.com; 6 Broadwick St, W1; 11am-7pm
Mon-Sat, noon-5pm Sun; Oxford Circus) For
women's lingerie designed to be worn and
seen, and certainly not hidden, pull up to
wonderful Agent Provocateur, started by
Joseph Corré, son of British fashion designer
Vivienne Westwood. Its sexy and playful cor-
sets, and bras and nighties for all shapes and
sizes, exude confident and positive sexuality.

Gosh!   Books

(Map p274; 020-7437 0187; www.goshlondon.
com; 1 Berwick St, W1; 10.30am-7pm; Piccadilly Circus) Gosh! pack a big pow into this small
space filled with prints, graphic novels, manga and children's books. Comics have taken
over the basement, where fans can geek out
over vintage editions and back issues.

Gay's the Word   Books

(Map p284; 020-7278 7654; www.gaystheword.
co.uk; 66 Marchmont St, WC1; 10am-6.30pm
Mon-Sat, 2-6pm Sun; Russell Sq) The UK's
first gay and lesbian bookstore, this London
institution has been selling LGBT+ works
since 1979. It has a superb selection and
a genuine community spirit, bolstered by
weekly and monthly discussion groups.

Browns   Clothing

(Map p278; 020-7514 0016; www.brownsfashion.
com; 23-27 South Molton St, W1; 10am-7pm
Mon-Wed & Sat, to 8pm Thu & Fri, noon-6pm Sun;
Bond St) Edgy and exciting, this series of
knocked-together shops on upmarket South
Molton St is full of luxury threads and shoes
from internationally renowned talent as well
as not-yet-noticed designers. Browns was
the first to bring Ralph Lauren and Calvin
Klein to the UK, and their exceptional selection still seeks the next big thing.

Reckless Records   Music

(Map p274; 020-7437 4271; www.reckless.co.uk;
30 Berwick St, W1; 10am-7pm; Oxford Circus
or Tottenham Court Rd) This small independent
record store has hardly changed since it
opened in 1984. Even this far into the 21st
century, Reckless is stuffed with people ri-
fling through second-hand records and CDs.

The shopfront was shown on iconic British
band Oasis' *(What's The Story) Morning
Glory?* album cover, on display in the front
window.

West London

Royal Trinity Hospice   Clothing

(Map p278; 020-7361 1530; www.royaltrinity
hospice.london/kensington; 31-33 Kensington
Church St, W8; 10am-6pm Mon-Sat, 11am-5pm
Sun; High St Kensington) For designer and
top-end items in women's clothing, shoes
and bags, it's well worth a browse through
this well-supplied charity shop on Kensington Church St. Fresh items are always
coming in, and the sister shop alongside has
menswear and further odds and ends.

Lutyens & Rubinstein   Books

(Map p278; 020-7229 1010; www.lutyens
rubinstein.co.uk; 21 Kensington Park Rd, W11;
10am-6pm Mon & Sat, to 6.30pm Tue-Fri,
11am-5pm Sun; Ladbroke Grove) Lutyens
& Rubinstein is a tremendous, discerning
bookshop. It's a squeeze, but its small size
pays dividends. Established by a company
of literary agents, the focus is on 'excellence
in writing', as determined by customers and
readers, so every book comes recommended. Don't expect huge piles of best-sellers.

Portobello Green Arcade   Clothing

(Map p278; 281 Portobello Rd, W10; 9am-6pm
Mon-Sat, 11am-6pm Sun; Ladbroke Grove) Portobello Green Arcade is home to some
cutting-edge clothing and jewellery designers as well as small, independent niche
shops, such as **Adam** (020-8960 6944; www.
adamoflondon.com; 10am-5.30pm Tue-Sat,
noon-5pm Sun) and **Chinese Tea Company**
(020-8960 0096; www.the-chinese-tea-
company.com; 11am-6pm Mon-Sat).

Rough Trade West   Music

(Map p278; 020-7229 8541; www.roughtrade.
com; 130 Talbot Rd, W11; 10am-6.30pm Mon-Sat,
11am-5pm Sun; Ladbroke Grove) Once home
to the eponymous post-punk label, this
compact shop offers vintage and alternative
vinyl and puts on the odd gig too.

Top Five London Souvenirs

Tea

The British drink par excellence, with plenty of iconic names to choose from. For lovely packaging too, try Fortnum & Mason (p183) or Harrods (p181; pictured above).

Vintage Clothes & Shoes

London vintage-fashion finds will forever be associated with your trip to the city. Start your search at the Sunday Upmarket (p75).

British Design

With its cool and understated chic, British design has made a name for itself worldwide. Try the Conran Shop (p181) or the Southbank Centre shop (p183).

Music

London is brilliant for buying records. Try Rough Trade East (p179) or Reckless Records (p186).

London Toys

Double-decker buses, Paddington Bears, guards in bearskin hats; London's icons make for great souvenirs. Hamleys (p143) is the place to go.

BAR OPEN

Afternoon pints, all-night clubbing
and beyond

Bar Open

You need only glance at William Hogarth's Gin Lane prints from 1751 to realise that Londoners and alcohol have had more than a passing acquaintance. The metropolis offers a huge variety of venues to wet your whistle in – from cosy neighbourhood pubs to glitzy all-night clubs, and everything in between.

In This Section

Opening Hours

Pubs traditionally open at 11am or noon and close at 11pm, with an earlier closing on Sunday. Some bars and pubs open later and remain open until around 2am or 3am on weekends. Clubs generally open at 10pm on the weekend and close between 3am and 7am.

Previous page: Ye Olde Mitre (p196)

North London
Atmospheric pubs and live music (p199)

Clerkenwell, Shoreditch & Spitalfields
Dozens of bars, pubs, clubs and everything in-between (p194)

West London
Traditional pubs, river views, relaxed evenings (p206)

East London
The new locus of London cool, with excellent bars (p196)

The West End
Legendary establishments, up-for-it crowds (p204)

The City
Post-work punters with some destination, skyscraper-roof bars, quiet after 10pm (p201)

Kensington & Hyde Park
Not London's oldest watering holes, but some charming pubs (p198)

The South Bank
Good, down-to-earth boozers and modern bars (p202)

Richmond, Kew & Hampton Court
Some of the capital's best, most historic riverside pubs (p200)
(9.5km)

River Thames

Greenwich & South London
A mix of historic riverside pubs and trendy microbreweries (p197)

Costs & Tipping

Many clubs are free or cheaper mid-week. If you want to go to a famous club on a Saturday night (*the* night for clubbing), expect to pay up to £25. Some places are considerably cheaper if you arrive earlier in the night.

Tipping isn't customary.

Useful Websites

Skiddle (www.skiddle.com) Comprehensive info on clubnights, DJs and events.

Time Out (www.timeout.com/london) Has details of bars, pubs and nightlife.

The Best...

Experience London's finest drinking establishments

Pubs

Lamb & Flag (p204) Just about everyone's West End favourite, so expect a scrum.

Tap on the Line (p200) Lovingly restored Victorian boozer in Kew.

Cat & Mutton (p196) Simultaneously traditional and hip, and always up for a party.

King's Arms (p203) Incredibly atmospheric setting, with coal fire in winter.

Cutty Sark Tavern (p197) A Greenwich institution, with wonderful views of the Thames.

Bars

American Bar (p204) Mayfair hotel bar with an art-deco ambience.

Cocktail Trading Co (p139) Classy and cool, with killer cocktails.

Bar Pepito (p199; pictured above) Pocket-sized Andalusian bar dedicated to lovers of sherry.

Gordon's Wine Bar (p205) Sip a glass of wine in the vaults under Charing Cross.

Cocktail Bars

Dukes London (p207; pictured above) Bond-worthy martinis in Ian Fleming's favourite St James's bar.

Zetter Townhouse Cocktail Lounge (p194) Louche, antique-filled lounge tucked away in Clerkenwell.

Satan's Whiskers (p196) Friendly crew swizzling up a storm in Bethnal Green.

Swift (p204) Pre-dinner or post-theatre tipples in Soho.

Clubs

Fabric (p194) Massive club with a global reputation.

XOYO (p139) Excellent and varied gigs, club nights and art events.

Heaven (p205) One of the best gay nightclubs in the capital, with a varied programme.

Craft Beer

Rake (p203) Way ahead of its time, and still one of the best.

Greenwich Union (p198) Choose from six or seven beers and settle in the lovely garden.

Euston Tap (p200) The place to go for beer aficionados; the choice is dazzling.

Views

Netil360 (p196) Uber-hip rooftop bar gazing over the East End to the City.

Oblix (p202; pictured above) It's not even halfway up the Shard, but the views are legendary.

Galvin at Windows (p204) Fabulous cocktails and views west across Hyde Park.

Sky Pod (p202) Sip a cocktail on a terrace, 35 floors above the city.

EDINBORO CASTLE

FREE BEER

Beer Gardens

Windsor Castle (p206) Come summer, regulars abandon the Windsor's historic interior for the chilled-out garden.

Edinboro Castle (p200) A festive place to stretch out on a summer evening.

Greenwich Union (p198) Work your way through the Meantime brews from a garden table.

★ Lonely Planet's Top Choices

American Bar (p204) Age-old elegance in Mayfair's Beaumont Hotel.

Netil360 (p196) Hip East Enders head to this rooftop eyrie for expansive views and rounds of croquet.

Little Bird (p207) South London distillery serving daytime cocktails to Maltby Street Market goers.

King's Arms (p203) A real, proper pub in Central London.

Cocktail Trading Co (p139) Drinking has never been classier – or more delicious.

🔆 Clerkenwell, Shoreditch & Spitalfields

Discount Suit Company   Cocktail Bar

(Map p280; 📞020-7247 8755; www.discountsuit company.co.uk; 29a Wentworth St, E1; ⏰5pm-midnight Mon-Thu, 2pm-1am Fri & Sat, 5-11pm Sun; Ⓤ Aldgate East) Tucked away, Discount Suit Company is one of the city's finest speakeasies – though on weekends you'll see that this closet-sized space is no secret. Superb, reasonably priced concoctions (a rarity in this area) are created behind the bar, originally a storeroom for the suit company above. Super-friendly staff and mixologists who'll happily go off-piste seal the deal.

Can't find it? Look for the 'City Wear' shop signs at the corner of Wentworth St and Bell Lane.

Fabric   Club

(Map p282; 📞020-7336 8898; www.fabriclondon. com; 77a Charterhouse St, EC1; ⏰11pm-7am Fri, to 8am Sat, to 5.30am Sun; Ⓤ Farringdon) The king of London's after-hours scene, Fabric is a huge subterranean rave cave housed in a converted meat cold store. Each room has its own sound system, which you'll really feel in Room One – it has a 'bodysonic' vibrating dance floor that's attached to 450 bass shakers, which emit low-end frequencies, so the music radiates into your muscles just by standing there.

Following a temporary closure in 2016 because of drug-related deaths in the club, Fabric operates a very strict door policy (you must be aged over 19 and have a formal ID) and a zero-tolerance policy towards drug use. Searches are thorough.

Annoyingly, there's a £15 minimum if you're paying for drinks by card. Bring cash.

Fox & Anchor   Pub

(Map p282; 📞020-7250 1300; www.foxand anchor.com; 115 Charterhouse St, EC1; ⏰7am-11pm Mon-Fri, from 8.30am Sat, from 11am Sun; 📶; Ⓤ Barbican) Behind the Fox & Anchor's wonderful 1898 art-nouveau facade is a stunning traditional Victorian boozer,

one of the last remaining market pubs in London that's permitted to serve alcohol before 11am. Fully celebrating its proximity to Smithfield Market, the grub is gloriously meaty. Only the most voracious of carnivores should opt for the City Boy Breakfast (£19.50), which comes with a pint of Guinness.

Zetter Townhouse Cocktail Lounge   Cocktail Bar

(Map p282; 📞020-7324 4545; www.thezetter townhouse.com/clerkenwell/bar; 49-50 St John's Sq, EC1; ⏰7am-midnight Sun-Wed, to 1am Thu-Sat; 📶; Ⓤ Farringdon) Behind an unassuming door on St John's Sq, this ground-floor bar is decorated with plush armchairs, stuffed animal heads and a legion of lamps. The cocktail list takes its theme from the area's distilling history – recipes of yesteryear plus home-made tinctures and cordials are used to create interesting and unusual tipples.

Gibson   Cocktail Bar

(Map p282; 📞020-7608 2774; www.thegibsonbar. london; 44 Old St, EC1; ⏰5pm-1am Mon-Thu, to 2am Fri & Sat, 1-10.30pm Sun; Ⓤ Old St) Hope you packed your explorer's hat, because the Gibson will take you on an adventure. The cocktail menu hops through the calendar month by month, and you decide what season to visit. Perhaps some hemp oil and cannabis jelly to forget February or flambéed pineapple skin or smoky mezcal and popping candy to heat up your summer?

Found   Cocktail Bar

(Map p282; www.foundthebar.com; 5 Ravey St, EC2; ⏰4-11pm Tue & Wed, to midnight Thu, to 1am Fri, 6pm-1am Sat, 6-10.30pm Sun; Ⓤ Old St) Single-handedly propping up Shoreditch's cocktail scene this side of Rivington St, speakeasy-style Found employs a decidedly simple equation for success: a well-priced curated cocktail list plus a friendly neighbourhood welcome. Don't be afraid to ask for recommendations or menu alterations. The come-as-you-are vibe is refreshing. Look for the yellow lamp painted with a black F outside the entrance.

Fox & Anchor

Black Rock   Bar

(Map p282; ☑020-7247 4580; www.blackrock. bar; 9 Christopher St, EC2; ⊗5pm-midnight Mon-Wed, to 2am Thu-Sat; Ⓤ Moorgate or Liverpool St) Whisky might not grow on trees, but at Black Rock, it sure grows in them. The centrepiece of this tiny bar is a 5m-long, 185-year-old oak tree that's been split in half and carved out to hold two rivers of whisky, which age as they're stored in the wood and are poured straight into your glass from taps at the end of the trunk.

Nude Espresso   Coffee

(Map p282; www.nudeespresso.com; 26 Hanbury St, E1; ⊗7.30am-5.30pm Mon-Fri, 9.30am-5pm Sat & Sun; Ⓤ Shoreditch High St) This simply styled, cosy coffee shop serves top-notch brews that are roasted across the street. Along with the usual options, Nude has rotating single-origin coffees as well as slow-brew and espresso-based blends. Pair your beans with a sweet treat or full brunch (served until a leisurely 2.30pm on weekdays and 3pm on weekends) to refuel while Brick Lane shopping.

Jerusalem Tavern   Pub

(Map p282; ☑020-7490 4281; www.stpeters brewery.co.uk; 55 Britton St, EC1; ⊗noon-11pm Mon-Fri; Ⓤ Farringdon) Housed in a building from 1720, this tiny, atmospheric pub covered in wood panelling, delft tiles and scuffed paintwork is the only London dispensary of the fantastic beers from St Peter's Brewery in Suffolk. Be warned: seating's limited and it's hugely popular. Arrive early to nab the raised 'pulpit' seats, but you'll likely be relegated to the overflow area in the street.

Hawksmoor
Spitalfields Bar   Cocktail Bar

(Map p282; ☑020-7426 4856; www.the hawksmoor.com; 157b Commercial St, E1; ⊗5.30-11pm Mon-Thu, to 1am Fri, 4pm-1am Sat; 🛜; Ⓤ Shoreditch High St) Black leather, bevelled mirror tiles and a copper wall gleam with candlelight in this darkly glamorous basement bar below the eponymous steak restaurant (p156). The adventurous cocktail list is matched with a good selection of beer and wine, which you can pair with tempting takes on classic North

The Pub

The pub (public house) is at the heart of London life and is one of the capital's great social levellers. Virtually every Londoner has a 'local' and looking for your own is a fun part of any visit to the capital.

Pubs in the City and other central areas are mostly after-work drinking dens, busy from 5pm onwards during the week. But in more residential areas, pubs come into their own at weekends, when long lunches turn into sloshy afternoons and groups of friends settle in for the night. Many also run popular quizzes on week nights. Other pubs entice punters through the doors with live music or comedy. Some have developed such a reputation for the quality of their food that they've been dubbed gastropubs (p153).

You can order almost any beverage you like in a pub. Some specialise in craft beer, offering drinks from local microbreweries, including real ale, fruit beers, organic ciders and other rarer beverages. Others, particularly the gastropubs, invest in a good wine list.

BIKEWORLDTRAVEL/SHUTTERSTOCK ©

American bar food (burgers, popcorn chicken and poutine) if you missed the meat feast upstairs.

Ye Olde Mitre   Pub

(Map p282; www.yeoldemitreholborn.co.uk; 1 Ely Ct, EC1; ⊘11am-11pm Mon-Fri; 🐾; ⓤFarringdon) A delightfully cosy historic pub with an extensive beer selection, tucked away in a backstreet off Hatton Garden, Ye Olde Mitre was originally built in 1546 for the servants of

Ely Palace. There's no music, so rooms echo only with chit-chat. Queen Elizabeth I danced around the cherry tree by the bar, they say.

❾ East London

Netil360   Rooftop Bar

(Map p285; www.netil360.com; 1 Westgate St, E8; ⊘noon-8.30pm Wed & Sun, to 10.30pm Thu-Sat Apr-Nov; 🐾; ⓤLondon Fields) Perched atop Netil House, this uber-hip rooftop cafe-bar offers incredible views over London, with brass telescopes enabling you to get better acquainted with workers in 'the Gherkin' building. In between drinks you can knock out a game of croquet on the Astroturf, or perhaps book a hot tub.

Cat & Mutton   Pub

(Map p285; ☏020-7249 6555; www.catand mutton.com; 76 Broadway Market, E8; ⊘noon-11pm Mon, to midnight Tue-Thu, to 1am Fri, 10am-1am Sat, noon-11.30pm Sun; ⓤLondon Fields) At this fabulous Georgian pub, Hackney locals sup pints under the watchful eyes of hunting trophies, black-and-white photos of old-time boxers and a large portrait of Karl Marx. If it's crammed downstairs head up the spiral staircase to the comfy couches. Weekends get rowdy, with DJs spinning their best tunes until late.

Satan's Whiskers   Cocktail Bar

(Map p285; ☏020-7739 8362; www.facebook. com/satanswhiskers; 343 Cambridge Heath Rd, E2; ⊘5pm-midnight; ⓤBethnal Green) Small neon red lettering is the only sign you're about to enter a world-class cocktail bar. With an ever-changing drinks menu, snug booths, crazy taxidermy and a killer soundtrack, it's a memorable stop on an East London bar hop.

Dove   Pub

(Map p285; ☏020-7275 7617; www.dovepubs.com; 24-28 Broadway Market, E8; ⊘noon-11pm Sun-Fri, 11am-11pm Sat; 🐾; ⓤLondon Fields) The Dove has a rambling series of wooden floorboard rooms and a wide range of Belgian Trappist, wheat and fruit-flavoured beers. Drinkers spill on to the street in warmer weather, or hunker down in the low-lit back room with board games when it's chilly. Pub meals with good vegetarian options are available too.

Last Tuesday Society — Club

(Map p285; ☏020-7998 3617; www.thelasttues daysociety.org; Viktor Wynd Museum of Curiosities, Fine Art & Natural History, 11 Mare St, E8; ⏱3-11pm Tue, noon-11pm Wed-Sat, to 10.30pm Sun; Ⓤ Bethnal Green) London's most curious cocktail bar and *wunderkabinett* of taxidermy, tribal masks and ephemera from across the globe, with experimental drinks starting with Absinthe Hour at 6pm weekdays. It's busy on weekends; call ahead if you want to book a table. It runs special events from masked balls (St Valentine's Day, Halloween) to Drink and Draw shibari (Japanese rope bondage) nights.

Dalston Superstore — Gay & Lesbian

(Map p285; ☏020-7254 2273; www.dalstonsuper store.com; 117 Kingsland High St, E8; ⏱11.45am-late; Ⓤ Dalston Kingsland) Dalston Superstore is hard to pigeonhole, which we suspect is the point. This two-level industrial space is open all day but comes into its own after dark when there are club nights in the basement.

Bethnal Green Working Men's Club — Club

(Map p285; ☏020-7739 7170; www.workersplay time.net; 42-44 Pollard Row, E2; ⏱pub 6pm-late Wed-Sat, club hours vary; Ⓤ Bethnal Green) As it says on the tin, this is a true working men's club. Except that this one has opened its doors and let in all kinds of club nights, including trashy burlesque, LGBT shindigs, retro nights, beach parties and bake-offs. Expect sticky carpets, a shimmery stage set and a space akin to a school-hall disco.

❾ Greenwich & South London

Cutty Sark Tavern — Pub

(Map p286; ☏020-8858 3146; www.cuttysarks e10.co.uk; 4-6 Ballast Quay, SE10; ⏱11.30am-11pm Mon-Sat, noon-10.30pm Sun; 🛜; Ⓤ Cutty Sark or Maze Hill) Housed in a delightful bow-windowed, wood-beamed Georgian

🍸 Clubbing

When it comes to clubbing, London is up there with the best of them. You'll probably know what you want to experience – it might be big clubs such as Fabric (p194), or sweaty shoebox clubs with the freshest DJ talent – but whether thumping techno, indie rock, Latin, ska, pop, dubstep, grime, R&B or hip-hop, there's something going on every night.

Thursdays are loved by those who want to have their fun before the office workers mob the streets on Fridays. Saturdays are the busiest and best if you're a serious clubber, and Sundays often see surprisingly good events, popular with hospitality workers who traditionally have Mondays off.

There are clubs across town, though it has to be said that the best of them are moving further out of the centre every year, so be prepared for a hike on a night bus. The East End is the top area for cutting-edge clubs, especially Shore ditch. Dalston and Hackney are popular for makeshift clubs in restaurant basements and former shops. Camden Town still favours the indie crowd, while King's Cross has a bit of everything. The gay party crowd mainly gravitates south of the river, especially Vauxhall, although a toehold is kept in the West and East Ends.

building directly on the Thames, this 200-year-old tavern is one of the few independent pubs left in Greenwich. Half a dozen cask-conditioned ales on tap line the bar, there's an inviting riverside seating area opposite and an upstairs dining room looking out on to glorious views. It's a 10-minute walk from the DLR station.

Greenwich Union   Pub

(Map p286; 020-8692 6258; www.greenwich union.com; 56 Royal Hill, SE10; noon-11pm Mon-Fri, 11.30am-11pm Sat, 11.30am-10.30pm Sun; Greenwich or Cutty Sark) The award-winning Union plies six or seven local microbrewery beers (it used to be owned by Greenwich-based Meantime Brewery) and a strong list of ales, plus bottled international brews. It's a handsome place with a welcoming long, narrow bar leading to a conservatory and beer garden at the rear.

Old Brewery   Bar

(Map p286; 020-3437 2222; www.oldbrewery greenwich.com; Pepys Bldg, Old Royal Naval College, SE10; 10am-11pm Mon-Sat, to 10.30pm Sun; Cutty Sark) Situated within the grounds of the Old Royal Naval College (p132), the Old Brewery once housed the working microbrewery of Meantime, one of London's earliest craft breweries. Now owned by Young's pub company, the site is still sublimely set inside the college grounds and offers pub food (mains £11 to £25) and a range of beers (from £5), best enjoyed in the huge beer garden.

Trafalgar Tavern   Pub

(Map p286; 020-3887 9886; www.trafalgar tavern.co.uk; 6 Park Row, SE10; noon-11pm Mon-Thu, noon-1am Fri, 10am-1am Sat, 10am-11pm Sun; Cutty Sark) This elegant tavern with big windows overlooking the Thames is steeped in history. Dickens apparently knocked back a few here – and used it as the setting for the wedding breakfast scene in *Our Mutual Friend* – and prime ministers Gladstone and Disraeli used to dine on the pub's celebrated whitebait. Food is served until 9pm.

Kensington & Hyde Park

Anglesea Arms   Pub

(Map p278; 020-7373 7960; www.anglesea arms.com; 15 Selwood Tce, SW7; 11am-11pm Mon-Sat, to 10.30pm Sun; South Kensington) Seasoned with age and decades of ale-quaffing patrons (including Charles

Trafalgar Tavern

DOUG MCKINLAY/LONELY PLANET ©

Dickens, who lived on the same road, and DH Lawrence), this old-school pub boasts considerable character and a strong showing of beers and gins (over two dozen), while the terrace out front swarms with punters in warmer months. Arch-criminal Bruce Reynolds masterminded the Great Train Robbery over drinks here.

Tomtom Coffee House   Cafe

(Map p278; ☎020-7730 1771; www.tomtom. co.uk; 114 Ebury St, SW1; ⊗8am-6pm Mon-Fri, 9am-6pm Sat & Sun; 🛜; ⓊVictoria) Tomtom has built its reputation on amazing coffee: not only are the drinks fabulously presented, but the selection is dizzying: from the usual espresso-based suspects to filter, and a full choice of beans. Take away or enjoy in the small interior or the tiny terrace outside if the weather's good.

The cafe also serves lovely food throughout the day, from breakfast and toasties on sourdough bread to homemade pies (from £6.20).

Queen's Arms   Pub

(Map p278; www.thequeensarmskensington. co.uk; 30 Queen's Gate Mews, SW7; ⊗noon-11pm Mon-Sat, to 10.30pm Sun; Ⓤ Gloucester Rd) Just around the corner from the Royal Albert Hall is this blue-grey-painted godsend. Located in an adorable cobbled-mews setting off bustling Queen's Gate, it beckons with a cosy interior, welcoming staff and a right royal selection of ales – including several from small, local cask brewers – and ciders on tap. In warm weather, drinkers stand outside in the mews (only permitted on one side).

The fine pub menu is good for lunch or dinner, with burger-and-a-beer offers on Mondays for £12.95.

❷ North London

Bar Pepito   Wine Bar

(Map p284; ☎020-7841 7331; www.camino. uk.com/location/bar-pepito; 3 Varnishers Yard, Regent Quarter, N1; ⊗5pm-midnight Mon-Fri, 6pm-midnight Sat; ⓊKing's Cross St Pancras) This tiny, intimate Andalusian bodega specialises

 Beer

The raison d'être of a pub is first and foremost to serve beer – be it lager, ale or stout, in a glass or a bottle. On draught (drawn from the cask), it is served by the pint (570mL) or half-pint (285mL) and, more occasionally, third-of-a-pint for real ale tasting.

Pubs generally serve a good selection of lager (highly carbonated and drunk cool or cold) and a smaller selection of real ales or 'bitter' (still or only slightly gassy, drunk at room temperature, with strong flavours). The best-known British lager brand is Carling, though you'll find everything from Fosters to San Miguel.

Among the multitude of ales on offer in London pubs, London Pride, Courage Best, Burton Ale, Adnam's, Theakston (in particular Old Peculier) and Old Speckled Hen are among the best. Once considered something of an old man's drink, real ale has enjoyed a renaissance among young Londoners, riding tandem with the current fashion for craft beer (small-batch beers from independent brewers). Staff at bars serving good selections of real ales and craft beers are often hugely knowledgeable, just like a sommelier in a restaurant, so ask them for recommendations if you're not sure what to order.

in sherry and tapas (£2.50 to £15). Novices fear not: the staff are on hand to advise. They're also experts at food pairings (top-notch ham and cheese selections). To go the whole hog, try a tasting flight of selected sherries with snacks to match.

Microbreweries

Numerous microbreweries have sprouted throughout London in recent years. Many of them offer drinking on the premises at weekends, and sometimes week nights too, such as Anspach & Hobday (p203).

Names to look out for when you're at the pub include Meantime, Sambrooks, Camden Town Brewery, London Fields Brewery, Five Points Brewing Co, Redchurch, Beavertown, Hackney Brewery, Partizan and the Kernel.

Beavertown beer cans
JOSH HARRISON/ALAMY STOCK PHOTO ©

Drink, Shop & Do　　　　　　　Bar
(Map p284; ☏020-7278 4335; www.drinkshopdo .co.uk; 9 Caledonian Rd, N1; ⊙10am-midnight Mon-Wed, to 1am Thu, to 2am Fri, 10.30am-2am Sat, to 6pm Sun; ☎; Ⓤ King's Cross St Pancras) This kooky outlet will not be pigeonholed. As its name suggests, it is many things: a bar, a cafe, an activities centre, even a disco. The idea is that there will always be drinking (be it tea or gin), music and things to do – anything from dancing to building Lego robots.

Euston Tap　　　　　　　　　　Bar
(Map p284; ☏020-3137 8837; www.eustontap. com; 190 Euston Rd, NW1; ⊙noon-late Mon-Sat, to 10pm Sun; Ⓤ Euston) This specialist drinking spot inhabits a monumental stone structure on the approach to Euston station. Craft-beer devotees can choose between 16 cask ales, 25 keg beers and 150 brews by the bottle. Grab a seat on the pavement, take the tight spiral staircase upstairs or buy a bottle to take away.

It's part of a twinset with the **East Lodge** across the street, with another 12 keg beers and eight cask ales on offer.

Edinboro Castle　　　　　　　Pub
(Map p284; www.edinborocastlepub.co.uk; 57 Mornington Tce, NW1; ⊙noon-11pm Mon-Sat, to 10.30pm Sun; ☎; Ⓤ Camden Town) Large and relaxed Edinboro offers a fun atmosphere and a fine bar and full menu. The highlight, however, is the huge beer garden, complete with warm-weather barbecues and decorated with coloured lights on long summer evenings. Patio heaters come out in winter.

FEST Camden　　　　　　　　Club
(Map p284; ☏020-7428 4922; www.festcamden. com; Chalk Farm Rd, NW1; ⊙noon-11pm Sun-Wed, to 2.30am Thu-Sat; Ⓤ Chalk Farm) Tucked away in what used to be the horse hospital in the stables (p182), this space now hosts a diverse range of events, from cinema nights to club nights and from cabaret to comedy.

EngineerPub　　　　　　　　Pub
(Map p284; ☏020-7483 1890; www.theengineer primrosehill.co.uk; 65 Gloucester Ave, NW1; ⊙noon-11pm Mon-Sat, to 10.30pm Sun; ☎; Ⓤ Camden Town or Chalk Farm) The dictionary definition of a beautiful backstreet boozer, the Engineer is all dark wood, cosy booths and unvarnished tables, and has a hidden garden dripping with vines and potted plants. Drinks range from standards to unexpected British craft brews and fine wines, and there's a posh pub food menu. A short walk from the tube station but a world away from Camden's madness.

🜨 Richmond, Kew & Hampton Court

Tap on the Line　　　　　　　Pub
(☏020-8332 1162; www.taponth*eline.co.uk; Station Approach, TW9; ⊙8.30am-11pm Mon-Thu, 8am-11pm Fri, 9am-11pm Sat, 10am-10.30pm Sun; ☎; Ⓡ Kew Gardens, Ⓤ Kew Gardens) Right by the platform at Kew Gardens station (the only London tube platform with its

own pub), this lovingly restored Victorian yellow-brick boozer is well worth a visit. With outside seating surrounded by foliage and twinkling fairy lights in the courtyard at the front, it's a fine haven for a pub lunch. There's live music on Saturdays from 7pm.

❸ The City

Nickel Bar   Cocktail Bar

(Map p280; ☎020-3828 2000; www.thened. com/restaurants/the-nickel-bar; 27 Poultry, EC2; ☺8am-2am Mon-Fri, 9am-3am Sat, to midnight Sun; 🛜; Ⓤ Bank) There's something *Great Gatsby*-ish about the Ned hotel: the elevated jazz pianists, the vast verdite columns, the classy gin cocktails. Of all the bars inside this magnificent former banking hall, the Nickel Bar soaks up the atmosphere best. Inspired by the glamorous American saloons of the 1930s and the elegance of SS *Normandie*, this is timeless nightcap territory.

Jamaica Wine House   Pub

(Map p280; ☎020-7929 6972; www.jamaica winehouse.co.uk; 12 St Michael's Alley, EC3; ☺11am-11pm Mon-Fri; Ⓤ Bank) Not a wine bar at all, the 'Jam Pot' is a historic wood-lined pub that stands on the site of what was London's first coffee house (1652). Reached by a narrow alley off Cornhill, its warmly lit streetlamp sign leads you to the age-old ambience of its darkened rooms.

City of London Distillery   Cocktail Bar

(Map p280; ☎020-7936 3636; www.cityoflondon distillery.com; 22-24 Bride Lane, EC4; ☺4-11pm Mon-Sat; Ⓤ Blackfriars) Hogarth's *Gin Lane* print provides a warning before you descend the stairs to one of the few bars in London to distil its own 'mother's ruin' on-site. It proudly displays its shiny distilling vats behind windows at the back of the bar. Tours (£25) and gin-making classes (£125) are available.

Ship   Pub

(Map p280; ☎020-7702 4422; www.shipec3. co.uk; 3 Hart St, EC3; ☺11.30am-11pm Mon-Fri; Ⓤ Tower Hill) Marooned among a sea of soulless office blocks a short walk from Tower

Jamaica Wine House

Hill, this slim, nautically themed 1802 pub has an ornately decorated facade and serves better-than-average pub grub.

Ye Olde Cheshire Cheese   Pub

(Map p280; 020-7353 6170; info@yeolde cheshirecheese.com; Wine Office Court, 145 Fleet St, EC4; noon-11pm Mon-Sat; Black-friars) Rebuilt in 1667 after the Great Fire, this is one of London's most famous pubs, accessed via a narrow alley off Fleet St. Thackeray and Dickens have supped in its gloomy surrounds, where crackling fires, rickety floorboards and low beams add to its appeal. The vaulted cellars are thought to be remnants of a 13th-century Carmelite monastery.

Sky Pod   Bar

(Map p280; 0333 772 0020; https://skygarden. london/sky-pod-bar; L35, 20 Fenchurch St, EC3; 7am-midnight Mon & Tue, to 1am Wed-Fri, 8am-1am Sat, 8am-midnight Sun; Monument) Prices at this decidedly average rooftop bar are a little on the steep side (spirits from £9.50; beers from £6), but it's got the best views in the business, and booking a table gives

access to **Sky Garden** (Map p280; 020-7337 2344; 10am-6pm Mon-Fri, 11am-9pm Sat & Sun) FREE even if tickets there have sold out. It's cold in winter. No shorts, sportswear, trainers or flip-flops after 5pm.

The South Bank

Oblix   Bar

(Map p280; www.oblixrestaurant.com; 32nd fl, Shard, 31 St Thomas St, SE1; noon-11pm; London Bridge) The views from Oblix on the 32nd floor of the Shard (p81) aren't quite as impressive as the panoramas from the 69th-floor viewing platform, but you'll still be wowed. Relax with a cocktail (from £13.50) in the stylish bar and enjoy views towards the City, East and South London. Live music or DJ most nights from 7pm. Smart dress recommended.

George Inn   Pub

(NT; Map p280; 020-7407 2056; www.national trust.org.uk/george-inn; 77 Borough High St, SE1; 11am-11pm Mon-Thu, to midnight Fri & Sat, noon-10.30pm Sun; London Bridge) This

Ye Olde Cheshire Cheese

magnificent galleried coaching inn is the last of its kind in London. The present building, owned by the National Trust, dates from 1677 and is mentioned in Charles Dickens' *Little Dorrit*. The picnic benches in the huge cobbled courtyard fill up on balmy evenings (no reservations), otherwise you can find a spot in the labyrinth of dark rooms and corridors inside.

King's Arms   Pub

(Map p280; ☎020-7207 0784; www.theking sarmslondon.co.uk; 25 Roupell St, SE1; ☺11am-11pm Mon-Sat, noon-10.30pm Sun; ⓤWaterloo) Relaxed and charming, this neighbourhood boozer is found at the corner of Roupell St (p199), a terraced Waterloo backstreet. The traditional bar area, complete with open fire in winter, serves up a changing selection of ales, bitters and bottled beers. It gets packed with after-work crowds between 6pm and 8pm.

Rake   Pub

(Map p280; ☎020-7407 0557; 14 Winchester Walk, SE1; ☺noon-11pm Mon-Thu, 11am-11pm Fri, 10am-11pm Sat, noon-10pm Sun; ⓤLondon Bridge) Look at the menus on-screen at the Rake or rely on the helpful bar staff to guide you in all things beer. There are 10 taps, and the selection of craft beers, real ales, lagers and ciders changes constantly. It's a teensy place yet always busy; the decking outside is especially popular.

Tanner & Co   Pub

(Map p280; ☎020-7357 0244; www.tannerandco. co.uk; 50 Bermondsey St; ☺8am-midnight Mon-Wed, to 1am Thu & Fri, 10am-1am Sat, to 11pm Sun; ⓤLondon Bridge) This converted warehouse is one of many lively pubs and bars on Bermondsey St, where the friendly bar staff are ready to mix up a cocktail, advise on your wine or pour you a beer (or a slushy if that takes your fancy). The decked outside seating area, lit by colourful string lights, is popular year-round.

Vaulty Towers   Bar

(Map p280; ☎020-7928 9042; www.vaultytowers. london; 34 Lower Marsh, SE1; ☺noon-11pm Sun-Wed, to 1am Thu-Sat; ⓤWaterloo) This

wacky bar and events space in the heart of Waterloo is filled with eccentric props, courtesy of its partner, nearby arts space the Vaults, and has a buzzing atmosphere with super-friendly staff. Food comes in the form of burgers and tacos, and is excellent quality.

Anspach & Hobday   Microbrewery

(Map p280; www.anspachandhobday.com; 118 Druid St, SE1; ☺5-9.30pm Fri, 10.30am-6.30pm Sat, 1-5pm Sun; ⓤLondon Bridge) Beer aficionados visiting Maltby Street Market (p164) will want to stop by this taproom and microbrewery in the railway arches. It serves an award-winning porter, along with IPA, various pale ales, craft beers and lager, all brewed on-site. Red and white wine also available.

Coffee House   Coffee

(The Gentlemen Baristas; Map p280; www. thegentlemenbaristas.com; 63 Union St, SE1; ☺7am-6pm Mon-Thu, to 11pm Fri, 8.30am-5pm Sat, to 4pm Sun; ☎; ⓤLondon Bridge or Borough) Slightly pretentious cafe that does very good coffee (£2 to £3), decent pastries and a small range of sandwiches. It attracts arty and media types who fill the tables in the red-brick room at the back.

Queen Elizabeth
Roof Garden   Rooftop Bar

(Map p280; www.southbankcentre.co.uk; Queen Elizabeth Hall, Southbank Centre, Belvedere Rd, SE1; ☺10am-10pm May-Sep; ⓤWaterloo) Amid the concrete jungle of the Queen Elizabeth Hall (p217) and the Hayward Gallery (p99) sits this unexpected rooftop garden cafe-bar. Find a spot and relax, surrounded by potted trees and planted 'wild meadows'. River views just add to the sense of wonder.

Scootercaffe   Cafe

(Map p280; 132 Lower Marsh, SE1; ☺8.30am-11pm Mon-Thu, to midnight Fri, 10am-midnight Sat, to 11pm Sun; ☎; ⓤWaterloo) This quirky cafe-bar, with its mishmash of furniture and uneven floor, has a lot of character. The slight smell of petrol and two scooters that form part of the decor are reminders of its previous role as a scooter-repair shop. It serves killer hot chocolates, coffee and decadent cocktails. House-roasted coffee available to buy.

⊖ The West End

American Bar   Bar

(Map p278; ☎020-7499 1001; www.thebeaumont
.com/dining/american-bar; Beaumont, Brown
Hart Gardens, W1; ⊙11.30am-midnight Mon-Sat,
to 11pm Sun; 🛜; Ⓤ Bond St) Sip a bourbon
or a classic cocktail in the 1920s art-deco
ambience of this stylish bar at the hall-
mark **Beaumont hotel** (d/studio/ste from
£550/865/1475; ❄🛜). It's central, glam and
like a private members' club, but far from
stuffy. Only a few years old, the American
Bar feels like it's been pouring drinks since
the days of the flapper and the jazz age.

American Bar   Cocktail Bar

(Map p274; ☎020-7836 4343; www.fairmont.
com/savoy-london/dining/americanbar; Savoy,
Strand, WC2; ⊙11.30am-midnight Mon-Sat, from
noon Sun; Ⓤ Temple, Charing Cross or Embankment) Home of the Hanky Panky, White Lady
and other classic cocktails created on-site,
the seriously dishy and elegant American
Bar – no relation to the American Bar in the
Beaumont – is a London icon, with soft blue
furniture, gleaming art-deco lines and live
piano music. Cocktails start at £18 and peak
at a stupefying £5000 (for the Sazerac, containing Sazerac de Forge cognac from 1858).

Lamb & Flag   Pub

(Map p274; ☎020-7497 9504; www.lamband
flagcoventgarden.co.uk; 33 Rose St, WC2;
⊙11am-11pm Mon-Sat, noon-10.30pm Sun;
Ⓤ Covent Garden) Perpetually busy pint-sized
Lamb & Flag is full of charm and history,
and has been a public house since at least
1772. Rain or shine, you'll have to elbow
your way through the merry crowd drinking
outside to the bar. The main entrance is at
the top of tiny, cobbled Rose St.

Swift   Cocktail Bar

(Map p274; ☎020-7437 7820; www.barswift.com;
12 Old Compton St, W1; ⊙3pm-midnight Mon-Sat,
3-10.30pm Sun; Ⓤ Leicester Sq or Tottenham
Court Rd) One of our favourite spots for a
tipple, Swift has a sleek, candlelit Upstairs
Bar designed for those who want a quick
drink before dinner or the theatre, while

the Downstairs Bar is a whisky-lover's
dream, with 250 bottles and counting, plus
art-deco-inspired sofas that invite lounging,
especially when live blues and jazz are
played on Friday and Saturday nights.

Galvin at Windows   Bar

(Map p278; ☎020-7208 4021; www.galvinat
windows.com; 28th fl, London Hilton on Park Lane,
22 Park Lane, W1; ⊙11am-1am Mon-Wed, to 2am
Thu-Sat, to 11pm Sun; 🛜; Ⓤ Hyde Park Corner)
From the top floor of the London Hilton on
Park Lane, this swish bar gazes on to awesome views, especially come dusk. Cocktail
prices reach similar heights, but the leather
seats are inviting and the marble bar is
gorgeous. The one-Michelin-star restaurant
with the same scenery offers a bargain
weekday lunch menu (two/three courses
£31/37). The dress code is smart casual.

Mr Fogg's Tavern   Bar

(Map p274; ☎020-7581 3992; www.mr-foggs.
com/mr-foggs-tavern; 58 St Martin's Lane, WC2;
⊙noon-11pm Mon-Sat, to 10pm Sun; Ⓤ Leicester
Sq) An unexpected oasis for the weary
Covent Garden visitor, Mr Fogg's is a themed
throwback to the drinking dens of yore.
Taking its inspiration from the protagonist of
Jules Verne's novel, this pub is filled with Union Flag bunting, costumed staff and kitschy
knick-knacks of a well-travelled Victorian. Gin
lovers are in for a treat.

Sketch   Cocktail Bar

(Map p274; ☎020-7659 4500; www.sketch.london;
9 Conduit St, W1; ⊙7am-2am Mon-Fri, 8am-2am
Sat, 8am-midnight Sun; Ⓤ Oxford Circus) If artists
operated an asylum, it might look something
like Sketch. Merrily undefinable, Sketch has
all at once a two-Michelin-starred restaurant, a millennial-pink dining room lined with
nonsensical cartoons by British artist David
Shrigley, a mystical-forest-themed bar with
a self-playing piano, and toilets hidden inside
gleaming white egg-shaped pods. We don't
know what's happening either, but we're
here for it.

Attendant   Coffee

(Map p274; ☎020-7580 3413; www.the-
attendant.com; 27a Foley St, W1; ⊙8am-5pm

Lamb & Flag

Mon-Fri, 9am-5pm Sat & Sun; [U]Goodge St) This abandoned Victorian public toilet got a flush of new life when this coffee shop opened here in 2013. The restroom has been sensitively restored (and fortunately deep-cleaned), and you can grab a stool at the urinal while waiting for your brew to arrive.

Craft Beer Co   Craft Beer

(Map p274; [J]020-7240 0431; www.thecraft beerco.com/covent-garden; 168 High Holborn, WC1; [clock]noon-midnight Sun-Wed, to 1am Thu-Sat; [U]Tottenham Court Rd) Incongruously carved out of a corner of a leisure centre, this branch of an eight-strong chain boasts 15 cask pumps from UK microbreweries, as well as 30 keg lines and a range of 200-plus beers in bottles and cans from around the world. Don't worry if the bar looks rammed; there's usually table space in the basement.

Cahoots   Cocktail Bar

(Map p274; [J]020-7352 6200; www.cahoots-london.com; 13 Kingly Ct, W1; [clock]5pm-1am Mon-Wed, 4pm-2am Thu, 4pm-3am Fri, 1pm-3am Sat, 3pm-midnight Sun; [U]Oxford St) All aboard the nostalgia train, and mind the gap: Cahoots

is a retro cocktail bar fashioned as an abandoned tube station during wartime London. Some cocktails come in teacups, and the bar snacks – crisps and salad cream sandwich, anyone? – in ration trays. It's madly popular, so book in advance.

Gordon's Wine Bar   Wine Bar

(Map p274; [J]020-7930 1408; https://gordons winebar.com; 47 Villiers St, WC2; [clock]11am-11pm Mon-Sat, noon-10pm Sun; [U]Embankment or Charing Cross) Quite possibly the oldest wine bar in London (opened in 1890), cavernous, candlelit and atmospheric Gordon's is a victim of its own success – it's relentlessly busy, and unless you arrive before the office crowd does, forget about landing a table. Nibble on cheese, bread and olives with your plonk – there's even a vegan wine list.

Heaven   Gay

(Map p274; [J]020-7930 2020; www.heaven nightclub-london.com; Villiers St, WC2; [clock]11pm-5am Mon, to 4am Thu & Fri, 10.30pm-5am Sat; [U]Embankment or Charing Cross) This perennially popular mixed/gay bar under the arches beneath Charing Cross station hosts excellent live gigs and club nights. Monday's Popcorn (mixed dance party, with an all-welcome door policy) offers one of the best weeknight's clubbing in the capital. The celebrated G-A-Y takes place here on Thursday (G-A-Y Porn Idol), Friday (G-A-Y Camp Attack) and Saturday (plain ol' G-A-Y).

Lamb   Pub

(Map p284; ☏020-7405 0713; www.thelamb london.com; 94 Lamb's Conduit St, WC1; ◷11am-11pm Mon-Wed, to midnight Thu-Sat, noon-10.30pm Sun; ⓤRussell Sq) The Lamb's central mahogany bar with beautiful Victorian 'snob screens' (so-called as they allowed the well-to-do to drink in private) has been a favourite with locals since the 1720s. Three centuries later, its popularity hasn't waned, so come early to bag a booth and sample its good selection of Young's bitters and genial atmosphere.

Yard   Gay

(Map p274; ☏020-7437 2652; www.yardbar. co.uk; 57 Rupert St, W1; ◷2-11.30pm Mon & Tue, noon-11.30pm Wed & Thu, noon-midnight Fri & Sat, noon-10.30pm Sun; ⓤPiccadilly Circus) This Soho favourite attracts a cross-section of the great and the good. It's fairly attitude-free, perfect for pre-club drinks or just an evening out. Grab a seat in the upstairs loft bar or join the friendly crowd in the open-air courtyard bar (heated in season) below.

Queen's Larder   Pub

(Map p284; ☏020-7837 5627; www.queenslarder. co.uk; 1 Queen Sq, WC1; ◷11.30am-11pm Mon-Fri, noon-11pm Sat, noon-10.30pm Sun; ⓤRussell Sq) Opposite Queen Square Gardens is this cosy pub, so-called because Queen Charlotte, wife of 'mad' King George III, rented part of the cellar to store special foods for him while he was being treated nearby for insanity. This watering hole is teensy, but there are a few outside tables and a dining room upstairs.

❷ West London

Troubadour   Bar

(Map p278; ☏020-7341 6333; www.troubadour london.com; 263-267 Old Brompton Rd, SW5;

◷cafe 9am-midnight, club 8pm-12.30am or 2am Mon-Sat, to 11.30pm Sun; ☎; ⓤEarl's Court) On a comparable spiritual plane to Paris' Shakespeare and Company bookshop, this eccentric, time-warped and convivial boho bar-cafe has been serenading drinkers since 1954. Adele, Ed Sheeran, Joni Mitchell, Jimi Hendrix and Bob Dylan have performed here, and there's still live music (largely jazz and folk) most nights downstairs. A wide-ranging wine list, Sunday roasts and a pleasant rear garden complete the picture.

Windsor Castle   Pub

(Map p278; www.thewindsorcastlekensington. co.uk; 114 Campden Hill Rd, W11; ◷noon-11pm Mon-Sat, to 10.30pm Sun; ☎; ⓤNotting Hill Gate) This classic tavern on the brow of Campden Hill Rd has history, nooks and charm on tap. Alongside a decent beer selection and a solid gastropub-style menu, there's a historic compartmentalised interior, a roaring fire (in winter), a delightful beer garden (in summer) and affable regulars (all seasons).

Earl of Lonsdale   Pub

(Map p278; 277-281 Portobello Rd, W11; ◷noon-11pm Mon-Fri, 10am-11pm Sat, noon-10.30pm Sun; ⓤNotting Hill Gate or Ladbroke Grove) For those traipsing Portobello Rd this is a good bolt-hole, named after the bon vivant founder of the AA (Automobile Association, *not* Alcoholics Anonymous). The Earl is peaceful during the day, with older locals and young hipsters inhabiting the reintroduced snugs. There are Samuel Smith ales, a pleasant back room with sofas, plus banquettes, open fires and a large beer garden.

Notting Hill Arts Club   Club

(Map p278; www.nottinghillartsclub.com; 21 Notting Hill Gate, W11; ◷hours vary; ☎; ⓤNotting Hill Gate) London wouldn't be what it is without places like NHAC, which mixes underground music with the odd big pop name. The small basement venue attracts a musically curious crowd, with live performances (usually 7pm to 10pm) and club nights (10pm to 2am) on Fridays and Saturdays and some week nights. Dress code: no suits and ties.

London in a Glass

Garnishes include
a slice of lime or lemon

Pour over as few or
as many ice cubes as
you like

Use a rocks glass
or a highball glass

Use a classic London
Gin such as Jensen,
Sacred or Sipsmith

Top up with tonic water

Gin & Tonic

PJOHNSON1/GETTY IMAGES ©

Gin was imported from Holland in the
17th century but Londoners quickly
adopted it as their own. In the 1850s,
Britons in the colonies had the enlight-
ened idea of mixing their daily quinine
dose (for malaria prevention) with gin –
and the gin and tonic was born. Gin has
experienced a boom in popularity over
the last decade and there are a number
of microdistilleries in London.

★ Top Three Spots for a G&T

Little Bird (www.littlebirdgin.com; Maltby
St, SE1; ◔5-10pm Thu & Fri, 10am-10pm
Sat, 11am-4pm Sun; Ⓤ London Bridge or
Bermondsey) This South London–based
gin distillery has a bar in the arches at
Maltby Street Market, ready to ply merry
punters with devilishly good cocktails
served in jam jars.

Jensen's (www.jensensgin.com; 55
Stanworth St, SE1; ◔10am-4pm Sat, from
11am Sun; Ⓤ London Bridge) A micro gin
distillery, open on weekends for tastings
and sales.

Dukes London (☏020-7491 4840; www.
dukeshotel.com/dukes-bar; Dukes Hotel, 35 St
James's Pl, SW1; ◔2-11pm Mon-Sat, 4-10.30pm
Sun; ☏; Ⓤ Green Park) This classic bar has
a gentlemen's-club-like ambience, where
white-jacketed masters mix up perfect
preparations.

SHOWTIME

From a night out at the theatre
to live-music venues

Showtime

Whatever it is that sets your spirits soaring or your booty shaking, you'll find it in London. The city has been a world leader in theatre ever since a young bard from Stratford-upon-Avon set up shop here in the 16th century. And if London started swinging in the 1960s, its live rock and pop scene has barely let up since.

In This Section

Tickets/Websites

Book well ahead for live performances and, if you can, buy directly from the venue.

You can buy discounted tickets up to two days in advance for West End productions from **Tkts Leicester Square** (www.officiallondontheatre.com/tkts).

National Theatre, designed by Sir Denys Lasdun (p216)

The Best...

Theatre

Shakespeare's Globe (p216) Shakespeare, as it would have been 400 years ago.
National Theatre (p216) Contemporary theatre on the South Bank.
Old Vic (p217) A heavy hitter in London's theatrical scene.
Royal Court Theatre (p214) Forward-thinking, promoting new voices.
Unicorn Theatre (p217) Because theatre isn't just for grown-ups!

Live Music

Royal Albert Hall (p214) Gorgeous, grand and spacious, yet strangely intimate.
KOKO (p214) Fabulously glitzy venue, showcasing original indie rock.
Ronnie Scott's (p218) The most famous jazz club in London, with reason.
Scala (p215) Great venue for intimate gigs.

✪ Clerkenwell, Shoreditch & Spitalfields

Rich Mix
Arts Centre

(Map p282; ☎020-7613 7498; www.richmix.org.
uk; 35-47 Bethnal Green Rd, E1; ⊙9am-11pm Mon-
Fri, 10am-11pm Sat & Sun; ⓤShoreditch High St)
Founded in 2006 in a converted garment
factory, this nonprofit cultural centre has a
three-screen cinema, a bar and a theatre.
Films shown run the gamut from mainstream to obscure film festivals, and the
programming for performing arts is hugely
eclectic, with anything from spoken word to
live music and comedy. It's open every day
except Christmas Day.

Sadler's Wells
Dance

(Map p282; ☎020-7863 8000; www.sadlerswells.
com; Rosebery Ave, EC1; ⓤAngel) A glittering
modern venue that was first established
in 1683, Sadler's Wells is the most eclectic
modern-dance and ballet venue in town,
with experimental dance shows of all genres
and from all corners of the globe. The Lilian
Baylis Studio stages smaller productions.

✪ East London

Cafe Oto
Live Music

(Map p285; www.cafeoto.co.uk; 18-22 Ashwin
St, E8; ⊙9.30am-late; ☎; ⓤDalston Junction)
Dedicating itself to promoting experimental and alternative musicians, this is
Dalston's premier venue for music nerds
to stroke their proverbial beards while
listening to electronic bleeps, Japanese
psychedelica or avant folk. Set in a
converted print warehouse, it's one of
London's most idiosyncratic live-music
venues. When there are no gigs on, it's
open as a cafe-bar.

Hackney Empire
Theatre

(Map p285; ☎020-8985 2424; www.hackney
empire.co.uk; 291 Mare St, E8; ⓤHackney
Central) One of London's most beautiful
theatres, this renovated Edwardian music
hall (1901) offers an extremely diverse
range of performances, from hard-edged
political theatre to musicals, opera and
comedy. It's one of the best places to
catch a pantomime at Christmas.

Darbar Festival at Sadler's Wells

Arcola Theatre
Theatre

(Map p285; ☎020-7503 1646; www.arcola theatre.com; 24 Ashwin St, E8; ⓤDalston Junction) Dalston is a fair schlep from the West End, but drama buffs still flock to this innovative theatre for its adventurous and eclectic productions. A unique annual feature is **Grimeborn**, an opera festival focusing on lesser-known or new works – it's Dalston's answer to East Sussex's world-famous Glyndebourne opera festival, taking place around the same time (August).

Vortex Jazz Club
Jazz

(Map p285; ☎020-7254 4097; www.vortexjazz. co.uk; 11 Gillett Sq, N16; ⓢ8pm-midnight; ⒭Dalston Kingsland) With a fantastically varied menu of jazz, the Vortex hosts an outstanding line-up of musicians, singers and songwriters from the UK, the US, Europe, Africa and beyond. It's a small venue so make sure you book if there's an act you particularly fancy.

✪ Greenwich & South London

Oliver's Jazz Bar
Jazz

(Map p286; ☎020-8858 3693; www.olivers jazzbar.com; 9 Nevada St, SE10; cover charge £5-8; ⓢ4pm-midnight Mon-Sat, 5-8pm Sun; ⓤGreenwich or Cutty Sark) This 1960s-style basement jazz bar has been a Greenwich institution for years, hidden away on a backstreet near the entrance to Greenwich Park. There's live jazz every night of the week, with many players affiliated with the Trinity Laban Conservatoire nearby.

Up the Creek
Comedy

(Map p286; ☎020-8584 4581; www.up-the-creek.com; 302 Creek Rd, SE10; tickets £5-20; ⓢ7-11pm Thu & Sun, to 2am Fri & Sat; ⓤCutty Sark) Bizarrely enough, the hecklers can be funnier than the acts at this great club. Mischief, rowdiness and excellent comedy are the norm, with the Blackout open-mic night on Thursdays (www.the-blackout. co.uk; £6) and Sunday specials

✦ Classical Music, Ballet & Opera

With multiple world-class orchestras and ensembles, quality venues, reasonable ticket prices and performances covering the whole musical gamut from traditional crowd-pleasers to innovative compositions, London will satisfy even the fussiest classical-music buff. The Southbank Centre (p217), Barbican Centre (p215), Royal Albert Hall (p214). The Proms is the year's biggest event.

Opera and ballet lovers should make a night at the Royal Opera House (p65) a priority – the setting and quality of the programming are truly world-class.

Opera at the Royal Opera House (p65)

(www.sundayspecial.co.uk; £7). There's an after-party on Fridays and Saturdays.

✪ Kensington & Hyde Park

Pheasantry
Live Music

(Map p278; ☎020-7439 4962; www.pizza expresslive.com/venues/chelsea-the-pheasantry; 152-154 King's Rd, SW3; from £12; ⓢ11.30am-11pm; ⓤSloane Sq or South Kensington) Currently run by PizzaExpress, the Pheasantry on King's Rd is a 19th-century building that has been a ballet academy, a boho bar and a nightclub (where Lou Reed once sang). These days it ranges over three floors, with a lovely garden at the front for al fresco dining, but the crowd-puller is the live cabaret and jazz in the basement.

Exterior of the Royal Albert Hall

Royal Albert Hall · Concert Venue

(Map p278; ☑0845 401 5034; www.royalalbert
hall.com; Kensington Gore, SW7; Ⓤ South
Kensington) This splendid Victorian concert
hall hosts classical music, rock and other
performances, but is famously the venue
for the BBC-sponsored Proms. Booking is
possible, but from mid-July to mid-
September Promenaders queue for £5
standing tickets that go on sale one hour
before curtain-up. Otherwise, the box
office and prepaid-ticket collection counter
are through door 12 (south side of the hall).

Royal Court Theatre · Theatre

(Map p278; ☑020-7565 5000; www.royalcourt
theatre.com; Sloane Sq, SW1; tickets £12-38;
Ⓤ Sloane Sq) Equally renowned for staging
innovative new plays and old classics,
the Royal Court is among London's most
progressive theatres and has continued
to foster major writing talent across
the UK for over 60 years. There are two
auditoriums: the main Jerwood Theatre
Downstairs, and the much smaller studio
Jerwood Theatre Upstairs. Tickets for
Monday performances are £12.

✪ North London

Cecil Sharp House · Traditional Music

(Map p284; www.cecilsharphouse.org; 2 Regent's
Park Rd, NW1; ⊗9am-11pm; Ⓤ Camden Town)
Home to the English Folk Dance and Song
Society, this institute keeps all manner
of folk traditions alive. Performances and
classes range from traditional British
music and cèilidh dances to clog stamping,
bell-jingling Morris dancing, all held in its
mural-covered Kennedy Hall. The dance
classes are oodles of fun and there's a real
community vibe; no experience necessary.

KOKO · Live Music

(Map p284; www.koko.uk.com; 1a Camden High St,
NW1; Ⓤ Mornington Cres) Once the legendary
Camden Palace, where Charlie Chaplin and
the Sex Pistols performed, and where Prince
played surprise gigs, KOKO is maintaining
its reputation as one of London's better gig
venues. The theatre has a dance floor and
decadent balconies, and attracts an indie
crowd. There are live bands most nights and
hugely popular club nights on Saturdays.

Scala — Live Music

(Map p284; ☎020-7833 2022; www.scala.co.uk; 275 Pentonville Rd, N1; Ⓤ King's Cross St Pancras) Opened in 1920 as a salubrious golden-age cinema, Scala slipped into porn-movie hell in the 1970s, only to be reborn as a club and live-music venue in the early 2000s. It's one of the top places in London to catch an intimate gig and is a great dance space too, hosting a diverse range of club nights.

Green Note — Live Music

(Map p284; ☎020-7485 9899; www.greennote. co.uk; 106 Parkway, NW1; ⊗7-11pm; Ⓤ Camden Town) Camden may be the home of punk, but it also has the Green Note: one of the best places in London to see live folk and world music, with gigs every night of the week. The setting is intimate: a tiny bare-brick room with mics set up in a corner, backdropped by red curtains.

Jazz Cafe — Live Music

(Map p284; ☎020-7485 6834; www.thejazzcafe london.com; 5 Parkway, NW1; ⊗live shows from 7pm, club nights 10.30pm-3am; Ⓤ Camden Town) The name would have you think jazz is the main staple, but it's only a small slice of what's on offer here. The intimate club-like space also serves up funk, hip-hop, R&B, soul and rare groove, with big-name acts regularly dropping in. Saturday club night is soul night, with live sets from the house band.

Regent's Park Open Air Theatre — Theatre

(Map p284; ☎0844 826 4242; www.openair theatre.org; Queen Mary's Gardens, Regent's Park, NW1; ⊗May-Sep; ♿; Ⓤ Baker St) A popular and very atmospheric summertime fixture in London, this 1250-seat outdoor auditorium plays host to four productions a year: famous plays, new works, musicals and usually one production aimed at families.

✪ The City

Barbican Centre — Performing Arts

(Map p282; ☎020-7638 8891; www.barbican. org.uk; Silk St, EC2; ⊗box office 10am-8pm

Live Music

Musically diverse and defiantly different, London is a hotspot of musical innovation and talent. It leads the world in articulate indie rock, in particular, and tomorrow's guitar heroes are right-this-minute paying their dues on sticky-floored stages in Camden Town, Shoreditch and Dalston.

Monster international acts see London as a crucial stop on their transglobal stomps, but be prepared for tickets selling out faster than you can find your credit card. The city's beautiful old theatres and music halls play host to a constant roster of well-known names in more intimate settings. In summer, giant festivals take over the city's parks, including **Wireless** (www.wirelessfestival.co.uk; Finsbury Park, N4; ⊗Jul) in Finsbury Park.

If jazz or blues are your thing, London has some excellent clubs and pubs where you can catch classics and contemporary tunes. The city's major jazz event is the **London Jazz Festival** (www.efglondon jazzfestival.org.uk; ⊗Nov) in November.

Wireless Festival

Mon-Sat, 11am-8pm Sun; Ⓤ Barbican) Home to the London Symphony Orchestra and the BBC Symphony Orchestra, the **Barbican** (Map p282; ☎020-7638 4141; tours adult/child £12.50/10; ⊗9am-11pm Mon-Sat, 11am-11pm Sun) also hosts scores of other concerts, focusing on jazz, folk, world and soul artists. Dance is also performed here, while the cinema screens recent releases as well as film festivals.

✪ The South Bank

Shakespeare's Globe   Theatre
(Map p280; ☎020-7401 9919; www.shakespeares globe.com; 21 New Globe Walk, SE1; seats £20-45, standing £5; Ⓤ Blackfriars or London Bridge) If you love Shakespeare and the theatre, the Globe will knock your theatrical socks off. This authentic Shakespearean theatre is a wooden 'O' without a roof over the central stage area, and although there are covered wooden bench seats in tiers around the stage, many people (there's room for 700) do as 17th-century 'groundlings' did, and stand in front of the stage.

You may have to wrap up, as the building is quite open to the elements. Groundlings note: umbrellas are not allowed, but cheap raincoats are on sale. Unexpected aircraft noise is unavoidable too.

The theatre season runs from late April to mid-October and includes works by Shakespeare and his contemporaries, such as Christopher Marlowe.

If you don't like the idea of standing in the rain or sitting in the cold, opt for an indoor candlelit play in the **Sam Wanamaker Playhouse**, a Jacobean theatre similar to the one Shakespeare would have used in winter. The programming also includes opera.

National Theatre   Theatre
(Map p280; ☎box office 020-7452 3000; www. nationaltheatre.org.uk; South Bank, SE1; 👪; Ⓤ Waterloo) The architecture of the nation's flagship theatre is considered an icon of the brutalist school. The complex comprises three auditoriums for performances. Fantastic **backstage tours** lasting up to 1½ hours (adult/child £11/9) are available daily. Every tour is different, but you can expect to go into at least one auditorium and may be able to see rehearsals and changes of sets, visit the prop room or bump into actors. Book ahead via the website.

Unicorn Theatre   Theatre
(Map p280; ☎020-7645 0560; www.unicorn theatre.com; 147 Tooley St, SE1; 👪; Ⓤ London Bridge) Hosting 10 to 15 different shows a year, Unicorn Theatre aims to offer quality performances for children, aged from six months to the late teens. Productions are

Unicorn Theatre

wide-ranging and perfectly tailored to their target audience.

Southbank Centre Concert Venue

(Map p280; ☎020-3879 9555; www.southbank centre.co.uk; Belvedere Rd, SE1; ☺10am-8pm; Ⓤ Waterloo) The Southbank Centre comprises several venues – **Royal Festival Hall, Queen Elizabeth Hall** and Purcell Room – hosting a wide range of performing arts. As well as regular programming, it organises fantastic festivals, including **Underbelly** (a summer festival of comedy, circus and family entertainment) and **Meltdown** (a music event curated by the best and most eclectic names in music).

Old Vic Theatre

(Map p280; ☎0844 871 7628; www.oldvictheatre. com; The Cut, SE1; Ⓤ Waterloo) Artistic director Matthew Warchus (who directed *Matilda the Musical* and the film *Pride*) aims to bring eclectic programming to the Old Vic theatre: expect new writing, as well as dynamic revivals of old works and musicals.

Young Vic Theatre

(Map p280; ☎020-7922 2922; www.youngvic.org; 66 The Cut, SE1; Ⓤ Southwark or Waterloo) This groundbreaking theatre is as much about showcasing and discovering new talent as it is about people discovering theatre. The Young Vic features actors, directors and plays from across the world, many tackling contemporary political and cultural issues, such as the death penalty, racism or corruption, and often blending dance and music with acting.

✪ The West End

Prince Charles Cinema Cinema

(Map p274; ☎020-7494 3654; www.princecharles cinema.com; 7 Leicester Pl, WC2; Ⓤ Leicester Sq) The last independent theatre in the West End, Prince Charles Cinema is universally loved for its show-anything attitude. Sing-a-longs and quote-a-longs (*Frozen*, *Elf* and *The Rocky Horror Picture Show* are perennial faves), all-nighter movie marathons (including Disney PJ parties) and anniversary and

Theatre

A night out at the theatre is as much a must-do London experience as a trip on the top deck of a double-decker bus. London's Theatreland in the dazzling West End – from Aldwych in the east, past Shaftesbury Ave to Regent St in the west – has a concentration of theatres only rivalled by New York's Broadway. It's a thrillingly diverse scene, encompassing Shakespeare's classics performed with old-school precision, edgy new works, raise-the-roof musicals and some of the world's longest-running shows.

CHRISPICTURES/SHUTTERSTOCK ©

special-format screenings regularly grace its listings. Arriving in costumed character is encouraged.

Wigmore Hall Classical Music

(Map p278; ☎020-7935 2141; www.wigmore-hall. org.uk; 36 Wigmore St, W1; Ⓤ Bond St) Wigmore Hall, built in 1901 as a piano showroom, is one of the best and most active classical-music venues in town (with more than 460 concerts a year), not only because of its fantastic acoustics, beautiful Arts and Crafts–style cupola over the stage and great variety of concerts, but also because of the sheer standard of the performances.

Ronnie Scott's Jazz

(Map p274; ☎020-7439 0747; www.ronnie scotts.co.uk; 47 Frith St, W1; ☺6pm-3am Mon-Sat, noon-4pm & 6.30pm-midnight Sun; Ⓤ Leicester Sq or Tottenham Court Rd) Ronnie Scott's jazz club opened in 1959 and became widely known as Britain's best,

Prince Charles Cinema (p217)

hosting such luminaries as Miles Davis, Charlie Parker, Ella Fitzgerald, Count Basie and Sarah Vaughan. The club continues to build upon its formidable reputation by presenting a range of big names and new talent. Book in advance, or come for a more informal gig at Upstairs @ Ronnie's.

PizzaExpress Jazz Club   Jazz

(Map p274; ☎020-7439 4962; www.pizzaexpress live.com/venues/soho-jazz-club; 10 Dean St, W1; Ⓤ Tottenham Court Rd) It might seem odd to pair a chain pizza place with smooth sax, but this spot has been one of the best jazz venues in London since opening in 1976. The club is hugely popular and has live music every night of the week. Artists such as Norah Jones, Gregory Porter and the late Amy Winehouse played here in their early days.

Comedy Store   Comedy

(Map p274; ☎0844 871 7699; www.thecomedy store.co.uk; 1a Oxendon St, SW1; Ⓤ Piccadilly Circus) This was one of the first (and is still one of the best) comedy clubs in London. The Comedy Store Players, the most famous improvisation outfit in town, take the stage on Wednesday and Sunday nights, featuring the wonderful Josie Lawrence, a veteran of the scene. On Thursdays, Fridays and Saturdays, Best in Stand Up features the best of London's comedy circuit.

Borderline   Live Music

(Map p274; ☎020-3871 7777; www.borderline. london; Orange Yard, off Manette St, W1; Ⓤ Tottenham Court Rd) Through the hard-to-find entrance off Orange Yard and down into the basement you'll find a packed, 300-capacity venue that's been the launch pad for a number of alt-rock and indie musicians. It has really punched above its weight: Blur, REM, Muse, the Wombats, Bloc Party, Mumford & Sons and many others all played early-career gigs here.

✪ West London

Puppet Theatre
Barge
Puppet Theatre

(Map p278; ☏020-7249 6876; www.puppet
barge.com; opposite 35 Blomfield Rd, W9; adult/
child £13/9; ◷Oct–mid-July; ⛾Warwick Avenue)
This utterly charming marionette (aka puppet) theatre can be found in a converted
barge moored in Little Venice – an area as
pretty as it sounds. The theatre has been
here for almost 40 years and holds regular
performances during weekends and school
holidays. Ducking into its interior to see a
show is an intimate, magical experience.

Bush Theatre
Theatre

(☏020-8743 5050; www.bushtheatre.co.uk;
7 Uxbridge Rd, W12; ◷10am-11pm Mon-Sat;
⛾Shepherd's Bush) This West London
theatre is renowned for encouraging new
writing. Its success since 1972 is down to
strong plays from the likes of Jonathan
Harvey, Conor McPherson, Stephen
Poliakoff and Mark Ravenhill. It also has an
excellent cafe and bar.

Gate Picturehouse
Cinema

(Map p278; ☏0871 902 5731; www.picture
houses.co.uk; 87 Notting Hill Gate, W11; tickets
£7.50-14.10; ⛾Notting Hill Gate) Opened in
1911, the single-screen Gate has one of
London's most charming art-deco cinema
interiors, with director Q&As and a wealth
of cinema clubs, including the E4 Slackers
Club (students) and Silver Screen
(over-60s). The cheapest tickets are on
Mondays. Sink a drink in the foyer bar before or after your film (a mix of art-house
and mainstream).

Electric Cinema
Cinema

(Map p278; ☏020-7908 9696; www.electric
cinema.co.uk; 191 Portobello Rd, W11; tickets
£10-40; ⛾Ladbroke Grove) Having notched
up its centenary in 2011, the Electric is one
of the UK's oldest cinemas, updated. Avail
yourself of the luxurious leather armchairs,
sofas, footstools and tables for food and
drink in the auditorium, or select one of
the six front-row double beds! Tickets are
cheapest on Mondays.

Opera Holland Park
Opera

(Map p278; ☏0300 999 1000; www.opera
hollandpark.com; Holland Park, W8; tickets
£20-80; ⛾High St Kensington or Holland
Park) Sit under the 1000-seat canopy,
temporarily erected every summer for a
nine-week season in the middle of Holland
Park (p145), for a mix of crowd-pleasers
and more obscure works. Four operas are
generally performed each year.

ACTIVE LONDON

Exploring the city on two wheels and more

Active London

London boasts highly developed infrastructure for participatory and spectator sports, with world-famous sporting venues scattered around the city. London also has a huge amount of green space for weekend warriors to work up a sweat in, while cyclists will find good provisions for visitors on two wheels, as an activity in itself or for simply getting about.

In This Section

Sports Seasons

Rugby The Six Nations, rugby's annual competition between England, Scotland, Wales, Ireland, France and Italy, runs across five weekends in February and March.

Football The Premier League runs from August to May (p227).

Tennis London is gripped by Wimbledon fever in July.

ArcelorMittal Orbit, designed by Anish Kapoor and Cecil Balmond, at the Queen Elizabeth Olympic Park (p225)

The Best...

Best Sporty Parks

Queen Elizabeth Olympic Park (p225) Major venues for football, swimming and cycling, plus canal cruises, abseiling and a giant slide.

Hyde Park (p100) Popular for jogging, horse riding, tennis, cycling, swimming and boating.

Hampstead Heath (p83) Lots of room for joggers, plus sports fields and swimming ponds.

Best For Adrenalin

ArcelorMittal Orbit (p225) Free-fall abseil off the tower or take a 178m slide to the ground.

Thames Rockets (p225) Blast along the Thames, James Bond–style, in a rigid inflatable speedboat.

Up at the O2 (p227) Scale the heights of the O2 Arena.

➊ Walking Tours

Hidden London   Tours

(☎020-7565 7298; www.ltmuseum.co.uk/whats-on/hidden-london; tours £35-85) Get under the skin of London on an incredible insider-access tour run by the London Transport Museum. Excursions take you to the depths of the city's abandoned tube stations, which have been film sets for a number of flicks including Skyfall and V for Vendetta, and to the heights of London's first skyscraper at 55 Broadway, Transport for London's HQ.

Sign up for email alerts to get notice of when the next tours are going on sale, and book early.

Shoreditch Street Art Tours   Walking

(Map p282; ☎07834 088533; www.shoreditch streetarttours.co.uk; tours start at Goat Statue, Brushfield St, E1; adult/child under 16 £15/10; ⊙tours usually 10am or 1.30pm Fri-Sun; ⓤLiverpool St) The walls of Brick Lane and Shoreditch are an ever-changing open-air gallery of street art, moonlighting as the canvas for legends such as Banksy and Eine as well as more obscure artists. Passionate guide Dave, bored of his job in the City, once spent his lunch breaks roaming these streets, but he now helps translate the stunning pieces to a rapt audience.

Tours must be booked online in advance, but you pay (cash only) in person at the start.

Guide London   Tours

(Association of Professional Tourist Guides; ☎020-7611 2545; www.guidelondon.org.uk; half-/full day £165/270) Hire a prestigious Blue Badge Tourist Guide, know-it-all guides who have studied for two years and passed a dozen written and practical exams to do their job. They can tell you stories behind the sights that you'd only hear from them or whisk you on a themed tour (eg royalty, the Beatles, parks, shopping). Go by car, public transport, bike or on foot.

Unseen Tours   Walking

(☎07514 266774; www.sockmobevents.org. uk; tours £12) See London from an entirely different angle on one of these award-winning neighbourhood tours led by the London homeless (60% of the tour price goes to the guide). Tours cover Covent Garden, Soho, Brick Lane, Shoreditch and London Bridge.

Open House London   Tours

(☎020-7383 2131; www.openhouselondon.org. uk) The annual free Open House London weekend event during the third week of September sees over 800 buildings open to the public. Open House London is run by Open City, a charity promoting cities with a year-round programme of events and initiatives, including talks and architectural tours on foot, boat and bike to various parts of London.

➊ Bus Tours

Original Tour   Bus

(www.theoriginaltour.com; adult/child £32/15; ⊙8.30am-8.30pm) A 24-hour hop-on, hop-off bus service with a river cruise thrown in, as well as three themed walks: Changing of the Guard, Rock 'n' Roll and Jack the Ripper. Buses run every five to 15 minutes; you can buy tickets on the bus or with online discounts. Also available are 48-hour tickets (adult/child £42/20) and 72-hour tickets (adult/child £52/25).

Big Bus Tours   Bus

(☎020-7808 6753; www.bigbustours.com; adult/child £37/19; ⊙every 5-20min 8.30am-6pm Apr-Sep, to 5pm Oct & Mar, to 4.30pm Nov-Feb) Informative commentaries in 12 languages, along four bus routes. The ticket includes a free river cruise with City Cruises and three thematic walking tours. The ticket is valid for 24 hours; for an extra £7 (£3 for children), you can upgrade to a 48-hour ticket (cheaper if bought online). Onboard wi-fi.

Kew Explorer   Bus

(☎020-8332 5648; www.kew.org/kew-gardens/whats-on/kew-explorer-land-train; Kew Gardens, TW9; adult/child £5/2; ⊞Kew Gardens, ⓤKew Gardens) For a good overview of the Kew

Gardens (p134), jump aboard this road train that allows you to hop on and off at stops along the way, on a 40-minute itinerary. There are seven stops in all along a route that runs in a long loop from the main Victoria Gate, returning to its departure point. The Explorer is also available for private hire.

Boat Tours

London Waterbus Company   Cruise
(Map p278; ☎07917 265114; www.london waterbus.com; 32 Camden Lock Pl, NW1; adult/child one-way £10/8, return £15/13; ⊗hourly 10am-5pm Apr-Oct, weekends only & less frequent departures other months; ⓤWarwick Ave or Camden Town) These enclosed barges take enjoyable 50-minute trips on Regent's Canal between Little Venice and Camden Lock, passing by Regent's Park and stopping at London Zoo. There are fewer departures outside high season; check the website for schedules. One-way tickets (adult/child £29/23) including zoo entry allow passengers to disembark within the zoo grounds. Buy tickets on board.

Thames Rockets   Boating
(Map p280; ☎020-7928 8933; www.thames rockets.com; Boarding Gate 1, London Eye, Waterloo Millennium Pier, Westminster Bridge Rd, SE1; adult/child from £44.95/29.95; ⊗10am-6pm; ⛟; ⓤWaterloo or Westminster) Thames Rockets run several different speedboat experiences, reaching 30 knots along the high-speed section of the Thames. The Ultimate London Adventure and Captain Kidd's Canary Wharf Voyage are both 50 minutes long and suitable for families. For something a little more grown-up, try Thames Lates in summer (including a cocktail), or there's Break the Barrier for those that love speed.

Alfred Le Roy   Cruise
(Map p285; www.alfredleroy.com; Queen's Yard, White Post Lane, E9; from £13; ⊗Sat & Sun; ⓤHackney Wick) When it's not moored as a floating bar outside Crate Brewery, this

Queen Elizabeth Olympic Park

The glittering centrepiece of London's 2012 Olympic Games, the **Queen Elizabeth Olympic Park** (Map p285; www.queenelizabetholympicpark.co.uk; E20; ⓤStratford) is vast 227-hectare expanse includes the main Olympic venues as well as playgrounds, walking and cycling trails, gardens, and a diverse mix of wetland, woodland, meadow and other wildlife habitats – an environmentally fertile legacy for the future. The main focal point is London Stadium. It had a Games capacity of 80,000, which was scaled back to 54,000 seats for its new role as the home ground for West Ham United FC.

Other signature buildings include the London Aquatics Centre, Lee Valley VeloPark, ArcelorMittal Orbit and the Copper Box Arena, a 7000-seat indoor venue for sports and concerts. Then there's the BeachEast, an artificial sandy beach on the River Lea, and Here East, a vast 'digital campus' covering an area equivalent to 16 football fields.

narrow boat heads out on booze cruises by Queen Elizabeth Olympic Park. On Saturdays it heads upriver to Springfield Park at noon, and downriver to Limehouse Basin at 3.30pm. Two-hour Sunday cruises offer a £25 all-you-can-drink prosecco, Bloody Mary and mimosa add-on. Book online.

Swimming & Spa

Hampstead Heath Ponds   Swimming
(www.cityoflondon.gov.uk; Hampstead Heath, NW5; adult/child £2/1; ⊗from 7am, closing times vary with season; ⓤHampstead Heath) Set in the midst of the gorgeous heath, Hampstead's three bathing ponds (men's, women's and mixed) offer a cooling dip in murky brown water. Despite what you might think from

🚲 Santander Cycles

London's cycle-hire scheme is called **Santander Cycles** (🗐0343 222 6666; www.tfl.gov.uk/modes/cycling/santander-cycles). The bikes have proved as popular with visitors as with Londoners.

The idea is simple: pick up a bike from one of the 750 docking stations dotted around the capital. Cycle. Drop it off at another docking station.

The access fee is £2 for 24 hours. All you need is a credit or debit card. The first 30 minutes are free; it's then £2 for any additional period of 30 minutes.

You can take as many bikes as you like during your access period (24 hours), leaving five minutes between each trip.

The pricing structure is designed to encourage short journeys rather than longer rentals; for those, go to a hire company. You'll also find that although easy to ride, the bikes only have three gears and are quite heavy. You must be aged 18 to buy access and at least 14 to ride a bike.

Santander Bike station
COWARDLION/SHUTTERSTOCK ©

its appearance, the water is tested daily and meets stringent quality guidelines.

Porchester Spa   Spa
(Map p278; 🗐020-7313 3858; www.porchesterspatreatments.co.uk; Porchester Centre, Queensway, W2; entry £28.90; ⊙10am-10pm; Ⓤ Bayswater or Royal Oak) Housed in a gorgeous, art-deco building, the Porchester is a no-frills spa run by Westminster Council. With a 30m swimming pool, a large Finnish-log sauna, two steam rooms, three Turkish hot

rooms and a massive plunge pool, there are plenty of affordable treatments on offer, including massages and male and female pampering/grooming sessions.

It's women-only on Tuesdays, Thursdays and Fridays all day and between 10am and 2pm on Sundays; and men-only on Mondays, Wednesdays and Saturdays. Couples are welcome from 4pm to 10pm on Sundays.

London Aquatics Centre   Swimming
(🗐020-8536 3150; www.londonaquaticscentre.org; Carpenters Rd, E20; adult/child from £5.20/3; ⊙6am-10.30pm; Ⓤ Stratford) The sweeping lines and wavelike movement of Zaha Hadid's award-winning Aquatics Centre make it the architectural highlight of Queen Elizabeth Olympic Park (www.queenelizabetholympicpark.co.uk; E20; Ⓤ Stratford). Bathed in natural light, the 50m competition pool beneath the huge undulating roof (which sits on just three supports) is an extraordinary place to swim. There's also a second 50m pool, a diving area, a gym, a crèche and a cafe.

🚴 Cycling

London Bicycle Tour   Cycling
(🗐020-7928 6838; www.londonbicycle.com; 74 Kennington Rd, SE11; tour incl bike adult/child from £26.95/22.95, bike hire per day £20; Ⓤ Lambeth North) Three-hour tours begin in Lambeth and take in London's highlights on both sides of the river; the classic tour is run in six languages. A night ride is available. You can also hire traditional or specialty bikes, such as tandems and folding bikes, by the hour or day.

Lee Valley VeloPark   Cycling
(Map p285; 🗐0300 003 0613; www.visitleevalley.org.uk/velopark; Abercrombie Rd, E20; 1hr taster £40, pay & ride from £4, bike & helmet hire adult/child from £12/8; ⊙9am-10pm; Ⓤ Stratford International) The beautifully designed, cutting-edge velodrome at Queen Elizabeth Olympic Park is open to the public – either to wander through and

watch the pros tear around the steep-sloped circuit, or to have a go yourself. Both the velodrome and the attached BMX park offer taster sessions. Mountain bikers and road cyclists can attack the tracks on a pay-and-ride basis.

Tennis

Wimbledon Championships
Spectator Sport

(📞020-8944 1066; www.wimbledon.com; Church Rd, SW19; grounds admission £8-25, tickets £33-225; 🚆493, Ⓤ Southfields) For two weeks each June and July, the sporting world's attention is fixed on the quiet southern suburb of Wimbledon, as it has been since 1877. Most show-court tickets for the Wimbledon Championships are allocated through public ballot, applications for which begin in early August of the preceding year and close at the end of December.

The ballot is famously oversubscribed and entry by no means guarantees a ticket. A quantity of court, grounds and late-entry tickets are available if you queue very early on the day of play. If you want a show-court ticket it is recommended you camp out the night before in the queue – a great experience in itself! See the website for details.

🧗 Climbing

Up at the O2
Adventure Sports

(www.theo2.co.uk/upattheo2; O2, Greenwich Peninsula, SE10; from £30; 🕑 hours vary; Ⓤ North Greenwich) Pull on a climbing suit and harness and scale the famous **O2** entertainment venue to reach a viewing platform perched 52m above the Thames with sweeping views of Canary Wharf, the river, Greenwich and beyond. Hours vary depending on the season (sunset and twilight climbs also available). They also run wheelchair-accessible climbs and can accommodate most guests with disabilities.

 Football

Football (soccer) is at the very heart of English sporting culture. Of the many London clubs in the Premier League (www.premierleague.com), Arsenal, Chelsea and Tottenham Hotspur have the strongest following. The competition runs from August to May, although it can be difficult for visitors to secure tickets to matches (they are usually all snapped up by season-ticket holders). Consider taking a tour at one of the main stadiums instead. Or watch a game at the pub.

Wembley (📞0800 169 9933; www.wembley stadium.com; tours adult/child £22/14; Ⓤ Wembley Park) The city's landmark national stadium, where England traditionally plays its international matches and where the FA Cup Final is contested.

London Stadium (📞020-8522 6157; www.london-stadium.com; Queen Elizabeth Olympic Park, E20; tours adult/child £19/11; 🕑 tours 10am-4.15pm; Ⓤ Pudding Mill Lane) Still known to most Londoners as the Olympic Stadium, it is now the home ground for West Ham United FC.

Arsenal Emirates Stadium (📞020-7619 5000; www.arsenal.com/tours; Hornsey Rd, N5; self-guided tours adult/child £23/15, guided tours £40; 🕑 10am-5pm Mon-Fri, 9.30am-6pm Sat, 10am-4pm Sun; Ⓤ Holloway Rd) Home ground for Arsenal since 2006.

Stamford Bridge (📞0371 811 1955; www.chelseafc.com; Stamford Bridge, Fulham Rd, SW6; tours adult/child £24/15; 🕑 museum 9.30am-5pm, tours 10am-3pm; Ⓤ Fulham Broadway) Hallowed turf for Chelsea fans.

Tottenham Hotspur Stadium (📞034-4499 5000; http://new-stadium.tottenham hotspur.com/; 782 High Road, Tottenham, N17; Ⓤ Tottenham Hale) Spurs' new stadium, opened in April 2019, is the largest club stadium in London, with the world's first dividing, retractable pitch (to allow for other events). It was not yet open for tours at the time of writing.

REST YOUR HEAD

Top tips for the best accommodation

RITZ CIGARS

Rest Your Head

Landing the right accommodation is integral to your London experience, and the city offers no shortage of choice. There's some fantastic accommodation, from party-oriented hostels to stately top-end hotels.

Budget is likely to be your main consideration, given how pricey London accommodation is, but you should also think about the neighbourhood you'd like to stay in. Are you a culture vulture? Do you want to walk (or take a quick cab ride) home after a night out? Are you after village charm or cool cachet? Think your options through and book ahead: London is busy year-round.

In This Section

Prices & Tipping

A 'budget hotel' in London generally costs up to £100 per night for a standard double room with bathroom. For a midrange option, plan on spending £100 to £200. Luxury options run £200 and higher.

Tipping isn't expected in hotels in London, except perhaps for porters in top-end hotels (although it remains discretionary).

Previous page: Exterior of the Ritz Hotel on Piccadilly

SSOKOLOV/SHUTTERSTOCK ©

Reservations

° Book rooms as far in advance as possible, especially for weekends and holiday periods.

° Visit London (www.visitlondon.com) offers a free accommodation booking service and has a list of family-friendly accommodation.

° Most hotels will match prices on booking sites if you book directly, and this may come with extra perks such as free breakfast or late checkout.

Useful Websites

° **Lonely Planet** (www.lonelyplanet. com/london) Hundreds of properties, from budget hostels to luxury apartments.

° **London Town** (www.londontown. com) Excellent last-minute offers on boutique hotels and B&Bs.

° **Sawdays** (www.sawdays.co.uk) Handpicked selection of bolt-holes in the capital.

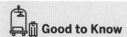 **Good to Know**

Value-added tax (VAT; 20%) is added to hotel rooms. Some hotels include this in their advertised rates, some don't.

Breakfast may be included in the room rate. Sometimes this is a continental breakfast; full English breakfast might cost extra.

Hotels

London has a grand roll call of stately hotels and many are experiences in their own right. Standards at the top end are high, but so are the prices. Quirkiness and individuality can be found in abundance, alongside dyed-in-the-wool traditionalism. While a rung or two down in overall quality and charm, midrange chain hotels generally offer good locations and dependable comfort. A new trend is for smart hotels with tiny but well-designed rooms and larger communal spaces for spreading out in; prices often start extremely reasonably for these but rise sharply for last-minute bookings. Demand can often outstrip supply – especially on the bottom step of the market – so book ahead, particularly during holiday periods and in summer.

B&Bs

Bed and breakfasts generally come in at a tier below hotels, often promising boutique-style charm and a more personal level of service. Handy B&B clusters appear in Paddington, South Kensington, Victoria and Bloomsbury.

Hostels

Generally the cheapest form of accommodation, hostels can be both an affordable and a sociable option. They vary widely in quality, so choose carefully. Those with a reputation as party hostels can be a lot of fun, but don't expect to get much sleep. As well as dorm rooms, many also offer twin and double rooms, sometimes with en suite bathrooms. These private rooms are often better than what you'd get for an equivalent price in a budget hotel.

Long-Term Rentals

If you're in London for a week or more, try a short-term or serviced apartment; rates at the bottom end are comparable to a B&B, you can manage your budget more carefully by eating in, and you'll feel like a local.

Neighbourhoods with a great vibe include Notting Hill, Hackney, Bermondsey, Pimlico and Camden, where you'll find plenty of food markets, great local pubs and lots of boutiques. Traditional accommodation is limited in this area, but many travellers can find places to stay on the usual home-sharing services.

For something a little more hotel-like, serviced apartments are a great option. The following are in the centre: **Cheval Three Quays** (020-3725 5333; www. chevalresidences.com; 40 Lower Thames St, EC3; apt from £369; ❄ ☎; Ⓤ Tower Hill), and **No 5 Maddox Street** (020-7647 0200; www. living-rooms.co.uk/hotel/no-5-maddox-st; 5 Maddox St, W1; 1-/2-/3-bed apt from £325/650/895; ❄ ☎; Ⓤ Oxford Circus).

Where to Stay

Neighbourhood	For	Against
The West End	Great transport links; wide range of accommodation; good restaurants.	Busy tourist areas; expensive.
The City	Central location; good transport links; quality hotels; cheaper weekend rates.	Quiet at weekends; high prices during the week.
The South Bank	Cheaper than West End; excellent pubs and views.	Many chain hotels; choice limited.
Kensington & Hyde Park	Excellent for museums and shopping; great accommodation range; stylish area; good transport.	Quite expensive; drinking and nightlife options limited.
Clerkenwell, Shoreditch & Spitalfields	Hip area with great bars and nightlife; excellent for boutique hotels.	Few top sights.
East London	Markets, multicultural feel; great restaurants and traditional pubs.	Few sleeping options; can be less safe at night.
North London	Vibrant nightlife; pockets of village charm; boutique hotels and hostels; quiet during the week.	Noncentral and away from main sights.
West London	Good shopping, markets and pubs; boutique hotels; good transport.	Pricey; light on top sights.
Greenwich & South London	Great boutique options; leafy escapes; near top Greenwich sights.	Sights spread out; transport limited.
Richmond, Kew & Hampton Court	Smart riverside hotels; semirural pockets; quiet; fantastic riverside pubs.	Sights spread out; far from central London.

Crossrail Place at Canary Wharf station, architect Foster and Partners

In Focus

Flags at anti-Brexit protest

London Today

London has led a relatively charmed life, always overcoming its challenges. Even after the plagues, the Great Fire of London and the Blitz bombings, the city carried on. Spiralling property prices and Brexit uncertainties are small fry in comparison. The economy remains buoyant despite the weak pound, new buildings vie for attention on the skyline, and major investments have been made in public transport.

Out the Door

Arguably *the* topic of the moment is Brexit, the UK's departure from the EU, which was approved by the electorate in a June 2016 referendum. The referendum was approved by a 52% to 48% margin nationwide, revealing a divide between London (which voted to remain by 60% to 40%) and many other parts of the country.

Brexit negotiations have been protracted and convoluted, the fallout dividing families and friends, and bleak predictions of a post-Brexit apocalypse have filled the pages of pro-EU newspapers across the nation. Some Londoners fret about the city losing its multicultural edge (270 nationalities speaking some 300 different languages). Others worry about a sudden house-price crash that may follow a 'no deal' Brexit (departing from the EU with no agreement with the EU) and the predicted economic chaos that many say

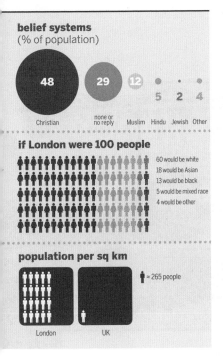

belief systems
(% of population)

48 — Christian
29 — none or no reply
12 — Muslim
5 — Hindu
2 — Jewish
4 — Other

if London were 100 people

60 would be white
18 would be Asian
13 would be black
5 would be mixed race
4 would be other

population per sq km

London | UK

† ≈ 265 people

will follow. Others are more stoic or have simply reached saturation point, having had enough of the ceaseless white noise of Brexit. But whatever their perspective, Londoners all care about the future of London and hope the city can preserve its much-cherished influence, attractiveness and dynamism.

Going Up & Up & Up

Throughout the 2010s, London was a city in transition. What was once a relatively low-level place has soared ever upwards. For many years vertical growth was contained to the City of London and Canary Wharf in the Docklands. By the end of the decade some 435 buildings of over 20 storeys were in the pipeline – double the amount of just two years before – and most are in East London, the Greenwich Peninsula and the South Bank. Only time will tell how the city responds. Keeping pace with the rising skyline until recently were property prices, which increased at eye-watering rates for the better part of 20 years.

All Change

The former mayor of London, Boris Johnson, left office after two terms to join Theresa May's Conservative party as foreign secretary (only to resign in 2018). The capital rejected his party's new mayoral candidate, Zac Goldsmith, in favour of Sadiq Khan, a Labour MP who was born in Tooting in South London to a working-class British Pakistani family and is a practising Muslim, making him the world's first elected leader of that faith in any Western city. His performance in office has been well received overall, notably his response to the 2017 terrorist attacks in London and Manchester. Khan's term comes to an end in 2020; he has indicated that he will stand for re-election.

Way To Go

Some of the brightest news coming out of London is Crossrail. Now officially named the Elizabeth Line, Crossrail is an ambitious (delayed and over-budget) underground and overground transport system that will stretch for 73 miles east and west and through central London, linking Reading with Shenfield. The new line will increase central London rail capacity by 10% and bring an extra 1.5 million people to within 45 minutes of central London.

Even better news is the so-called Night Tube, with the Victoria and Jubilee Lines, plus most of the Piccadilly, Central and Northern Lines, running all night on weekends. The service has been extended to include the London overground between Highbury & Islington and New Cross Gate, and other lines are expected to follow suit in the next few years.

Buckingham Palace (p48)

LUKASZ PAJOR/SHUTTERSTOCK ©

History

London's history is a long and turbulent narrative spanning more than two millennia. Over those years there have been good times of strength and economic prosperity, and horrific times of plague, fire and war. But even when down on its knees, London has always been able to get up, dust itself off and move on, constantly reinventing itself along the way.

AD 43

The Romans invade Britain, led by Emperor Claudius; they mix with the local Celtic tribespeople and stay for almost four centuries.

852

Vikings settle in London; a period of great struggle between the kingdoms of Wessex and Denmark begins.

1066

Following his decisive victory at the Battle of Hastings, William, Duke of Normandy, is crowned king of England in Westminster Abbey.

Hampton Court Palace (p124)

KIEVVICTOR/SHUTTERSTOCK ©

Londinium

The Celts were the first to arrive in the area that is now London, some time around the 4th century BC. The river was twice as wide as it is today and probably served as a barrier separating tribal groups.

It was the Romans, however, who established a real settlement in AD 43, the port of Londinium. They slung a wooden bridge over the Thames (near the site of today's London Bridge) and created a thriving colonial outpost.

By the middle of the 3rd century, Londinium was home to some 30,000 people of various ethnic groups, with temples dedicated to a large number of cults. When Emperor Constantine converted to Christianity in 312, the fledgling religion became the empire's – and London's – official cult, seeing off its rival, Mithraism.

In the 4th century, the Roman Empire in Britain began to decline. The Romans abandoned Britain for good in 410, and Londinium was reduced to a sparsely populated backwater.

1215
King John signs the Magna Carta, an agreement forming the basis of constitutional law in England.

1290
King Edward I issues an edict expelling all Jews from England; the banishment remains in effect for more than 360 years.

1348
Rats on ships from Europe bring the 'Black Death', a plague that eventually wipes out half of the city's residents.

Westminster Abbey (p36)

GRZEGORZ_PAKULA/SHUTTERSTOCK ©

Saxon & Norman London

Saxon settlers, who colonised the southeast of England from the 5th century onwards, established themselves outside the city walls due west of Londinium in Lundenwic. This trading community grew in importance and attracted the attention of the Vikings in Denmark. They attacked in 842 and again nine years later, burning Lundenwic to the ground. Under the leadership of King Alfred the Great of Wessex, the Saxon population fought back, driving the Danes out in 886.

Saxon London grew into a prosperous and well-organised town segmented into 20 wards, each with its own alderman and resident colonies of German merchants and French vintners. But attacks by the Danes continued apace, and the Saxon leadership was weakening; in 1016 Londoners were forced to accept the Danish leader Canute as king of England. With the death of Canute's brutal son Harthacanute in 1042, the throne passed to the Saxon Edward the Confessor, who went on to found a palace and an abbey at Westminster.

On his deathbed in 1066, Edward anointed Harold Godwinson, the Earl of Wessex, as his successor. This enraged William, Duke of Normandy, who claimed that Edward had promised him the throne. William mounted a massive invasion from France, and on 14 October defeated (and killed) Harold at the Battle of Hastings, before marching on London to claim his prize. William, now dubbed 'the Conqueror', was crowned king of England in Westminster Abbey on 25 December 1066, ensuring the Norman conquest was complete.

Medieval & Tudor London

Successive medieval kings were happy to let the City of London keep its independence as long as its merchants continued to finance their wars and building projects.

Fire was a constant hazard in the cramped and narrow houses and lanes of 14th-century London, but disease caused by unsanitary living conditions and impure drinking water

1558	1605	1665
The first detailed map of London is commissioned by a group of German merchants; Queen Elizabeth I takes the throne.	A Catholic plot to blow up James I is foiled; Guy Fawkes, one of the alleged plotters, is executed the following year.	The Great Plague ravages London, wiping out a quarter of the population. It was one of Europe's last outbreaks of the disease.

from the Thames was the greatest threat. In 1348 rats on ships from Europe brought the Black Death, a bubonic plague that wiped out almost half the population of about 80,000 over the next year and a half.

With their numbers down, there was growing unrest among labourers, for whom violence became a way of life, and rioting was commonplace. The Peasants' Revolt in 1381 lasted months and cost the Archbishop of Canterbury and several ministers their heads.

London gained wealth and stature under the Houses of Lancaster and York in the 15th century, but their struggle for ascendancy led to the catastrophic Wars of the Roses. The century's greatest episode of political intrigue occurred during this time: in 1483 the 12-year-old Edward V of the House of York reigned for only two months before vanishing with his younger brother into the Tower of London, never to be seen again. Whether or not their uncle, Richard III – who became the next king – murdered the boys has been the subject of much conjecture over the centuries (Shakespeare would have us believe he did the evil deed).

Tudor London

During the Tudor dynasty, which coincided with the discovery of the Americas and thriving world trade, London became one of the largest and most important cities in Europe. Henry VIII reigned from 1509 to 1547, built palaces at Whitehall and St James's, and bullied his lord chancellor, Cardinal Thomas Wolsey, into giving him the one Wolsey had built at Hampton Court.

The most momentous event of his reign, however, was his split from the Catholic Church in 1534 after the Pope refused to annul his marriage to Catherine of Aragon, who had borne him only one surviving daughter after 24 years of marriage.

The 45-year reign (1558–1603) of Henry's daughter Elizabeth I is still regarded as one of the most extraordinary periods in English history. During these four decades English literature reached new heights, and religious tolerance gradually grew. With the defeat of the Spanish Armada in 1588, England became a naval superpower, and London established itself as the premier world trade market with the opening of the Royal Exchange in 1570.

Civil Wars & a Republic

Elizabeth was succeeded by her second cousin James I, and then his son Charles I. The latter's belief in the 'divine right of kings' set him on a collision course with an increasingly confident parliament at Westminster and a powerful City of London. The latter two rallied behind Oliver Cromwell against royalist troops. Charles was defeated in 1646 and executed in 1649.

Cromwell ruled the country as a republic for the next 11 years. Under the Common-wealth of England, as the English republic was known, Cromwell banned theatre, dancing, Christmas and just about anything remotely fun.

1666	**1708**	**1759**
The Great Fire of London burns for five days, leaving four-fifths of the metropolis in smoking ruins.	The last stone of Christopher Wren's masterpiece, St Paul's Cathedral, is laid by his son and the son of his master mason.	The British Museum opens to the public for the first time, levying no admission fee to all 'studious and curious persons'.

What's in the Name?

Many of London's street names, especially in the City, recall the goods that were traded there: Poultry, Cornhill, Sea Coal Lane, Milk and Bread Sts, and the more cryptic Friday St, where you bought fish for that fasting day. Other meanings are not so obvious. The '-wich' or '-wych' in names such as Greenwich, Aldwych and Dulwich come from the Saxon word *wic,* meaning 'settlement'. *Ea* or *ey* is an old word for 'island' or 'marsh'; thus Chelsea (Island of Shale), Bermondsey (Bermond's Island), Battersea (Peter's Island) and Hackney (Haca's Marsh). In Old English *ceap* meant 'market'; hence Eastcheap is where the common people shopped, while Cheapside (originally Westcheap) was reserved for the royal household. 'Borough' comes from *burg,* Old English for 'fort' or 'town'. And the odd names East Ham and West Ham come from the Old English *hamm* or 'hem'; they were just bigger enclosed (or 'hemmed-in') settlements than the more standard hamlets.

After Cromwell's death in 1658, parliament restored the exiled Charles II to the throne in 1660. Charles II's reign witnessed two great tragedies in London: the Great Plague of 1665, which decimated the population, and the Great Fire of London, which swept ferociously through the city's densely packed streets the following year.

Fire & Plague

Crowded, filthy London had suffered from recurrent outbreaks of bubonic plague since the 14th century, but nothing had prepared it for the Great Plague of 1665, which dwarfed all previous outbreaks.

As the plague spread, families affected were forced to stay inside for 40 days' quarantine, until the victim had either recovered or died. Previously crowded streets were deserted, churches and markets were closed, and an eerie silence descended. To make matters worse, the mayor believed that dogs and cats were the spreaders of the plague and ordered them all killed, thus ridding the disease-carrying rats of their natural predators. By the time the winter cold arrested the epidemic, an estimated 100,000 people had perished – around a quarter of the city's population – their corpses collected and thrown into vast 'plague pits'.

But just a year later, the mother of all blazes broke out on 2 September 1666 in a bakery in Pudding Lane near London Bridge.

It didn't seem like much to begin with – the mayor himself dismissed it as 'something a woman might piss out' before going back to bed – but the unusual autumn heat combined with rising winds meant the fire raged out of control for four days, reducing 80% of London to ash. Only eight people died (officially at least), but most of medieval London was obliterated.

1838	1851	1884
The coronation of Queen Victoria ushers in a new era for London; the British capital becomes the economic centre of the world.	The Great Exhibition, the brainchild of Victoria's consort, Albert, opens to great fanfare in the Crystal Palace in Hyde Park.	Greenwich Mean Time is established, making Greenwich Observatory the centre of world time, according to which all clocks are set.

Wren's London

The wreckage of the inferno at least allowed master architect Christopher Wren to build his 51 magnificent churches. The crowning glory of the 'Great Rebuilding' was his St Paul's Cathedral, completed in 1708.

In 1685 some 1500 Huguenot (Protestant) refugees arrived in London, fleeing persecution in Catholic France; another 3500 would follow. Mainly artisans, many began manufacturing luxury goods such as silks and silverware in and around Spitalfields and Clerkenwell, which were already populated with Irish, Jewish and Italian immigrants and artisans. London was fast becoming one of the world's most cosmopolitan places. By 1700 it was Europe's largest city, home to some 600,000 people.

Georgian & Victorian London

While the achievements of the 18th-century Georgian kings were impressive (though 'mad' George III will forever be remembered as the king who lost the American colonies), they were overshadowed by those of the dazzling Victorian era, dating from Queen Victoria's ascension to the throne in 1837.

During the Industrial Revolution, London became the nerve centre of the largest and richest empire the world had ever witnessed, in an imperial expansion that covered a quarter of the earth's surface area and ruled over more than 500 million people.

New docks in East London were built to facilitate the booming trade with the colonies, and railways began to fan out from the capital. The world's first underground railway opened between Paddington and Farringdon in 1863 and was such a success that other lines quickly followed. Many of London's most famous buildings and landmarks were built at this time, including what is now officially named Elizabeth Tower but popularly known as Big Ben (1859), the Royal Albert Hall (1871) and the iconic Tower Bridge (1894).

Queen Victoria lived to celebrate her Diamond Jubilee in 1897, but died four years later aged 81 and was laid to rest beside her beloved consort, Prince Albert, at Windsor. Her reign is seen as the climax of Britain's world supremacy, when London was the de facto capital of the world.

Waves of immigrants, from Irish and Jews to Chinese and Indian sepoys (soldiers serving under British orders), arrived in London during the 19th century, when the population exploded from one million to well over six million people. This breakneck expansion was not beneficial to all – inner-city slums housed the poor in atrocious conditions of disease and overcrowding, while the affluent expanded to leafy suburbs.

The World Wars

Later known as the Great War, WWI broke out in August 1914, and the first German bombs fell from zeppelins near the Guildhall a year later, killing 39 people. Planes were soon

1908	**1940–41**	**1953**
London hosts the Olympic Games; a total of 22 teams take part and the entire budget is £15,000.	London is devastated by the Blitz, although St Paul's Cathedral and the Tower of London escape largely unscathed.	Queen Elizabeth II's coronation is broadcast live around the world on television; many English families buy their first TV.

A Golden Age for the Arts

Georgian London saw a great creative surge in music, art and architecture. Court composer George Frederick Handel wrote *Water Music* (1717) and *Messiah* (1741) after settling here at age 27, and in 1755 Dr Johnson published the first English-language dictionary. William Hogarth, Thomas Gainsborough and Joshua Reynolds produced some of their finest paintings and engravings, and many of London's most elegant buildings, streets and squares were erected or laid out by architects such as John Soane, his pupil Robert Smirke, and the prolific John Nash.

dropping bombs on the capital, killing in all some 670 Londoners (half the national total of civilian deaths).

Although the interwar years were beset with industrial strife, intellectually the 1920s were the heyday of the Bloomsbury Group, which counted writers Virginia Woolf and EM Forster and the economist John Maynard Keynes in its ranks. The spotlight shifted westwards to Fitzrovia in the following decade, when George Orwell and Dylan Thomas raised glasses with contemporaries at the Fitzroy Tavern on Charlotte St. Cinema, TV and radio arrived: the BBC aired its first radio broadcast from the roof of Marconi House on the Strand in 1922, and the first TV programme from Alexandra Palace 14 years later).

In the 1930s Prime Minister Neville Chamberlain's policy of appeasing Adolf Hitler proved misguided, as the German führer's lust for expansion appeared insatiable. When Nazi Germany invaded Poland on 1 September 1939, Britain declared war, having signed a mutual-assistance pact with the Poles only a few days before. World War II (1939–45), which would prove to be Europe's darkest hour, had begun.

Winston Churchill, prime minister from 1940, orchestrated much of the nation's war strategy from the Cabinet War Rooms deep below Whitehall, lifting the nation's spirit from here with his stirring wartime speeches. By the time Nazi Germany capitulated in May 1945, up to a third of the East End and the City of London had been flattened by bombs, almost 30,000 Londoners had been killed and a further 50,000 seriously wounded.

Monarchy Turmoil

1936 will remain in the annals of royal history as the year of the three kings. The monarchy took a knock when Edward VIII, who was to become king after his father George V died, abdicated to marry a woman who was not only twice divorced but – egad! – an American. His brother, George VI (father of the current queen Elizabeth II) took over instead, propelling the then relatively anonymous princess Elizabeth to heir to the throne.

Postwar London

Once the celebrations of Victory in Europe (VE day) had died down, the nation began to confront the war's appalling toll and to rebuild. The years of austerity had begun, with rationing

1959	**1981**	**2000**
The Notting Hill Carnival is launched by Claudia Jones to promote better race relations following the riots of 1958.	Brixton sees the worst race riots in London's history.	Ken Livingstone is elected mayor of London as an independent.

of essential items, and high-rise residences sprouting up from bombsites. Rationing of most goods ended in 1953, the year Elizabeth II was crowned following the death the year before of her father King George VI.

Immigrants from around the world – particularly the former colonies – flocked to post-war London, where a dwindling population had generated labour shortages, and the city's character changed forever. The place to be during the 1960s, 'Swinging London' became the epicentre of cool in fashion and music, its streets awash with colour and vitality.

The ensuing 1970s brought glam rock, punk, economic depression and the country's first female prime minister in 1979. In power for the entire 1980s and pushing an unprecedented programme of privatisation, the late Margaret Thatcher is easily the most significant of Britain's postwar leaders. Opinions about 'Maggie' still polarise the Brits today.

While poorer Londoners suffered under Thatcher's significant trimming back of the welfare state, things had rarely looked better for the wealthy, as London underwent explosive economic growth. In 1992, much to the astonishment of most Londoners, the Conservative Party was elected for their fourth successive term in government, despite Mrs Thatcher being jettisoned by her party a year and a half before. By 1995 the writing was on the wall for the Conservative Party, as the Labour Party, apparently unelectable for a decade, came back with a new face.

London in the New Century

Invigorated by its sheer desperation to return to power, the Labour Party elected the thoroughly telegenic Tony Blair as its leader; he managed to ditch some of the more socialist-sounding clauses in its party credo and reinvent it as New Labour, leading to a landslide win in the May 1997 general election. The Conservatives atomised nationwide; the Blair era had begun in earnest.

Most importantly for London, Labour recognised the demand the city had for local government, and created the London Assembly and the post of mayor. In Ken Livingstone, London elected a mayor who introduced a congestion charge and sought to update the ageing public-transport network. In 2008 he was defeated by his arch-rival, Conservative Boris Johnson.

Johnson won his second term in 2012, the year of the Olympic Games (overwhelmingly judged an unqualified success) and the Queen's Diamond Jubilee (the 60th anniversary of her ascension to the throne).

Since the Olympics, both the nation and the city have changed leadership (Theresa May replacing David Cameron as prime minister, Sadiq Khan taking over as mayor from Boris Johnson), and the Brexit referendum blowing a wind of change (panic?) through the city.

2005	**2012**	**2017**
A day after London is awarded the 2012 Olympics, 52 people are killed in a series of suicide bombings on London's transport network.	Boris Johnson narrowly beats Ken Livingstone to win his second mayoral election; London hosts the 2012 Olympics and Paralympics.	A fire in West London's public-housing Grenfell Tower kills 71 people, symbolising the capital's growing inequality.

London Skyline

GANGLIUIO/GETTY IMAGES ©

Architecture

Unlike many other world-class cities, London has never been methodically planned. It has developed in an organic fashion. London retains architectural reminders from every period of its long history. This is a city for explorers; seek out part of a Roman wall enclosed in the lobby of a modern building, for example, or a coaching inn dating to the Restoration tucked away in a courtyard off Borough High St.

Ancient London

London's architectural roots lie within the walled Roman settlement of Londinium, established in AD 43 on the northern banks of the River Thames where the City of London is located. Few Roman traces survive outside museums, though a Temple of Mithras (or Mithraeum), built in AD 240 and excavated in 1954, has moved to the eastern end of Queen Victoria St in the City following completion of the Bloomberg headquarters at Walbrook Sq. Stretches of the Roman wall remain as foundations to a medieval wall outside Tower Hill tube station and in a few sections below Bastion Highwalk, next to the Museum of London.

The Saxons, who moved into the area after the decline of the Roman Empire, found Londinium too small, all but ignored what the Romans had left behind and built their communities further up the Thames. Excavations carried out during renovations at the Royal Opera House in the late 1990s uncovered extensive traces of the Saxon settlement of Lundenwic, including some houses of wattle and daub. All Hallows by the Tower, northwest of the Tower of London, shelters an important archway, the walls of a 7th-century Saxon church and a Roman pavement. St Bride's, Fleet St, has a similar pavement.

With the arrival of William the Conqueror in 1066, the country received its first example of Norman architecture with the White Tower, the sturdy keep at the heart of the Tower of London. The church of St Bartholomew-the-Great at Smithfield also has Norman arches and columns supporting its nave. The west door and elaborately moulded porch at Temple Church (shared by Inner and Middle Temple), the undercroft at Westminster Abbey and the crypt at St-Mary-le-Bow are other outstanding examples of Norman architecture.

Open House London

If you want to see the inside of buildings whose doors are normally shut tight, visit London on the third weekend in September. That's when the charity Open House London (p224) arranges for the owners of over 800 private and public buildings to let the public in free of charge. Major buildings (eg the Gherkin, City Hall, Lloyd's of London, Royal Courts of Justice, BT Tower) have participated in the past; the full programme becomes available in August.

Medieval London

Traces of medieval London are hard to find thanks to the devastating Great Fire of 1666. There are a few treasures scattered around, including the mighty Tower of London, parts of which date back to the late 11th century. Westminster Abbey and Temple Church are 12th- to 13th-century creations.

Noteworthy medieval secular structures include the 1365 Jewel Tower, opposite the Houses of Parliament, and Westminster Hall, both surviving chunks of the medieval Palace of Westminster.

The finest London architect of the first half of the 17th century was Inigo Jones (1573–1652), who spent a year and a half in Italy and became a convert to the Renaissance-style architecture of Andrea Palladio. His *chefs d'œuvre* include Banqueting House (1622) in Whitehall and Queen's House (1635) in Greenwich. Often overlooked is his much plainer church of St Paul's in Covent Garden, which Jones designed in the early 1630s.

After the Great Fire

After the 1666 fire, Christopher Wren was commissioned to oversee reconstruction, but his vision of a new city layout of broad, symmetrical avenues never made it past the planners. His legacy lives on, however, in St Paul's Cathedral (1708), in the maritime precincts at Greenwich and in numerous City churches.

Nicholas Hawksmoor joined contemporary James Gibb in taking Wren's English baroque style even further; one great example is St Martin-in-the-Fields in Trafalgar Sq.

Like Wren before him, Georgian architect John Nash aimed to impose some symmetry on unruly London and was slightly more successful in achieving this, through grand creations such as Trafalgar Sq and the elegantly curving arcade of Regent St. Built in similar style, the surrounding squares of St James's remain some of the finest public spaces in London – little wonder then that Queen Victoria decided to move into the recently vacated Buckingham Palace in 1837.

The Gherkin

Towards Modernity

The Victorians replaced grand vision with pragmatism; they desired ornate civic buildings that reflected the glory of empire but were open to the masses, too. The Victorian-style turrets, towers and arches are best exemplified by the flamboyant Natural History Museum (Alfred Waterhouse), St Pancras Chambers (George Gilbert Scott) and the Houses of Parliament (Augustus Pugin and Charles Barry), the latter replacing the Palace of Westminster that had largely burnt down in 1834.

The Victorians and Edwardians were also ardent builders of functional and cheap terraced houses, many of which became slums, but today house London's urban middle classes.

The first decade of the 20th century and the interwar years were relatively quiet for British architecture. A couple of notable exceptions include the superb art-nouveau Michelin House (1911) on Fulham Road, and Bush House, at the end of the Strand, designed by US architect Harvey Wiley Corbett (1873–1954): built between 1923 and 1935, it was the home of the BBC World Service until 2012 and is now part of King's College London.

A flirtation with art deco and the great suburban residential building boom of the 1930s was followed by a utilitarian modernism after WWII. Hitler's bombs wrought the worst destruction on London since the Great Fire of 1666, and the immediate postwar problem was a chronic housing shortage. As the city rushed to build new housing to replace terraces lost in the Blitz, low-cost developments and unattractive high-rise housing were thrown up on bombsites; many of these blocks still fragment the London horizon today.

Brutalism – a hard-edged and uncompromising architectural style that flourished from the 1950s to the 1970s, favouring concrete and reflecting socialist utopian principles – worked better on paper than in real life, but made significant contributions to London's architectural melange. Denys Lasdun's National Theatre, begun in 1966, is representative of the style.

Little building was undertaken in the 1970s apart from roads, and the recession of the late 1980s and early 1990s brought much development and speculation to a standstill.

Postmodernism & Beyond

The next big wave of development arrived in the derelict wasteland of the former London docks, which were emptied of their terraces and warehouses and rebuilt as towering skyscrapers and 'loft' apartments. Taking pride of place in the Docklands was Cesar Pelli's 244m-high 1 Canada Square (1991), commonly known as Canary Wharf and easily visible from central London. The City was also the site of architectural innovation, including the centrepiece 1986 Lloyd's of London, Richard Rogers' 'inside-out' masterpiece of ducts, pipes, glass and stainless steel.

But London's very first postmodern building (designed in the late 1980s by James Stirling but not completed till 1998) is considered to be No 1 Poultry, a playful shiplike City landmark faced with yellow and pink limestone. The graceful British Library (Colin St John Wilson, 1998), with its warm red-brick exterior, Asian-inspired touches and wonderfully bright interior, initially met a very hostile reception but has now become a popular landmark.

Contemporary Architecture

The end of the 1990s was marked by a glut of millennium projects, with new structures built and others rejuvenated: the London Eye, Tate Modern and the Millennium Bridge all spiced up the South Bank, while Norman Foster's iconic 30 St Mary Axe, better known as the Gherkin, started a new wave of skyscraper construction in the City. Even the once-mocked Millennium Dome won a new lease of life as the O2 concert and sports hall.

By the middle of the decade, London's biggest urban-development project ever was under way, the 200-hectare Queen Elizabeth Olympic Park in the Lea River Valley near Stratford in East London, where most of the events of the 2012 Summer Olympics and Paralympics took place. But the park would offer few architectural surprises – except for Zaha Hadid's stunning London Aquatics Centre, a breathtaking structure suitably inspired by the fluid geometry of water; and the ArcelorMittal Orbit, a zany public work of art with viewing platforms, designed by the sculptor Anish Kapoor.

The spotlight may have been shining on East London, but the City and South London have also undergone energetic developments. Most notable is the so-called Shard, at 310m the EU's tallest building, completed in 2012. In the City, the Walkie Talkie has divided opinions, but its junglelike Sky Garden on levels 35 to 37 is universally loved.

In the City, 1 Undershaft will almost match the Shard for height – the maximum currently permissible – and become (some time around 2023) the tallest in the Square Mile at 73 floors.

Shakespeare's Globe (p216)

Literary London

For over six centuries, London has been the setting for works of prose. Indeed, the capital has been the inspiration for the masterful imaginations of such eminent wordsmiths as Shakespeare, Defoe, Dickens, Orwell, Conrad, Eliot, Greene and Woolf (even though not all were native to the city, or even British).

It's hard to reconcile the bawdy portrayal of London in Geoffrey Chaucer's *Canterbury Tales* with Charles Dickens' bleak hellhole in *Oliver Twist,* let alone Daniel Defoe's plague-ravaged metropolis in *Journal of the Plague Year* with Zadie Smith's multiethnic romp *White Teeth.* Ever-changing, yet somehow eerily consistent, London has left its mark on some of the most influential writing in the English language.

Chaucerian London

The first literary reference to London appears in Chaucer's *Canterbury Tales,* written between 1387 and 1400: the 29 pilgrims of the tale gather for their trip to Canterbury at the Tabard Inn in Talbot Yard, Southwark, and agree to share stories on the way there and back. The inn burned down in 1676; a blue plaque marks the site of the building today.

Shakespearian London

Born in Warwickshire, William Shakespeare (1564–1616) spent most of his life as an actor and playwright in London around the turn of the 17th century. He trod the boards of several theatres in Shoreditch and Southwark and wrote his greatest tragedies, among them *Hamlet, Othello, Macbeth* and *King Lear,* for the original Globe theatre on the South Bank. Although London was his home for most of his life, Shakespeare set nearly all his plays in foreign or imaginary lands. Only *Henry IV: Parts I & II* include a London setting – a tavern called the Boar's Head in Eastcheap.

Defoe & 18th-Century London

Daniel Defoe might be classified as the first true London writer, both living in and writing about the city during the early 18th century. He is most famous for his novels *Robinson Crusoe* (1719–20) and *Moll Flanders* (1722), which he wrote while living in Church St in Stoke Newington. Defoe's *Journal of the Plague Year* is his most absorbing account of London life, documenting the horrors of the Great Plague during the summer and autumn of 1665, when the author was just five years old.

Dickensian & 19th-Century London

Two early 19th-century Romantic poets drew inspiration from London. John Keats, born above a Moorgate public house in 1795, wrote 'Ode to a Nightingale' while living near Hampstead Heath in 1819 and 'Ode on a Grecian Urn' reportedly after viewing the Parthenon frieze in the British Museum the same year. William Wordsworth discovered inspiration for the poem 'Upon Westminster Bridge' while visiting London in 1802.

Charles Dickens was the definitive London author. When his father and family were interned at Marshalsea Prison in Southwark for not paying their debts, 12-year-old Charles was forced to fend for himself on the streets. That grim period provided a font of experiences from which to draw. His novels most closely associated with London are *Oliver Twist,* with its gang of thieves led by Fagin in Clerkenwell, and *Little Dorrit,* whose hero was born in the Marshalsea. The house in Bloomsbury where he wrote *Oliver Twist* and two other novels now houses the expanded Charles Dickens Museum.

Arthur Conan Doyle (1858–1930) portrayed a very different London. His pipe-smoking, cocaine-injecting sleuth, Sherlock Holmes, came to exemplify a cool and unflappable Englishness. Letters to the mythical hero and his admiring friend, Dr Watson, still arrive at 221b Baker St.

London at the end of the 19th century appears in many books, but especially those of Somerset Maugham. His first novel, *Liza of Lambeth,* was based on his experiences as an intern in the slums of South London, while *Of Human Bondage* provides a portrait of late-Victorian London.

American Writers & London in the 20th Century

Among Americans who lived in and wrote about London at the turn of the 20th century, Henry James stands supreme with his *Daisy Miller* and *The Europeans. The People of the Abyss*, by socialist writer Jack London, is a sensitive portrait of poverty and despair in the East End. St Louis–born TS Eliot moved to London in 1915, where he published his poem

Charles Dickens Museum interior (p45)

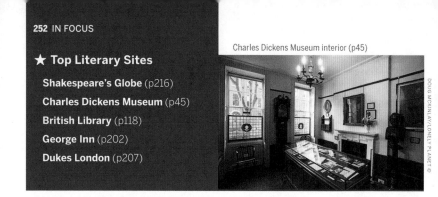

★ **Top Literary Sites**

Shakespeare's Globe (p216)

Charles Dickens Museum (p45)

British Library (p118)

George Inn (p202)

Dukes London (p207)

'The Love Song of J Alfred Prufrock' almost immediately and moved on to his ground-breaking epic 'The Waste Land', in which London is portrayed as an 'unreal city'.

Interwar Developments

Between the world wars, PG Wodehouse depicted London high life with his hilarious lampooning of the English upper classes in the Jeeves stories. Quentin Crisp, the self-proclaimed 'stately homo of England', provided the flipside, recounting in his ribald and witty memoir *The Naked Civil Servant* (not published until 1968) what it was like to be openly gay in sexually repressed prewar London. George Orwell's experience of living as a beggar and manual labourer in London's East End coloured his book *Down and Out in Paris and London* (1933).

The Modern Age

The End of the Affair, Graham Greene's novel chronicling a passionate and doomed romance, takes place in and around Clapham Common just after WWII, while Elizabeth Bowen's *The Heat of the Day* is a sensitive, if melodramatic, account of living through the Blitz.

Colin MacInnes described the bohemian, multicultural world of 1950s Notting Hill in *Absolute Beginners*, while Doris Lessing captured the political mood of 1960s London in *The Four-Gated City*, the last of her five-book *Children of Violence* series. Lessing also provided some of the funniest and most vicious portrayals of 1990s London in *London Observed*. Nick Hornby, nostalgic about his days as a young football fan in *Fever Pitch* and obsessive about vinyl in *High Fidelity*, found himself the voice of a generation.

This period is marked by the emergence of multicultural voices. Hanif Kureishi explored London from the perspective of young Pakistanis in his best-known novels *The Black Album* and *The Buddha of Suburbia,* while Timothy Mo's *Sour Sweet* is a poignant and funny account of a Chinese family in the 1960s trying to adjust to English life.

The decades leading up to the turn of the millennium were great ones for British literature, bringing a dazzling new generation of writers to the fore, such as Martin Amis *(Money, London Fields)*, Julian Barnes *(Metroland, Talking it Over)*, Ian McEwan *(Enduring Love, Atonement)* and Salman Rushdie *(Midnight's Children, The Satanic Verses)*.

Millennium London

Helen Fielding's *Bridget Jones's Diary* and its sequel, *Bridget Jones: The Edge of Reason*, launched the 'chick lit' genre; *Bridget Jones* transcended the travails of a young single Londoner to become a worldwide phenomenon.

Peter Ackroyd named the city as the love of his life; *London: the Biography* was his inexhaustible paean to the capital. Iain Sinclair is the bard of Hackney, who, like Ackroyd, has spent his life obsessed with and fascinated by the capital. His acclaimed and ambitious *London Orbital*, a journey on foot around the M25, London's mammoth motorway bypass, is required London reading.

New, diverse voices also emerged, including Monica Ali, who brought the East End to life in *Brick Lane*, and Zadie Smith, whose incisive wit and wacky East London characters in *White Teeth* conquered millions.

Literary Blue Plaques

The very first of London's Blue Plaques was put up in 1867, identifying the birthplace of the poet Lord Byron at 24 Holles St, W1, off Cavendish Sq. Since then a large percentage – some 25% of the 900-odd in place – have honoured writers and poets. The locations include everything from the offices of publisher Faber & Faber at 24 Russell Sq, where TS Eliot worked, to the Primrose Hill residence of Irish poet and playwright WB Yeats at 23 Fitzroy Rd, NW1 (where, incidentally, the US poet Sylvia Plath also briefly lived and committed suicide in 1963).

The Current Scene

Home to most of the UK's major publishers and its best bookshops, London remains a vibrant place for writers and readers alike. 'Rediscovered' author Howard Jacobson, variously called the 'Jewish Jane Austen' and the 'English Philip Roth', won the Man Booker Prize in 2010 for *The Finkler Question*, the first time the prestigious award had gone to a comic novel in a quarter-century. Literary titan and huge commercial success Hilary Mantel, author of *Wolf Hall*, won the same award for her historical novel *Bring up the Bodies* two years later.

London continues to inspire Zadie Smith with *NW* (2012), which chronicles the life of four characters in northwest London, and *Swing Time* (2016), which recounts the tale of two mixed-race girls from North London. Elif Shafak's *Honour* tells of how traditional practices shatter and transform the lives of Turkish immigrants in 1970s East London, while Jake Arnott's *The Long Firm* is an intelligent Soho-based gangster yarn.

Every bookshop in town has a London section, where you will find many of these titles and lots more.

National Gallery (p56)

ZABOTNOVA INNA/SHUTTERSTOCK ©

Art

When it comes to art, London has traditionally been overshadowed by other European capitals. Yet many of history's greatest artists have spent time in London, including the likes of Monet and Van Gogh and, in terms of contemporary art, there's a compelling argument for putting London at the very top of the European pack.

Holbein to Turner

It wasn't until the rule of the Tudors that art began to take off in London. The German Hans Holbein the Younger (1497–1543) was court painter to Henry VIII, and one of his finest works, *The Ambassadors* (1533), hangs in the National Gallery. A batch of great portrait artists worked at court during the 17th century, the best being Anthony van Dyck (1599–1641), who painted the *Equestrian Portrait of Charles I* (1638), also in the National Gallery. Charles I was a keen collector of art and it was during his reign that the Raphael Cartoons (1515), now in the Victoria & Albert Museum, came to London.

Local artists began to emerge in the 18th century, including portrait and landscape painter Thomas Gainsborough (1727–88); William Hogarth (1697–1764), whose much-reproduced social commentary *A Rake's Progress* (1733) hangs in Sir John Soane's Museum; and poet, engraver and watercolourist William Blake (1757–1827). A superior visual artist to Blake, John

Constable (1776–1837) studied the clouds and skies above Hampstead Heath, sketching hundreds of scenes that he'd later match with subjects in his landscapes.

JMW Turner (1775–1851), with oils and watercolours, represented the pinnacle of 19th-century British art. Through innovative use of colour and gradations of light, he created a new atmosphere that captured the wonder, sublimity and terror of nature. His later works, including *The Fighting Temeraire* (1839), *Snow Storm: Steam-Boat off a Harbour's Mouth* (1842), *Peace – Burial at Sea* (1842) and *Rain, Steam and Speed – the Great Western Railway* (1844), now in the Tate Britain and the National Gallery, were increasingly abstract, and although widely vilified at the time, later inspired the Impressionist works of Claude Monet.

The Pre-Raphaelites to Hockney

The brief but splendid flowering of the pre-Raphaelite Brotherhood (1848–54) took its inspiration from the Romantic poets, abandoning the pastel-coloured rusticity of the day in favour of big, bright and intense depictions of medieval legends and female beauty. The movement's main proponents were William Holman Hunt, John Everett Millais and Dante Gabriel Rossetti; artists Edward Burne-Jones and Ford Madox Brown were also strongly associated with the pre-Raphaelites. Works by all can be found at Tate Britain, with highlights being Millais' *Mariana* (1851) and *Ophelia* (1851–2), Rossetti's *Ecce Ancilla Domini!* (The Annunciation, 1850), John William Waterhouse's *The Lady of Shalott* (1888) and William Holman Hunt's *The Awakening Conscience* (1853).

In the early 20th century, cubism and futurism helped generate the short-lived Vorticists, a modernist group of London artists and poets, led by the dapper Wyndham Lewis (1882–1957), that sought to capture dynamism in artistic form. Sculptors Henry Moore (1898–1986) and Barbara Hepworth (1903–75) both typified the modernist movement in British sculpture. You can see examples of their work in the gardens of Kenwood House in Hampstead Heath.

After WWII, art transformed yet again. In 1945 the tortured, Irish-born painter Francis Bacon (1909–92) caused a stir when he exhibited his contorted *Three Studies for Figures at the Base of a Crucifixion* – now on display at the Tate Britain – and afterwards continued to spook the art world with his repulsive yet mesmerising visions. Also at the Tate Britain is Bacon's *Triptych – August 1972*, painted in the aftermath of his lover George Dyer's suicide.

The late art critic Robert Hughes once eulogised Bacon's contemporary, Lucian Freud (1922–2011), as 'the greatest living realist painter'. Freud's early work was often surrealist, but from the 1950s the bohemian Freud exclusively focused on pale, muted portraits – often nudes, and frequently of friends and family (although he also painted the Queen).

Also prominent in the 1950s was painter and collage artist Richard Hamilton (1922–2011), whose work includes the cover design of the Beatles' 1968 *White Album*. London in the swinging '60s was perfectly encapsulated by pop art, best articulated by David Hockney, born in 1937 and still very active at the time of writing. Hockney gained a reputation as one of the leading pop artists (although he rejected the label) through his early use of magazine-style images, but after a move to California, his work became increasingly naturalistic. Two of his most famous works are the Tate-owned *Mr and Mrs Clark and Percy* (1971) and *A Bigger Splash* (1974).

Gilbert & George were quintessential English conceptual artists of the 1960s. The Spitalfields odd couple are still at the heart of the British art world, now a part of the establishment.

Brit Art

Despite its incredibly rich art collections, Britain had never led, dominated or even really participated in a particular artistic epoch or style as Paris had in the 1920s or New York in the 1950s. That all changed in the twilight of the 20th century, when 1990s London became the beating heart of the art world.

The Vendramin Family by Titian, National Gallery (p56)

★ **Best for British Art**

Tate Britain (p54)

National Gallery (p57)

National Portrait Gallery (p57)

Summer Exhibition, Royal Academy of Arts (p51)

Brit Art sprang from a show called *Freeze,* which was staged in a Docklands warehouse in 1988, organised by artist and showman Damien Hirst and largely featuring his fellow graduates from Goldsmiths College. Influenced by pop culture and punk, this loose movement was soon catapulted to notoriety by the advertising guru Charles Saatchi, who bought an extraordinary number of works and came to dominate the scene.

Brit Art was brash, decadent, ironic, easy to grasp and eminently marketable. Hirst chipped in with a sliced cow preserved in formaldehyde; flies buzzed around another cow's head and were zapped in his early work *A Thousand Years*. Chris Ofili provoked with *The Holy Virgin Mary,* a painting of the black Madonna made partly with elephant excrement; brothers Jake and Dinos Chapman produced mannequins of children with genitalia on their heads; and Marcus Harvey created a portrait of notorious child-killer Myra Hindley entirely with children's handprints, whose value skyrocketed when it was repeatedly vandalised by the public.

The areas of Shoreditch, Hoxton, Spitalfields and Whitechapel – where many artists lived, worked and hung out – became the epicentre of the movement, and a rash of galleries moved in. For the 10 years or so that it rode a wave of publicity, the defining characteristics of Brit Art were notoriety and shock value. Its two biggest names, Hirst and Tracey Emin, inevitably became celebrities.

Some critics argued the hugely hyped movement was the product of a cultural vacuum, an example of the emperor's new clothes, with people afraid to criticise the works for fear they'd look stupid. Others praised its freshness and ingenuity.

Beyond Brit Art

On the fringes of Brit Art are a lot of less stellar but equally inspiring artists exploring other directions. A highlight is Richard Wilson's memorable installation *20:50* (1987) – a room filled waist-high with recycled oil. Entering down the walkway, you feel as if you've just been shot out into space. In Douglas Gordon's most famous work, *24 Hour Psycho* (1993), the Scottish video artist slowed Alfred Hitchcock's masterpiece so much it was stripped of its narrative and viewed more like a moving sculpture. Gary Hume first came to prominence with his *Doors* series: full-size paintings of hospital doors, which can be seen as powerful allegorical descriptions of despair – or just perfect reproductions of doors.

Today London counts some 1500 galleries, and its art scene is one of the world's biggest, with an international reach that rivals traditional hubs such as New York and Paris. Most of the established galleries are in districts like Mayfair, but for more cutting-edge work head for Hackney in East London and Bermondsey south of the river.

The biggest date on the art calendar is the controversial Turner Prize at the Tate Britain. Any British visual artist under the age of 50 is eligible to enter, although there is a strong preference for conceptual art. For many years, the prize was met with annual demonstrations by 'the Stuckists', who oppose conceptual art.

London buses near Big Ben (p52)

SAMOT/SHUTTERSTOCK ©

Survival Guide

Directory A–Z

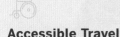

Accessible Travel

For travellers with access needs, London is a frustrating mix of user-friendliness and head-in-the-sand disinterest. New hotels and modern tourist attractions are legally required to be accessible to people in wheelchairs, but many historic buildings, B&Bs and guesthouses are in older buildings, which are hard or prohibitively expensive to adapt. Similarly, visitors with vision, hearing or cognitive impairments will find their needs met in a piecemeal fashion.

Transport is hit-and-miss too:

○ Around a quarter of tube stations, half of overground stations and all DLR and Queen Elizabeth line stations have step-free access.

○ Buses can be lowered to street level when they stop and wheelchair users travel free.

○ All black cabs are wheelchair-accessible.

○ Guide dogs are universally welcome on public transport and in hotels, restaurants, attractions etc.

Useful Resources

VisitLondon (www.visitlondon.com/traveller-information/essential-information/accessible-london) The tourist board's accessible-travel page has useful links and information on accessible shops, hotels and toilets.

Accessible London (http://www.disabledgo.com/accessible-london-visit-london) Professionally audited guide, produced by DisabledGo, to access in the city.

Transport for London (www.tfl.gov.uk/transport-accessibility/) All the information you'll need to get around London on public transport.

Customs Regulations

Until Brexit comes into force, the UK distinguishes between goods bought duty-free outside the EU and those bought in another EU country, where taxes and duties will have already been paid.

If you exceed your duty-free allowance, you will have to pay tax on the items. For European goods, there is officially no limit to how much you can bring, but customs uses certain guidelines to distinguish between personal and commercial use.

Discount Cards

The **London Pass** (1/2/3/6/10 days £75/99/125/169/199) is worthwhile for visitors who want to take in lots of paid sights in a short time. The pass offers free entry and queue-jumping to all major attractions, and can be adapted to include use of the Underground and buses. Child passes are available too. Check the website for details.

You can download the app to your smartphone or collect your pass from the **London Pass Redemption Desk** (☏020-7293 0972; www.londonpass.com; 11a Charing Cross Rd, WC2; ☉10am-4.30pm; ⓤLeicester Sq), near Leicester Sq.

Emergency

Dial ☏999 to call the police, fire brigade or an ambulance in case of an emergency.

Entry & Exit Formalities

UK immigration authorities are stringent and methodical, so queues can get long at passport control.

Electricity

**Type G
230V/50Hz**

Etiquette

Although largely informal in their everyday dealings, Londoners do observe some (unspoken) rules of etiquette.

Strangers Unless asking for directions, British people generally won't start a conversation at bus stops or on tube platforms. More latitude is given to non-British people.

Greetings When meeting someone formally for the first time, shake hands.

Queues The British don't tolerate queue jumping. Any attempt to do so will receive tutting and protest.

Tube Stand on the right and pass on the left while riding an Underground escalator.

Bargaining Haggling over the price of goods (but not food) is OK in markets, but non-existent in shops.

Punctuality It's not good form to turn up more than 10 minutes late for drinks or dinner. If you're unavoidably late, keep everyone in the loop.

Apologise The British love apologising. If you bump into someone on the tube, say sorry; they may apologise back, even if you are to blame.

Health

EU nationals can obtain free emergency treatment (and, in some cases, reduced-cost healthcare) on presentation of a **European Health Insurance Card** (www.ehic.org.uk). It's still too early to say what will happen to the EHIC card after the UK leaves the EU, but it would be advisable to check before travelling to London.

Reciprocal arrangements with the UK allow Australians, New Zealanders and residents and nationals of several other countries to receive free emergency medical treatment and subsidised dental care through the National Health Service. They can use hospital emergency departments, GPs and dentists. For a full list visit the 'Services near you' section of the NHS website.

Hospitals

A number of hospitals have 24-hour accident and emergency departments. Centrally located hospitals:
University College London Hospital (020-3456 7890; www.uclh.nhs.uk; 235 Euston Rd, NW1; Warren St or Euston Sq)

Guy's Hospital (020-7188 7188; www.guysandstthomas.nhs.uk; Great Maze Pond, SE1; London Bridge)

Insurance

Travel insurance is advisable as it offers greater flexibility over where and how you're treated and covers expenses for an ambulance and repatriation that will not be picked up by the NHS.

It will also cover mishaps such as loss of baggage, cancelled flights and so forth.

Book Your Stay Online

For more accommodation reviews by Lonely Planet authors, check out http://hotels.lonelyplanet.com/london. You'll find independent reviews, as well as recommendations on the best places to stay. Best of all, you can book online.

Pharmacies

The main pharmacy chains in London are Boots and Superdrug; a branch of either – or both – can be found on virtually every high street.

Internet Access

● Virtually every hotel in London now provides wi-fi free of charge.

● A huge number of cafes, and many restaurants, offer free wi-fi to customers, including major chain cafes. Cultural venues such as the Barbican and the Southbank Centre also have free wi-fi.

Legal Matters

Should you face any legal difficulties while in London, visit a branch of the Citizens Advice Bureau (www.citizensadvice.org.uk), or contact your embassy.

Drugs

Illegal drugs of every type are widely available in London, especially in clubs. Nonetheless, all the usual drug warnings apply. If you're caught with marijuana, you're likely to be arrested. Possession of harder drugs, including heroin and cocaine, is always treated seriously.

Searches on entering clubs are common.

Fines

In general you rarely have to pay on the spot for an offence. The exceptions are trains, the tube and buses, where people who can't produce a valid ticket for the journey when asked to by an inspector can be fined there and then.

LGBT+ Travellers

Protection from discrimination is enshrined in law, and same-sex couples have the right to marry. That's not to say that homophobia does not exist. Always report homophobic crimes to the police.

Useful Resources

60by80 (www.60by80.com/london) Gay travel information.

Boyz (www.boyz.co.uk) Weekly magazine covering the bar and club scenes.

Diva (www.divamag.co.uk) Monthly lesbian magazine.

Gay Times (www.gaytimes.co.uk) Long-standing monthly gay men's mag.

Pride Life (www.pridelife.com) Quarterly news and lifestyle magazine.

QX (www.qxmagazine.com) Another weekly mag devoted mainly to men's venues.

Time Out London LGBT (www.timeout.com/london/lgbt) Bar, club and events listings.

Money

ATMs are widespread. Major credit cards are accepted everywhere. The best place to change money is in post-office branches, which do not charge a commission.

Currency

The pound sterling (£) is the unit of currency. One pound sterling is made up of 100 pence (called 'pee', colloquially).

Notes come in denominations of £5, £10, £20 and £50, while coins are 1p ('penny'), 2p, 5p, 10p, 20p, 50p, £1 and £2.

Credit & Debit Cards

● Credit and debit cards are accepted almost universally in London, from restaurants and bars to shops and by some taxis.

● American Express and Diners Club are far less widely used than Visa and MasterCard.

● Contactless cards and payments (which do not require a chip and pin or a signature) are increasingly widespread (watch for the wi-fi-like symbol on cards, shops, taxis, buses, the Underground, rail services and other transport options). Transactions are limited to a maximum of £30.

Opening Hours

The following are standard opening hours.

Banks 9am–5pm Monday–Friday

Post offices 9am–5.30pm Monday–Friday and 9am–noon Saturday

Pubs & bars 11am–11pm (many are open later)

Restaurants noon–2.30pm and 6–11pm

Sights 10am–6pm

Shops 9am–7pm Monday–Saturday, noon–6pm Sunday

Public Holidays

Most attractions and businesses close for a couple of days over Christmas and sometimes Easter. Places that normally shut on Sunday will probably close on bank-holiday Mondays.

New Year's Day 1 January

Good Friday Late March/April

Easter Monday Late March/April

May Day Holiday First Monday in May

Spring Bank Holiday Last Monday in May

Summer Bank Holiday Last Monday in August

Christmas Day 25 December

Boxing Day 26 December

Practicalities

Weights & Measures The UK uses a confusing mix of metric and imperial systems.

Smoking & Vaping Forbidden in all enclosed public places. Most pubs have some sort of smoking area outside. Some pubs and restaurants have a no-vaping policy (so check for each establishment); vaping is not allowed on buses, the tube or trains in London.

Safe Travel

London is a fairly safe city for its size, but exercise common sense.

• Terrorist attacks have afflicted London in recent years, but risks to individual visitors are remote. Report anything suspicious to the police by calling ☑999 (emergency) or ☑101 (non-emergency).

• Keep an eye on your handbag/wallet, especially in bars and nightclubs, and in crowded areas such as the Underground.

• Be discreet with your tablet/smartphone – snatching happens.

• If catching a cab after a night's clubbing, get a black taxi or licensed minicab.

• Victims of rape and sexual abuse can contact **Rape Crisis England & Wales** (☑0808 802 9999, noon-2.30pm & 7-9.30pm; www.rapecrisis.org.uk); anyone in emotional distress can contact **Samaritans** (☑

116 123 toll free, 24 hours; www.samaritans.org).

Telephone

Buy local SIM cards for European and Australian phones, or a pay-as-you-go phone. Set other phones to international roaming. EU users do not pay roaming charges.

Useful Numbers

London's area code	☑020
International access code	☑00
Police, fire or ambulance	☑999
Reverse charge/ collect calls	☑155

Toilets

Train stations, bus terminals and attractions generally have good facilities, providing also for people with disabilities and those with young children. You'll also find public toilets across the city, some operated by local councils, others automated and self-cleaning. Most charge 50p. Department stores and museums generally have toilets. It's now an offence to urinate in the streets. To locate your nearest toilet, consult the Great British Public Toilet Map (www.toiletmap.org.uk), or download one of several toilet-finding apps to your smartphone.

Tourist Information

Visit London can fill you in on everything from tourist attractions and events (Changing the Guard, Chinese New Year parade etc) to river trips and tours, accommodation, eating, theatre, shopping, children's activities and LGBT+ venues. Kiosks are dotted about the city and can provide maps and brochures; some branches book theatre tickets.

Heathrow Airport (www.visit london.com/tag/tourist-information-centre; Terminal 1, 2 & 3 Underground station concourse; ⊗7.30am-8.30pm)

King's Cross St Pancras Station (www.visitlondon.com/tag/tourist-information-centre; Western Ticket Hall, Euston Rd, N1; ⊗8am-6pm)

Liverpool Street Station (www.visitlondon.com/tag/tourist-information-centre;

Liverpool St tube station, EC2; ⊗8am-5pm; ⓤLiverpool St)

Victoria Station (www.visit london.com/tag/tourist-information-centre; Victoria Station; ⊗8am-6pm; ⓤVictoria)

Visas

Not required for Australian, Canadian, New Zealand and US visitors, as well as several other nations, for stays of up to six months.

Immigration to the UK is becoming tougher, particularly for those seeking to work or study. The exit of the UK from the EU is planned for 2019 and entry requirements for EU nationals may change. Make sure you check the website of the UK Border Agency (www.gov.uk/check-uk-visa) or with your local British embassy or consulate for the most up-to-date information.

Women Travellers

Female visitors to London are unlikely to have many problems, provided they take the usual big-city precautions. Don't get into an Underground carriage with no one else in it or with just one or two men. And if you feel unsafe, you should take a taxi or licensed minicab.

Transport

Arriving in London

Most people arrive in London by air, but an increasing number of visitors coming from Europe let the *Eurostar* (the Channel Tunnel train) take the strain, while buses from the continent are also an option.

The city has five airports: Heathrow, which is the largest, to the west; Gatwick to the south; Stansted to the northeast; Luton to the northwest; and London City in the Docklands.

Flights, cars and tours can be booked online at lonelyplanet.com.

Heathrow Airport

Some 15 miles west of central London, Heathrow Airport (LHR; www.heathrowairport.com) is one of the world's busiest international airports; it has four terminals, numbered 2 to 5 – Terminal 1 was closed in 2015.

Train

Three Underground stations on the **Elizabeth and Piccadilly lines** serve Heathrow: one for Terminals 2 and 3, another for Terminal 4, and the terminus for

Terminal 5. The Elizabeth Line is the cheapest and quickest way of getting to Heathrow (30 minutes to central London), with stops in west London (Paddington), the West End (Bond Street and Tottenham Court Rd), the city (Liverpool St), and Canary Wharf (the financial district) among others. It runs from around 5am to midnight, with trains every few minutes. You can get your Oyster Card (travel card for all London transport) at the station.

Bus

National Express (www.nationalexpress.com) coaches (one-way from £6, 35 to 90 minutes, every 30 minutes to one hour) link the Heathrow Central bus station with London Victoria Coach Station.

Taxi

A metered black-cab trip to/from central London will cost between £48 and £90 and take 45 minutes to an hour, depending on traffic and your departure point.

Gatwick Airport

Located some 30 miles south of central London, Gatwick (LGW; www.gatwickairport.com) is smaller than Heathrow and is Britain's number-two airport, mainly for international flights. The North and South Terminals are linked by a 24-hour shuttle train, with the journey time about three minutes.

Train

National Rail (www.nationalrail.co.uk) Regular train services to/from London Bridge (30 minutes, every 15 to 30 minutes), London King's Cross (55 minutes, every 15 to 30 minutes) and London Victoria (30 minutes, every 10 to 15 minutes). Fares vary depending on the time of travel and the train company, but allow £10 to £20 for a single trip.

Gatwick Express (www.gatwickexpress.com; one way/return adult £19.90/36.70, child £9.95/18.35) Trains run every 15 minutes from the station near the Gatwick South Terminal to London Victoria. Services run from around 5am to about 11pm. The journey takes 30 minutes; book online for the best deals.

Bus

National Express (www.nationalexpress.com) coaches run throughout the day from Gatwick to London Victoria Coach Station (one-way from £8). Services depart hourly around the clock. Journey time is between 80 minutes and two hours, depending on traffic.

Taxi

A metered black-cab trip to/from central London costs around £100 and takes just over an hour. Minicabs are usually cheaper.

Stansted Airport

Stansted (www.stanstedairport.com) is 35 miles northeast of central London in the direction of Cambridge. An international airport, Stansted serves a multitude of mainly European destinations and is used primarily by low-cost carriers such as Ryanair.

Train

Stansted Express (☎0345 600 7245; www.stanstedexpress.com; one-way/return £17/29) This rail service (45 minutes, every 15 to 30 minutes) links the airport and Liverpool St station. From the airport, the first train leaves at 5.30am, the last at 12.30am. Trains depart Liverpool St station from 4.40am (on some days at 3.40am) to 11.25pm.

Bus

National Express (www.nationalexpress.com) coaches run around the clock, offering more than 100 services per day.

Airbus A6 Runs to Victoria Coach Station (around one hour to 1½ hours, every 20 minutes) via Marble Arch, Paddington, Baker St and Golders Green (one way from £10).

Airbus A7 Also runs to Victoria Coach Station (around one hour to 1½ hours, every 20 minutes), via Waterloo and Southwark (one-way from £10).

Airbus A8 Runs to Liverpool St station (one-way from £6, 60 to 80 minutes, every 30 minutes), via Bethnal Green, Shoreditch High St and Mile End.

EasyBus (www.easybus.co.uk) Runs services to Baker St and Old St tube stations every 15 minutes. The journey (one-way from £4.95) takes one hour from Old St, 1¼ hours from Baker St.

Climate Change & Travel

Every form of transport that relies on carbon-based fuel generates CO_2, the main cause of human-induced climate change. Modern travel is dependent on aeroplanes, which might use less fuel per kilometre per person than most cars but travel much greater distances. The altitude at which aircraft emit gases (including CO_2) and particles also contributes to their climate change impact. Many websites offer 'carbon calculators' that allow people to estimate the carbon emissions generated by their journey and, for those who wish to do so, to offset the impact of the greenhouse gases emitted with contributions to portfolios of climate-friendly initiatives throughout the world. Lonely Planet offsets the carbon footprint of all staff and author travel.

Terravision (www.terravision. eu) Links Stansted to Liverpool St station (one-way from £9, 55 minutes) and Victoria Coach Station (from £10, two hours) every 20 to 40 minutes between 6am and 1am. All buses have wi-fi.

Taxi

A metered black-cab trip to/from central London costs around £130. Minicabs are cheaper.

Luton Airport

A smallish airport 32 miles northwest of London, Luton (LTN; www.london-luton. co.uk) generally caters for cheap charter flights and discount airlines.

Train

National Rail (www.national rail.co.uk) Has 24-hour services (one-way from £14.70, 26 to 50 minutes, departures every six minutes to one hour) from London St Pancras International to Luton Airport Parkway station, from where an airport shuttle bus (one-way/return £2.30/3.60) will take you to the airport in 10 minutes.

Bus

Airbus A1 (www.national express.com; one-way from £11) Runs over 60 times daily to London Victoria Coach Station (one-way £11), via Portman Square, Baker Street, St John's Wood, Finchley Road and Golders Green. It takes around 1½ hours.

Green Line Bus 757 (☑0344 800 4411; www.greenline.co.uk; one-way/return £11/17) Runs to Luton Airport from London Victoria Coach Station (one-way £11) every 30 minutes on a 24-hour service via Marble Arch, Baker St, Finchley Rd and Brent Cross.

Taxi

A metered black-cab trip to/from central London costs about £110.

London City Airport

Its proximity to central London, which is just 6 miles to the west, as well as to the commercial district of the Docklands, means **London City Airport** (☑020-7646 0088; www.londoncityairport. com; Hartmann Rd, E16; ☎; Ⓤ London City Airport) is predominantly a gateway airport for business travellers.

Train

Docklands Light Railway (DLR; www.tfl.gov.uk/dlr) Stops at the London City Airport station (one-way £2.80 to £3.30). The journey to Bank takes just over 20 minutes.

Taxi

A metered black-cab trip to the City/Oxford St/ Earl's Court costs about £25/35/50.

St Pancras International Train Station

The arrival point for the **Eurostar** (www.eurostar. com) trains to/from Europe, including Paris, Brussels, Lille, Amsterdam and Rotterdam, is connected by many Underground lines to the rest of the city.

Getting Around

The tube, DLR and Overground networks are ideal for zooming across the city; buses, cycling or walking are great for shorter journeys.

Underground

The London Underground ('the tube'; 11 colour-coded lines) is part of an integrated-transport system that also includes the Elizabeth Line (a fast rail link), Docklands Light Railway (DLR; www.tfl.gov.uk/dlr; a driverless overhead train operating in the eastern part of the city) and Overground network (mostly outside of Zone 1 and sometimes underground). It is overall the quickest and easiest way of getting around the city, if not the cheapest.

The first trains operate from around 5.30am Monday to Saturday and 6.45am Sunday. The last trains leave around 12.30am Monday to Saturday and 11.30pm Sunday.

Additionally, selected lines (the Victoria and Jubilee lines, plus most of the Piccadilly, Central and Northern lines) run all night on Friday and Saturday to get revellers home (on what is called the 'Night Tube'), with trains every 10 minutes or so. Fares are off-peak.

During weekend closures, schedules, maps and alternative route suggestions are posted in every station, and staff are at hand to help redirect you.

Some stations, most famously Leicester Sq and Covent Garden, are much closer in reality than they appear on the map.

Fares

○ London is divided into nine concentric fare zones.

○ It will always be cheaper to travel with an Oyster Card or a contactless card than a paper ticket.

○ Children under the age of 11 travel free; 11- to 15-year-olds are half-price if registered on an accompanying adult's Oyster Card (register at Zone 1 or Heathrow tube stations).

Bus

London's ubiquitous red double-decker buses afford great views of the city, but be aware that the going can be slow, thanks to traffic jams and dozens of commuters getting on and off at every stop.

There are excellent bus maps at every stop detailing all routes and destinations served from that particular area (generally a few bus stops within a two- to three-minute walk, shown on a local map).

Bus services normally operate from 5am to 11.30pm.

Night Bus

○ More than 50 night-bus routes (prefixed with the letter 'N') run from around 11.30pm to 5am.

○ There are also another 60 bus routes operating 24 hours; the frequency decreases between 11pm and 5am.

Oyster Card

The Oyster Card is a smart card on which you can store credit towards 'prepay' fares, as well as Travelcards. Oyster Cards are valid across the entire public-transport network in London.

All you need to do when entering a station is touch your card on a reader (which has a yellow circle with the image of an Oyster Card on it) and then touch again on your way out. The system will then deduct the appropriate amount of credit from your card. For bus journeys, you only need to touch once upon boarding.

Oyster Cards ensure you will never pay more than the appropriate Travelcard (peak or off-peak) once the daily 'price cap' has been reached.

Oyster Cards can be bought (£5 refundable deposit required) and topped up at any Underground station, travel information centre or shop displaying the Oyster logo. To get your deposit back along with any remaining credit, simply return your Oyster Card at a ticket booth.

Contactless cards (which do not require chip and pin or a signature) can now be used directly on Oyster Card readers and are subject to the same Oyster fares. Foreign visitors should bear in mind the cost of card transactions.

Fares

Cash cannot be used on London's buses. Instead you must pay with an Oyster Card, Travelcard or a contactless payment card. Bus fares are a flat £1.50, no matter the distance travelled.

Children aged under 11 years travel free; 11- to 15-year-olds are half-price if registered on an accompanying adult's Oyster Card (register at Zone 1 or Heathrow tube stations).

Taxis

Black Cabs

The black cab is as much a feature of the London cityscape as the red double-decker bus.

◦ Cabs are available for hire when the yellow sign above the windscreen is lit; just stick your arm out to signal one.

◦ Fares are metered, with a flagfall charge of £2.60 (covering the first 235m during a weekday), rising by increments of 20p for each subsequent 117m.

◦ Fares are more expensive in the evenings and overnight.

◦ Apps such as **mytaxi** use your smartphone's GPS to locate the nearest black cab. You only pay the metered fare.

Minicabs

◦ Minicabs, which are licensed, are cheaper (usually) competitors of black cabs.

◦ Unlike black cabs, minicabs cannot legally be hailed on the street; they must be hired by phone or directly from one of the minicab offices (every high street has at least one and most clubs work with a minicab firm to send revellers home safely).

◦ Don't accept unsolicited offers from individuals claiming to be minicab drivers – they are just guys with cars.

◦ Minicabs don't have meters; there's usually a fare set by the dispatcher. Make sure you ask before setting off.

◦ Your hotel or host will be able to recommend a reputable minicab company in the neighbourhood; every Londoner has the number of at least one company.

◦ Apps such as Uber allow you to book a minicab in double-quick time and can save you money.

Boat

One of several companies operating boats along the River Thames, **Thames Clippers** (www.thames clippers.com; all zones adult/ child £9.90/4.95) offers proper commuter services. It's fast, pleasant and you're almost always guaranteed a seat and a view. Boats run every 20 minutes from 6am to between 10pm and 11pm. The route goes from London Eye Millennium Pier to Woolwich Arsenal Pier, with boats west to Putney, too.

Cycling

The **Santander Cycle** (☏0343 222 6666; www.tfl.gov. uk/modes/cycling/santander-cycles) scheme is a great, affordable and fun way to get around London.

Walking

You can't beat walking for neighbourhood exploration. There are plenty of bridges across the Thames and a couple of pedestrian tunnels beneath the river too.

Behind the Scenes

Acknowledgements

Climate map data adapted from Peel MC, Finlayson BL & McMahon TA (2007) 'Updated World Map of the Köppen-Geiger Climate Classification', Hydrology and Earth System Sciences, 11, 163344.

Cover photograph: St Paul's Cathedral reflected in the glass of One New Change shopping centre. David Jackson/Alamy ©

Illustration pp68-9 by Javier Zarracina.

This Book

This 4th edition of Lonely Planet's *Best of London* guidebook was curated by Emilie Filou, and researched and written by Emilie, Peter Dragicevich, Megan Eaves, Dan Fahey, Steve Fallon, Damian Harper, Lauren Keith, Claire Naylor, Niamh O'Brien, Tanya Parker, James Smart and Tasmin Waby. The previous three editions were also written by Emilie, Damian, Peter and Steve. This guidebook was produced by the following:

Destination Editor Cliff Wilkinson

Senior Product Editors Sandie Kestell, Genna Patterson

Regional Senior Cartographers Mark Griffiths, Alison Lyall

Product Editor Amy Lynch

Book Designers Aomi Ito, Virginia Moreno

Assisting Editors Janice Bird, Nigel Chin, Kate Mathews, Sam Wheeler

Cover Researcher Brendan Dempsey-Spencer

Thanks to Ronan Abayawickrema, Gwen Cotter, Liz Heynes, Will Jones, Alison Ridgway

---

Send Us Your Feedback

We love to hear from travellers – your comments keep us on our toes and help make our books better. Our well-travelled team reads every word on what you loved or loathed about this book. Although we cannot reply individually to postal submissions, we always guarantee that your feedback goes straight to the appropriate authors, in time for the next edition. Each person who sends us information is thanked in the next edition, the most useful submissions are rewarded with a selection of digital PDF chapters.

Visit lonelyplanet.com/contact to submit your updates and suggestions or to ask for help. Our award-winning website also features inspirational travel stories, news and discussions.

Note: We may edit, reproduce and incorporate your comments in Lonely Planet products such as guidebooks, websites and digital products, so let us know if you don't want your comments reproduced or your name acknowledged. For a copy of our privacy policy visit lonelyplanet.com/privacy.

Index

Canary Wharf financial district

London Maps

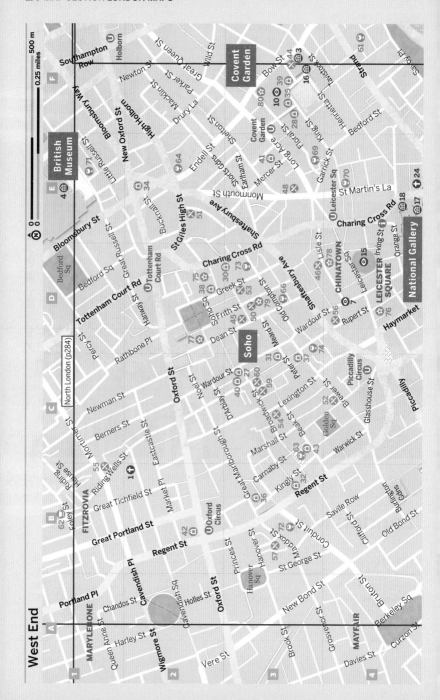

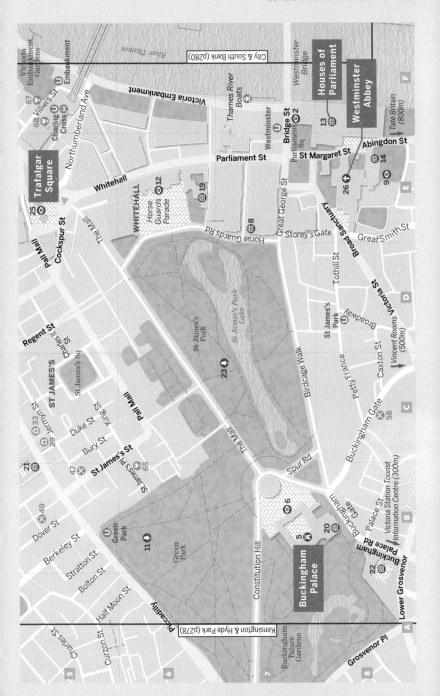

River Thames

City & South Bank (p280)

Victoria Embankment Gardens

Embankment

Villiers St

67

Charing Cross

68

Northumberland Ave

Victoria Embankment

Thames River Boats

Westminster Bridge

Houses of Parliament

Westminster Abbey

Westminster

Bridge St

2

Parliament Sq

13

St Margaret St

Abingdon St

14

9

26

Tate Britain (800m)

Parliament St

Great George St

Whitehall

Trafalgar Square

25

Cockspur St

Pall Mall

The Mall

WHITEHALL

Horse Guards Parade

12

19

8

Horse Guards Rd

Storey's Gate

Broad Sanctuary

Great Smith St

Tothill St

St James's Park Lake

St James's Park

St James's Park

Birdcage Walk

Broadway

Victoria St

Vincent Rooms (500m)

Regent St

Charles II St

St James's Sq

ST JAMES'S

Jermyn St

33 St

29

Duke St

King St

Pall Mall

Bury St

23

The Mall

Petty France

Caxton St

Buckingham Gate

21

47

St James's St

St James's St

65

Spur Rd

Victoria Station Tourist Information Centre (300m)

Buckingham Gate

58

49

Dover St

Green Park

Green Park

11

Constitution Hill

6

5

20

Buckingham Palace

Buckingham Palace Rd

Palace St

22

Lower Grosvenor Pl

Berkeley St

Stratton St

Bolton St

Half Moon St

Piccadilly

Kensington & Hyde Park (p278)

Buckingham Palace Gardens

Grosvenor Pl

Charles St

Curzon St

West End

◉ Sights

1	All Saints Margaret Street	B2
2	Big Ben	F7
3	Bond In Motion	F3
4	British Museum	E1
5	Buckingham Palace	B7
6	Changing the Guard	B7
7	Chinatown Gate	D4
8	Churchill War Rooms	E7
9	College Garden	E8
10	Covent Garden Piazza	F3
11	Green Park	B6
12	Horse Guards Parade	E6
13	Houses of Parliament	F8
14	Jewel Tower	E8
15	Leicester Square	D4
16	London Transport Museum	F3
17	National Gallery	E4
18	National Portrait Gallery	E4
19	No 10 Downing Street	E6
20	Queen's Gallery	B8
21	Royal Academy of Arts	B5
22	Royal Mews	B8
23	St James's Park	C7
24	St Martin-in-the-Fields	E4
25	Trafalgar Square	E5
26	Westminster Abbey	E8

ⓐ Shopping

27	Agent Provocateur	C3
28	Cambridge Satchel Company	F3
29	Fortnum & Mason	C5
30	Foyles	D3
31	Gosh!	C3
	Grant & Cutler	(see 30)
32	Hamleys	B3
33	Hatchards	C5
34	James Smith & Sons Umbrellas	E2
35	Karen Millen	F3
36	Liberty	B3
37	Lina Stores	C3
38	Milroy's of Soho	D2
39	Molton Brown	F3
	Ray's Jazz	(see 30)
40	Reckless Records	C3
41	Stanfords	E3
42	Topshop	B2
43	We Built This City	C3

⊗ Eating

44	Balthazar	F3
45	Barrafina	D3
46	Beijing Dumpling	D3
47	Cafe Murano	B5
48	Dishoom	E3
49	Gymkhana	B5
50	Hoppers	D3
51	Kanada-Ya	E2
52	Kiln	C4
53	Lina Stores	D3
54	Mildreds	C3
55	Mortimer House Kitchen	B1
56	Palomar	D4
57	Pollen Street Social	B3
	Portrait	(see 18)
58	Quilon	C8
59	Temper	C3
60	Yauatcha	C3

ⓓ Drinking & Nightlife

61	American Bar	F4
62	Attendant	B1
63	Cahoots	C3
64	Craft Beer Co	E2
65	Dukes London	B6
66	French House Soho	D3
67	Gordon's Wine Bar	F5
68	Heaven	F5
69	Lamb & Flag	E3
70	Mr Fogg's Tavern	E4
71	Museum Tavern	E1
72	Sketch	B3
73	Swift	D3
74	Yard	D3

ⓔ Entertainment

75	Borderline	D2
76	Comedy Store	D4
77	PizzaExpress Jazz Club	D2
78	Prince Charles Cinema	D4
79	Ronnie Scott's	D3
80	Royal Opera House	F3

Kensington & Hyde Park

◉ Sights
1 Albert Memorial E4
2 Apsley House..H4
3 Design Museum C5
4 Diana, Princess of Wales
    Memorial Fountain...................................F4
5 Holland Park B4
6 Hyde Park F3
7 Italian Gardens...E3
8 Kensington Gardens...................................E3
9 Kensington Palace......................................D4
10 Michelin House..F6
11 Natural History Museum E5
12 Portobello Road Market.............................B2
13 Science Museum E5
14 Sensational Butterflies E5
15 Serpentine Gallery......................................E4
16 Serpentine Lake..F4
17 Serpentine Sackler Gallery.......................F3
18 Speakers' Corner..G2
19 Victoria & Albert Museum F5
    Wildlife Photographer of
    the Year..(see 11)

◉ Activities, Courses & Tours
20 London Waterbus Company......................D1
21 Porchester Spa D2

◎ Shopping
22 Adam...B2
23 Browns H2
    Chinese Tea Company.....................(see 22)
    Conran Shop......................................(see 10)
24 Harrods G5
25 Harvey Nichols... G4
26 Honest Jon's..B1
27 Jo Loves H5
28 John Sandoe Books....................................G6
29 Lutyens & Rubinstein.................................B2
30 Peter Harrington...E6
31 Pickett G6
    Portobello Green Arcade ....(see 22)
32 Rough Trade West.......................................B2

33 Royal Trinity Hospice.................................C4
34 Selfridges H2

◈ Eating
35 Acklam Village Market...............................B2
    Chucs..(see 17)
36 Cockney's Pie and Mash B1
37 Comptoir Libanais......................................F5
38 Dinner by Heston Blumenthal...................G4
39 Foyer & Reading Room at
    Claridge's H2
40 Geales..C3
41 Kensington Palace Pavilion.......................D4
42 Ledbury C2
43 Lowry & Baker A1
44 Mazi..C3
45 Orangery..D3
46 Rabbit F6
47 Taquería C2
48 Tom's Kitchen..F6
    V&A Cafe...(see 19)
49 Wulf & Lamb G5

◉ Drinking & Nightlife
50 American Bar...H2
51 Anglesea Arms E6
52 Earl of Lonsdale..B2
53 Galvin at Windows......................................H4
54 Notting Hill Arts Club.................................C3
55 Queen's Arms E5
56 Tomtom Coffee House................................H5
57 Troubadour D6
58 Windsor Castle C4

◉ Entertainment
59 Electric Cinema B2
60 Gate Picturehouse C3
61 Opera Holland Park.....................................B4
62 Pheasantry...F6
63 Puppet Theatre Barge................................D1
64 Royal Albert Hall...E4
65 Royal Court Theatre G6
66 Wigmore Hall H2

Kensington & Hyde Park

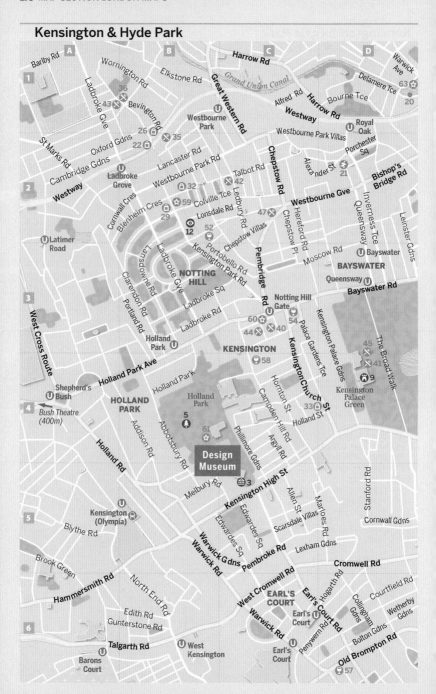

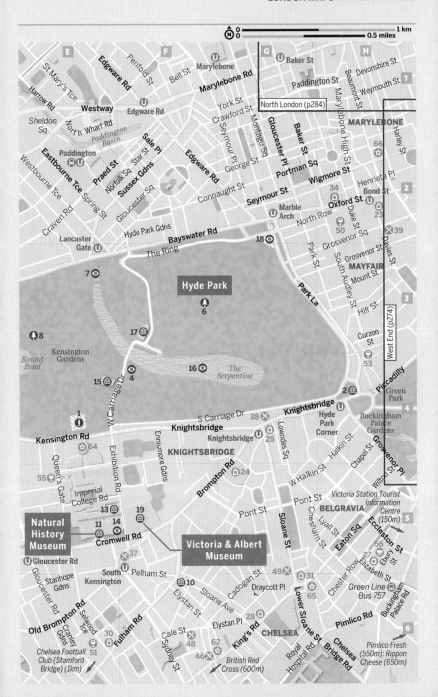

N

0 _____ 1 km
0 _____ 0.5 miles

E · F · G · H · 1

Penfold St

St Mary's Tce

Edgware Rd

Bell St

Marylebone

Marylebone

Marylebone Rd

Baker St

Paddington St

Devonshire St

Weymouth St

Harrow Rd

Westway

Edgware Rd

York St

Crawford St

Beaumont St

Marylebone High St

Harley St

MARYLEBONE

Sheldon Sq

North Wharf Rd

Paddington Basin

Sale Pl

Seymour Pl

Montagu Pl

Gloucester Pl

Baker St

66

Paddington

Praed St

Star St

Norfolk Sq

Sussex Gdns

George St

Portman Sq

Wigmore St

Henrietta Pl

Bond St

Eastbourne Tce

Westbourne Tce

Spring St

Gloucester St

Edgware Rd

Connaught St

Seymour St

Oxford St

Duke St

23

Craven Rd

Hyde Park Gdns

Marble Arch

North Row

50

Grosvenor Sq

Davies St

39

Lancaster Gate

Bayswater Rd

18

MAYFAIR

The Ring

Park St

South Audley St

7

Hyde Park

Park La

Mount St

Hill St

8

Kensington Gardens

6

West End (p274)

Curzon St

Round Pond

17

53

15

4

16

The Serpentine

Piccadilly

Green Park

2

1

S Carriage Dr

38

Knightsbridge

Hyde Park Corner

Buckingham Palace Gardens

Grosvenor Pl

Kensington Rd

64

Knightsbridge

Ennismore Gdns

W Carriage Dr

Knightsbridge

25

Lowndes Sq

Halkin St

Chapel St

Wilton Pl

55

Queen's Gate

Exhibition Rd

Imperial College Rd

KNIGHTSBRIDGE

Brompton Rd

24

W Halkin St

Pont St

BELGRAVIA

Victoria Station Tourist Information Centre (150m)

13

19

Natural History Museum

11

14

Cromwell Rd

Victoria & Albert Museum

Pont St

Sloane St

Lyall St

Cadogan St

Eaton Sq

27

Eccleston St

Gloucester Rd

37

South Kensington

Pelham St

10

Draycott Pl

Cheham St

49

31

65

Elizabeth St

Ebury

Green Line Bus 757

Buckingham Palace Rd

55

Stanhope Gdns

Gloucester Rd

Selwood Tce

Old Brompton Rd

Cranley Gdns

30

Fulham Rd

Cale St

Sydney St

Elystan St

Sloane Ave

Elystan Pl

48

62

46

King's Rd

Lower Sloane St

28

CHELSEA

Royal Hospital Rd

Pimlico Rd

Chester Row

Chelsea Bridge Rd

Pimlico Fresh (550m); Rippon Cheese (650m)

Chelsea Football Club (Stamford Bridge) (1km)

51

British Red Cross (600m)

North London (p284)

City & South Bank

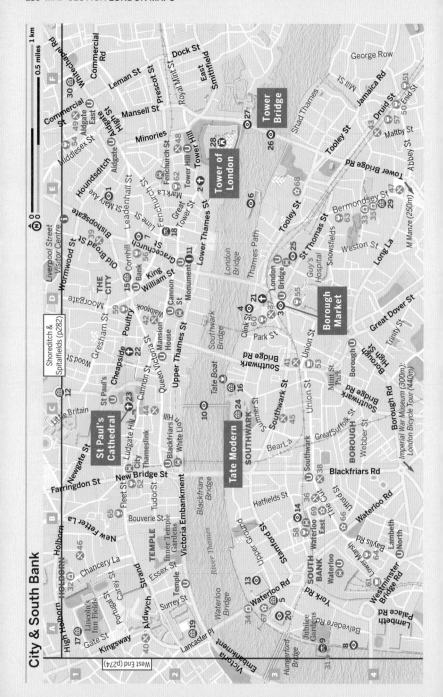

0 0 N

0 0.5 miles
0 1 km

West End (p274)

Shoreditch & Spitalfields (p282)

Liverpool Street Visitor Centre

St Paul's Cathedral

Tower of London

Tower Bridge

Tate Modern

Borough Market

Imperial War Museum (300m); London Bicycle Tour (440m)

M Manze (250m)

City & South Bank

◎ Sights
1	30 St Mary Axe	E1
2	All Hallows by the Tower	E2
3	Borough Market	D3
4	Golden Hinde	D3
5	Hayward Gallery	A3
6	HMS Belfast	E3
7	Leadenhall Market	E2
8	London Dungeon	A4
9	London Eye	A3
10	Millennium Bridge	C2
11	Monument	D2
12	Museum of London	C1
13	National Theatre	A3
14	Roupell St	B3
15	Royal Exchange	D2
16	Shakespeare's Globe	C3
17	Sir John Soane's Museum	A1
18	Sky Garden	E2
19	Somerset House	A2
20	Southbank Centre	A3
21	Southwark Cathedral	D3
22	St Mary-le-Bow	D2
23	St Paul's Cathedral	C2
24	Tate Modern	C3
25	The Shard	D3
26	Tower Bridge	E3
27	Tower Bridge Exhibition	F3
28	Tower of London	E2
29	White Cube Bermondsey	E4
30	Whitechapel Gallery	F1

⊕ Activities, Courses & Tours
31	Thames Rockets	A4

⊜ Shopping
32	London Silver Vaults	A1
33	Lovely & British	E4
34	South Bank Book Market	A3
	Southbank Centre Shop	(see 20)
35	Tin Lid	E4

⊗ Eating
36	Anchor & Hope	B3
37	Arabica Bar & Kitchen	D3
38	Baltic	B3
	Bar Tozino	(see 43)
	Café Below	(see 22)
39	City Social	E1
40	Counter at the Delaunay	A2
41	Flat Iron Square	C3
	Fortnum & Mason	(see 15)
42	Kym's	D2
43	Maltby Street Market	F4
44	Miyama	C2
	Padella	(see 3)
	Skylon	(see 20)
	The Delaunay	(see 40)
45	The Table Café	C3
46	Vanilla Black	B1
47	Watch House	E4
48	Wine Library	E2
49	Yuu Kitchen	F1

◉ Drinking & Nightlife
50	Anspach & Hobday	F4
51	Brew By Numbers	F4
52	City of London Distillery	B2
53	Coffee House	C3
54	Discount Suit Company	E1
55	George Inn	D3
56	Jamaica Wine House	D2
57	Jensen's	F4
58	King's Arms	B3
	Little Bird	(see 43)
59	Nickel Bar	D1
	Oblix	(see 25)
	Queen Elizabeth Roof Garden	(see 67)
60	Rake	D3
61	Scootercaffe	A4
62	Ship	E2
	Sky Pod	(see 18)
63	Tanner & Co	E4
64	Vaulty Towers	B4
65	Ye Olde Cheshire Cheese	B1

⊕ Entertainment
66	Old Vic	B4
67	Queen Elizabeth Hall	A3
	Royal Festival Hall	(see 20)
	Shakespeare's Globe	(see 16)
	Southbank Centre	(see 20)
68	Unicorn Theatre	E3
69	Young Vic	B3

Clerkenwell, Shoreditch & Spitalfields

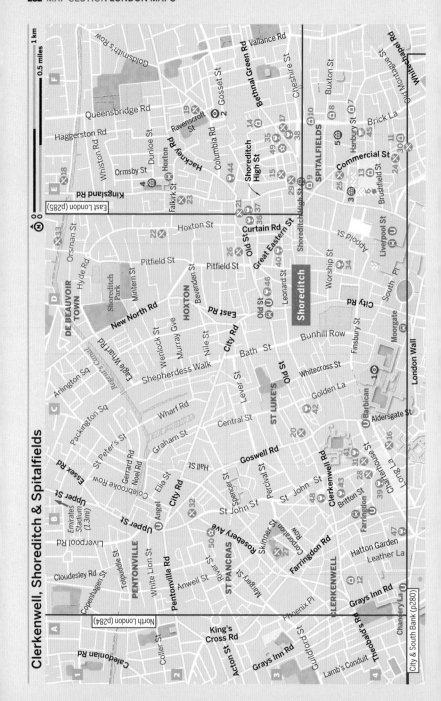

North London (p284)

East London (p285)

City & South Bank (p280)

Clerkenwell, Shoreditch & Spitalfields

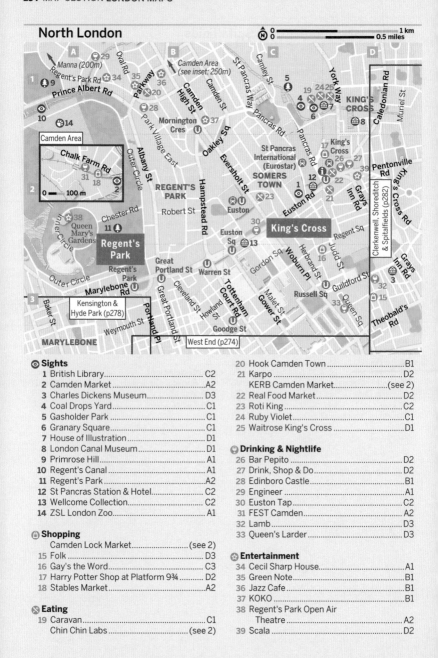

North London

East London

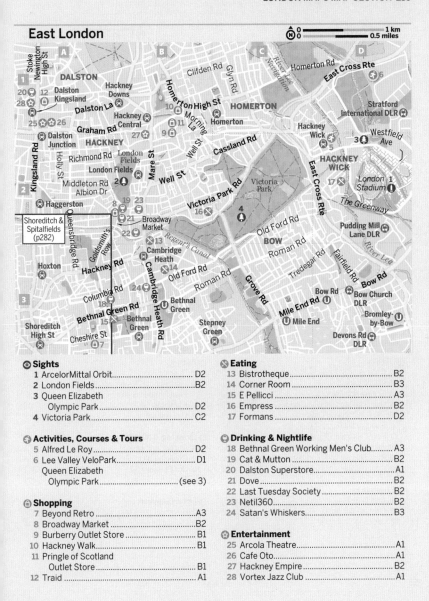

⊙ Sights

1 ArcelorMittal Orbit	D2
2 London Fields	B2
3 Queen Elizabeth Olympic Park	D2
4 Victoria Park	C2

⊙ Activities, Courses & Tours

5 Alfred Le Roy	D2
6 Lee Valley VeloPark	D1
Queen Elizabeth Olympic Park	(see 3)

⊙ Shopping

7 Beyond Retro	A3
8 Broadway Market	B2
9 Burberry Outlet Store	B1
10 Hackney Walk	B1
11 Pringle of Scotland Outlet Store	B1
12 Traid	A1

⊗ Eating

13 Bistrotheque	B2
14 Corner Room	B3
15 E Pellicci	A3
16 Empress	B2
17 Formans	D2

⊙ Drinking & Nightlife

18 Bethnal Green Working Men's Club	A3
19 Cat & Mutton	B2
20 Dalston Superstore	A1
21 Dove	B2
22 Last Tuesday Society	B2
23 Netil360	B2
24 Satan's Whiskers	B3

⊙ Entertainment

25 Arcola Theatre	A1
26 Cafe Oto	A1
27 Hackney Empire	B2
28 Vortex Jazz Club	A1

Greenwich

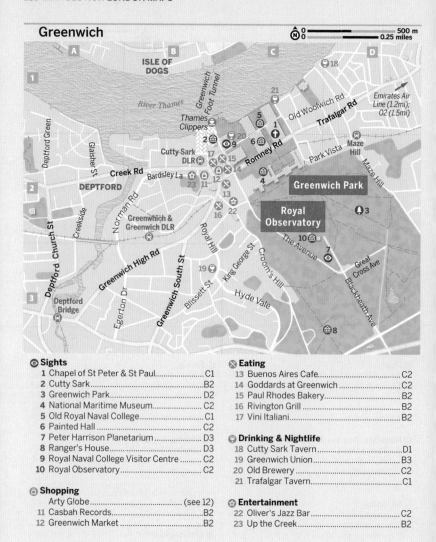

Symbols & Map Key

Look for these symbols to quickly identify listings:

- ◉ Sights
- ⊕ Activities
- ⊛ Courses
- ⊛ Tours
- ⊛ Festivals & Events
- ⊗ Eating
- ⊖ Drinking
- ⊛ Entertainment
- ⊖ Shopping
- ⊕ Information & Transport

These symbols and abbreviations give vital information for each listing:

🌱 Sustainable or green recommendation

FREE No payment required

- ☎ Telephone number
- ☺ Opening hours
- P Parking
- ⊖ Nonsmoking
- ✳ Air-conditioning
- @ Internet access
- 📶 Wi-fi access
- 🏊 Swimming pool

- 🚌 Bus
- ⛴ Ferry
- 🚋 Tram
- 🚆 Train
- 📋 English-language menu
- 🥗 Vegetarian selection
- 👪 Family-friendly

Find your best experiences with these Great For... icons.

 Art & Culture

 Beaches

 Budget

 Cafe/Coffee

 Cycling

 Detour

 Drinking

 Entertainment

 Events

Family Travel

🍽 Food & Drink

 History

 Local Life

 Nature & Wildlife

📷 Photo Op

🔭 Scenery

🛍 Shopping

 Short Trip

 Sport

🚶 Walking

❄ Winter Travel

Sights

- 🏖 Beach
- 🐦 Bird Sanctuary
- ⛩ Buddhist
- 🏰 Castle/Palace
- ✝ Christian
- ☯ Confucian
- 🕉 Hindu
- ☪ Islamic
- 卐 Jain
- ✡ Jewish
- 🗿 Monument
- 🏛 Museum/Gallery/ Historic Building
- 🏚 Ruin
- ⛩ Shinto
- ☬ Sikh
- ☯ Taoist
- 🍷 Winery/Vineyard
- 🐾 Zoo/Wildlife Sanctuary
- ◉ Other Sight

Points of Interest

- Bodysurfing
- Camping
- Cafe
- Canoeing/Kayaking
- Course/Tour
- Diving
- Drinking & Nightlife
- Eating
- Entertainment
- Sento Hot Baths/ Onsen
- Shopping
- Skiing
- Sleeping
- Snorkelling
- Surfing
- Swimming/Pool
- Walking
- Windsurfing
- Other Activity

Information

- 🏦 Bank
- Embassy/Consulate
- ✚ Hospital/Medical
- @ Internet
- Police
- Post Office
- Telephone
- Toilet
- ⓘ Tourist Information
- ● Other Information

Geographic

- Beach
- Gate
- Hut/Shelter
- Lighthouse
- Lookout
- ▲ Mountain/Volcano
- Oasis
- Park
-)(Pass
- Picnic Area
- Waterfall

Transport

- ✈ Airport
- Ⓑ BART station
- ⊗ Border crossing
- Ⓣ Boston T station
- 🚌 Bus
- Cable car/Funicular
- Cycling
- Ferry
- Ⓜ Metro/MRT station
- Monorail
- Ⓟ Parking
- Petrol station
- Ⓢ Subway/S-Bahn/ Skytrain station
- Taxi
- Train station/Railway
- Tram
- Ⓤ Underground/ U-Bahn station
- ● Other Transport

Our Story

A beat-up old car, a few dollars in the pocket and a sense of adventure. In 1972 that's all Tony and Maureen Wheeler needed for the trip of a lifetime – across Europe and Asia overland to Australia. It took several months, and at the end – broke but inspired – they sat at their kitchen table writing and stapling together their first travel guide, *Across Asia on the Cheap*. Within a week they'd sold 1500 copies. Lonely Planet was born.

Today, Lonely Planet has offices in Franklin, London, Melbourne, Oakland, Dublin, Beijing and Delhi, with more than 600 staff and writers. We share Tony's belief that 'a great guidebook should do three things: inform, educate and amuse'.

Our Writers

Emilie Filou

Emilie Filou is a freelance journalist specialising in business and development issues, with a particular interest in Africa. Born in France, Emilie is now based in London, UK, from where she makes regular trips to Africa. Her work has appeared in publications such as The *Economist*, The *Guardian*, the BBC, the *Africa Report* and the *Christian Science Monitor*. She has contributed to some 20 Lonely Planet guides, including *France*, *Provence*, *London*, *West Africa*, *Madagascar* and *Tunisia*. You can find out more on www.emiliefilou.com.

Damian Harper

Born off the Strand within earshot of Bow Bells (favourable wind permitting), Damian grew up in Notting Hill way before it was discovered by Hollywood. A onetime Shakespeare and Company bookseller and radio presenter, Damian has been authoring guidebooks for Lonely Planet since the late 1990s. He lives in South London with his wife and two kids, and frequently returns to China (his second home).

STAY IN TOUCH LONELYPLANET.COM/CONTACT

AUSTRALIA The Malt Store, Level 3, 551 Swanston St, Carlton, Victoria 3053
☎ 03 8379 8000,
fax 03 8379 8111

IRELAND Digital Depot, Roe Lane (off Thomas St), Digital Hub, Dublin 8, D08 TCV4, Ireland

USA 124 Linden Street, Oakland, CA 94607
☎ 510 250 6400,
toll free 800 275 8555,
fax 510 893 8572

UK 240 Blackfriars Road, London SE1 8NW
☎ 020 3771 5100,
fax 020 3771 5101

 twitter.com/ lonelyplanet

 facebook.com/ lonelyplanet

 instagram.com/ lonelyplanet

 youtube.com/ lonelyplanet

 lonelyplanet.com/ newsletter